Globalization, Trade and Poverty in Ghana

Edited by:
Charles Ackah and Ernest Aryeetey

International Development Research Centre
Ottawa · Cairo · Dakar · Montevideo · Nairobi · New Delhi · Singapore

First published in Ghana 2012 by
SUB-SAHARAN PUBLISHERS
P. O. BOX 358
LEGON-ACCRA
GHANA
Email: saharanp@africaonline.com.gh

ISBN: 978-9988-647-36-0

A co-publication with the
International Development Research Centre
P. O. Box 8500
Ottawa, ON K1G 3H9
Canada
www.idrc.ca / info@idrc.ca
ISBN (e-book) 978-1-55250-547-2

Typesetting by Kwabena Agyepong

Acknowledgments

This book is based on results of a research project carried out at the Institute of Statistical, Social and Economic Research (ISSER), University of Ghana, Legon. The project was generously funded by the International Development Research Centre (IDRC). We are deeply grateful to the IDRC for supporting this work. We also sincerely thank the chapter authors, editors, external reviewers, and the Project Advisory Committee for the work they did.

Contents

Foreword

The last 20 years have seen significant trade liberalisation across the world, and it is widely held that this has been beneficial for development, as suggested by large successful economies in Asia, including China, India, Bangladesh and Vietnam. These countries also have an impressive record in poverty reduction, though it is less clear to what extent this was a consequence of trade liberalisation.

Significant policy changes such as trade liberalisation will almost invariably have distributional consequences, with some gaining while others lose out, with probably differences in the short and longer term. The question of the impact of trade liberalisation on poverty was the subject of a review article in the Journal of Economic Literature, co-authored by Alan Winters, Neil McCulloch and myself. At that time empirical evidence on the question was very limited, with many of the articles we reviewed only covering specific aspects of it. Some more empirical evidence has accumulated over the subsequent eight years, though not so much for Africa.

This new study of Ghana, all chapters authored or co-authored by leading and emerging Ghanaian researchers, is a really welcome and valuable contribution to the literature. In depth country studies which look at different aspects of trade liberalisation are likely to be the most informative approach. And Ghana is an ideal focus. It has been one of the most successful African economies, which has achieved sustained growth over the past more than 25 years. Trade liberalisation and resulting export growth have been an important part of the story. Ghana also has had a very good record of poverty reduction, but to date there has been very little evidence as to whether trade liberalisation has been an important contributor to this.

The results presented in this study indeed confirm that trade liberalisation has had both positive and negative medium term impacts on different categories of households. Those engaged in exporting activities as well as skilled workers have benefited, but some poor and unskilled workers appear to have suffered, at least in the short to medium term. Trade liberalisation may therefore be a partial explanation for the increase in inequality Ghana has experienced in recent years. That said though the overall impact of trade liberalisation appears to have been positive in Ghana and to have contributed to poverty reduction over the longer term. But clearly appropriate complementary policies combined with institutional reforms are necessary to enable the benefits of trade liberalisation to be more widely shared than has been the case to date. These issues are likely to become all the more important as Ghana starts to extract its recently discovered oil.

Andy McKay
Professor of Development Economics
University of Sussex
United Kingdom
March 2012

List of Editors & Contributors

Charles Ackah – Research Fellow at the Institute of Statistical, Social and Economic Research (ISSER), University of Ghana.

Ernest Aryeetey – Vice Chancellor of the University of Ghana. At the time of writing, Director of the Institute of Statistical, Social and Economic Research (ISSER), University of Ghana.

Other Contributors:
Oliver Morrissey - School of Economics, University of Nottingham.
Simon Appleton - School of Economics, University of Nottingham.
Albert Laryea - Department of Economics, University of Ghana .
Sarah Akuoni - Department of Economics, University of Ghana.
William Baah-Boateng - Department of Economics, University of Ghana.
Kwadwo Opoku - Research Department, Bank of Ghana.
David Botchie - Institute of Statistical, Social and Economic Research, University of Ghana.
Vijay Bhasin - Department of Economics, University of Cape Coast.
Camara Kwasi Obeng - Department of Economics, University of Cape Coast.
William Gabriel Brafu-Insaidoo - Department of Economics, University of Cape Coast.

Introduction and Overview

Charles Ackah and Ernest Aryeetey

1. Introduction

The persistence of poverty in many developing countries, especially in Sub-Saharan Africa (SSA), in the face of increased globalisation and rapid trade liberalisation during the past two decades has inspired considerable debate on the impact of globalisation, in general, and trade liberalisation, in particular, on poverty. The standard argument, based on the Stolper-Samuelson theorem, is that global trade liberalisation would lead to a rise in the incomes of unskilled labour in developing countries. In other words, since developing countries are more likely to have a comparative advantage in producing unskilled labour-intensive goods, one would expect trade reforms in these countries to be inherently pro-poor (Krueger, 1983; Bhagwati and Srinivasan 2002; Bhagwati, 2004; Harrison, 2005). However, the experiences of many developing countries, particularly in SSA, have been disappointing and in many cases poverty has increased following trade liberalisation (Easterly, 2001). It is estimated that more than 1 billion people still live in extreme poverty (based on the US$1 per day poverty line), and half the world's population lives on less than US$2 a day.

In Ghana, as in many other SSA countries, poverty remains the fundamental problem confronting policy makers in the new millennium as highlighted in the Ghana Poverty Reduction Strategy (Government of Ghana, 2003) and Vision 2020: The First Medium-Term Development Plan (National Development Planning Commission,1977). Yet, between 1991 and 2006, the headcount index of poverty fell by 23.2 percentage points with the proportion of the population living below the national poverty line falling from 51.7% in 1991/92 to 28.5% in 2005/06. Poverty had fallen in the countryside as well as in the towns, though progress had been more rapid in rural areas. Research at ISSER (2006), suggests that this positive trend is likely to continue if Ghana maintains the average growth rates of the last few years making it likely that a number of targets contained in the Growth and Poverty Reduction Strategy II (GPRS2) will be achieved. This optimism is, however, tempered by the fact that while poverty declined, inequality increased significantly during the same period. The Gini index for consumption per equivalent adult increased from 0.353 in 1991/92 to 0.378 in 1998/99 and finally 0.394 in 2005/06. The evidence shows that the northern savannah area has been left behind in the national reduction in poverty, Large reductions in the incidence of poverty have occurred among private sector employees in both the formal and informal sectors, and among public sector wage employees, but export farmers have experienced the largest reduction in consumption poverty. Poverty reduction among the large numbers of food crop farmers, on the other hand, has been modest. Reductions in the incidence of poverty over the period have been smaller also for the non-farm self employed and informal sector wage employees. A recent publication by the World Bank suggests that had there been no change in inequality, the reduction in poverty would have reached 27.5 percentage points, so that Ghana would have achieved the Millenium Development Goal (MDG) target of reducing poverty by half in relation to its level of 1991/92.

These statistics have stimulated some concern about whether the poor gain from trade liberalisation, and under what circumstances it may actually hurt them. This is largely in view of the fact that most of the changes in the poverty data are associated with household involvement in international trade and also migration. It is not surprising that the impact of global integration on the welfare of the poor has become an important subject of ongoing interest to researchers and policy makers alike. While numerous studies have been conducted to examine the openness-growth-inequality-poverty linkages, little empirical evidence at the household level has been produced so far (McCulloch *et al.*, 2001; Winters *et al.*, 2004; Harrison, 2005).

In the last decade, in particular, considerable attempts have been made to measure the effects of both trade and trade policy on poverty. Winters *et al.* (2004), Goldberg and Pavcnik (2004), and Ravallion (2004) have provided excellent surveys of the evidence on the relationship between globalization and poverty. While the authors of these surveys acknowledge that there is mainly only *indirect* evidence regarding the linkages between globalization and poverty, the available evidence (Harrison, 2005) suggest that globalization produces both winners and losers and that the poor are more likely to share in the gains from globalization when there are complementary policies in place. Some studies (Dollar and Kraay 2000 and 2001) conclude that the poor benefit from trade since it stimulates economic growth without worsening income distribution whereas other studies argue that the poor may not be well placed to take advantage of the potential gains from globalization.

Thus, according to the latter studies, the benefits from globalization may accrue to those who are not particularly poor. A few other studies have actually reported adverse effects on poverty. However, empirical evidence is mixed and the globalization-poverty debate continues today. Accordingly, the issue of the impact of trade policy on poverty in developing countries has become the focus of recent research during which several methodological approaches have been deployed in the empirical literature.

In general, studies on the impact of trade liberalization on growth and/or poverty follow at least one of two broad methodological approaches cross-country and country-specific studies. It is worth noting that the cross-country studies almost all consider trade (policy) and growth, perhaps with inferences for impact on poverty predicated on an assumed link between growth to poverty reduction. Studies specifically looking at effects of trade (policy) on poverty/

welfare, on the other hand, are almost all country-specific. In spite of the numerous critiques of cross-country studies, they still have become, over the last decade, a major research tool for understanding the links between trade, growth and poverty. Most of the cross-country empirical literature seems to support the view that trade liberalisation (or openness) leads to more rapid growth and that economic growth results in poverty reduction, as exemplified in the influential papers by Jeffrey Sachs and Andrew Warner (1995) and David Dollar and Aart Kraay (2000 and 2001). However, these specific studies, or the general empirical approach, have come under severe criticism following the seminal work by Francisco Rodriguez and Dani Rodrik (2001). A number of methodological and econometric problems and the use of largely unsatisfactory trade policy measures have been identified as being responsible for the lack of robustness of these studies. In view of the major concerns over the methodologies deployed to study the impact of trade reforms, even some prominent proponents of free trade such as Srinivasan and Bhagwati (1999) have rejected cross-country regressions in favour of more in-depth case studies. Ravallion (2001:1813) quoted in Jenkins (2004:3) also points to the need for "more microeconomic and country-specific research on the factors determining why some poor people are able to take up the opportunities afforded by an expanding economy (…) while others are not." However, in spite of this call, empirical research on how trade policy reforms affect poverty at the household level is relatively scanty.

In the case of Ghana, for example, despite the general concerns expressed in many quarters, relatively little is known about the actual impact of trade liberalisation on the livelihoods of the poor. While some progress has been made in identifying the linkages between globalization and poverty outcomes in Ghana (Ocran *et al*. 2005; Oduro and Osei-Akoto, 2006; Aryeetey 2005; Aryeetey and McKay 2007), there is much that we do not know. We know very little about who gains and who loses as the Ghanaian economy becomes increasingly integrated into the world economy. In relation to gender impact, there is a general lack of empirical evidence to support or contest the apprehension that trade liberalisation may have increased the barriers to women's participation in the labour force. The lack of recent studies on the poverty impact of trade liberalisation (and globalisation, more generally) in Ghana is puzzling given its economic relevance, the availability of surveys and the fact that Ghana was 'adjustment's star pupil' (Alderman, 1994). Hence, any efforts directed at improving our understanding of the linkages between trade liberalisation and poverty in Ghana should be welcome.

This volume is one response to the challenge posed by the paucity of recent empirical evidence on the poverty and distributional impacts of trade policy reform in Ghana. The main objective of this volume is to contribute to our understanding of the poverty and distributional impact of trade policy reform in Ghana by analyzing how trade liberalisation affects the well-being of households and in particular, if the outcome it generates is pro-poor, with particular interest in the gender-differentiated impact. The volume attempts to answer the following questions:

- Who gains and who loses as the Ghanaian economy is opened to trade?
- In particular, what happens to poor households as Ghana becomes increasingly integrated into the global economy?
- Is there a close relationship between trade liberalisation and economic performance and have poor households benefited from trade related economic growth?
- Has the structure of protection and trade policy reforms in the last decade and a half been pro-poor?
- Has trade liberalisation in Ghana reduced or increased the barriers to women's participation in the labour force and have the trade net effects on poverty been positive?

2. Overview of the Volume

This volume combines both theory and quantitative econometric analysis to ascertain linkages between globalisation, trade and poverty in Ghana. The volume is divided into 11 chapters. The present chapter is prepared with the objective of serving as the introduction of the volume and overview of the subsequent chapters.

In Chapter 2, 'An overview of trade policies and development in Ghana', Laryea and Akuoni provide a background to the various transformations that Ghana's trade policy has undergone in the past up to the current export-led industrialisation strategy. They find that the outward-oriented policies adopted have helped integrate Ghana into the world economy, thereby providing a platform for the country to compete both domestically and in international markets. These policies have helped increase domestic competition and also improved opportunities for exporters. It is expected that Ghana will benefit greatly from the trade policies it has adopted.

In Chapter 3, 'Trends in growth, employment and poverty in Ghana', Ackah and Boateng find that Ghana has experienced impressive growth since the introduction of economic reforms in 1983. However, the benefits of this impressive growth have not been translated into the generation of quality employment. They find that the economy is still dominated by agriculture, vulnerable employment and poverty. Since 1991, a consistent decline of poverty has been noted. However, poverty is still endemic amongst food crop farmers who are excluded from minimum wage policies and government schemes for farmers. To curtail this problem they suggest that the participation of the poor should be taken into consideration when making policies.

In Chapter 4, 'Manufacturing employment and wage effects of trade liberalization', Ackah, Aryeetey and Opoku explore the impact of trade policy on wages and employment, paying particular attention to differences across key sectors, skills and overtime. They explore a potential match between the trends in trade liberalization and the trends in wages and employment. They find strong evidence that the growth of employment in the manufacturing sector in Ghana was significantly negatively impacted by the trade policy reforms of the 1990s and early 2000s, as high job losses occurred in sectors with the largest tariff cuts. The evidence suggests that trade protection creates more employment for unskilled labour than skilled labour in the manufacturing sector. Moreover, they find that trade liberalization in the manufacturing sector led to a fall in the average wage paid by manufacturing firms in Ghana, suggesting that workers employed in industries that were more exposed to liberalization experienced lower wages. They also find that greater openness is likely to be associated with significantly lower wages in firms which employ workers with low levels of education (the unskilled). This suggests that high trade protection that shields manufacturing firms from outside competition also protects the wages of unskilled workers.

In Chapter 5, 'Trade liberalization and the return to education in Ghana', Ackah, Morrissey and Opoku examine how income protection levels differ across households characterized by different skill levels. The positive effect of protection was disproportionately greater for low skilled labour households, suggesting that trade liberalization has an eroding effect on the welfare of unskilled labour households. In the short-run, all households regardless of skill type lose out from trade liberalization, but the poor unskilled households (because they are sector-specific and less mobile) would lose disproportionately, suggesting that within the same sector, a trade reform may lead to differing impacts on households with similar attributes but different skills. Education was found to be a fundamental household characteristic determining the probability that a household experiences poverty, *ceteris paribus*. From a policy standpoint, they concluded that contemplating trade liberalization without recognizing the complementary role of human capital investment may be a sub-optimal policy for the poor, at least in the short-run.

In Chapter 6, 'Trade liberalization and manufacturing firm productivity', Ackah, Aryeetey and Morrissey empirically investigate the effects of trade liberalization on firm-level productivity in Ghana. Controlling for observed and unobserved firm characteristics and industry heterogeneity, their findings show a strong negative impact of nominal tariffs on firm productivity. They also find large positive effects of tariff reductions on total factor productivity (TFP). These effects are consistent with the hypothesis that trade liberalization increases productivity in the domestic market, indicating that firms that are over-protected, as illustrated by high import tariffs pertaining to the industries in which they operate, have a lower level of TFP than firms that are exposed to competition. Additionally, strong effects of export intensity on productivity were found both on its own and in conjunction with lower tariffs. Exporters appeared to take greater advantage of foreign competition than non-exporters and were more sensitive to tariffs. The negative impact of trade protection on productivity is stronger for exporting firms (or firms that export larger shares of their output) relative to non-exporting firms.

In Chapter 7, 'The impact of elimination of trade taxes on poverty and income distribution in Ghana', Bhasin shows that elimination of trade-related import and export tariffs on agricultural goods and import tariffs on industrial goods in isolation or combined with foreign capital inflows and value-added tax reduces the incidence, depth, and severity of poverty of all categories of households, with the exception of the incidence of poverty of public sector employees and non-working people when import tariffs on industrial goods were eliminated in isolation. Regressive tax (VAT) as a revenue replacement made poor people better off due to neoclassical assumptions and transfers of VAT revenue to households. The impact of trade-related fiscal reforms on poverty and income differed across households. Mean incomes of private sector employees and non-working people improved to a large extent when trade liberalization in isolation was considered. Furthermore, a combination of foreign capital inflows and value-added tax improved the mean incomes of agricultural households to a large extent. It was suggested that the Government of Ghana should try to finance its unilateral trade liberalization through domestic resources instead of foreign resources in order to have greater impact on poverty reduction and improvement in the incomes of households.

In Chapter 8, 'Food prices, tax reforms and consumer welfare in Ghana during the 1990s', Ackah and Appleton analyse the effect of food price changes on household consumption in Ghana during the 1990s and assess the extent to which changes can be explained by trade and agricultural policy reforms. Demand for most food commodities in Ghana was found to be price sensitive, suggesting that Ghanaian household consumption did respond to relative price and real income changes. The burden of higher consumer food prices fell largely on the urban poor households. Trade liberalisation may not (for consumers) have been responsible for the welfare losses. The role of other factors and policies, such as the removal of fertilizer subsidies and exchange rate depreciation, could be decisive. The simulation exercise suggests that further tariff liberalisation would tend to offset the welfare losses of higher food prices for all household groups, although it is the poor and rural consumers that stand to gain the most. In sum, the results suggest, perhaps unsurprisingly, that although trade liberalisation may have a positive impact on welfare, at least from a consumption perspective, other factors may offset this, at least in the case of Ghana.

In Chapter 9, 'Effects of import liberalization on tariff revenue in Ghana', Insaidoo and Obeng examine the quantitative effect of import liberalization on import tariff yield in

Ghana. During the liberalisation period (post 1983), Ghana improved the generation of revenue from taxing imports although tariff revenue became less responsive to growth in imports in this period. Their findings suggested that import liberalization in Ghana is fiscally compatible although the impact of average official tariff rate reductions has been marginal. Inefficiencies in import tax administration, a clear identification of major sources of revenue leakage, the need for a review of the rationale for duty exemption programmes and a reduction of the range of items exempt from duty payments are some of the challenges of improving tariff revenue from taxing imports. Replacing of import tariff with the value-added tax and maintaining a liberal exchange rate regime are expected to enhance revenue generation from taxing imports. However, this can only be achieved through further improvements in customs administration and duty-collection mechanisms.

In Chapter 10, 'Cash cropping, gender and household welfare: evidence from Ghana', Ackah and Aryeetey examine how participation in cash cropping differs among women and men, and the ensuing implications for household welfare and food security among farm households in Ghana. They suggest that gender-related differences in the adoption of cocoa result from gender bias in access to complementary inputs such as land. Using propensity score matching techniques, the impact of cocoa adoption on farm household income and food security was examined. Their findings suggest that cocoa participation has a positive and statistically significant effect on household income and food security status. Commercial farming matters for poverty reduction in Ghana. Farmers that are able to adopt high-yield export crops such as cocoa are on average better off than farmers more oriented towards subsistence activities. Encouraging commercialization of farming in rural areas will help facilitate exports and reduce poverty. Gender bias in access to land, the most productive resource needed for participation in cash cropping in Ghana, appear to be the single most important constraint to female participation in cash cropping. Improvements in female access to land is seen to be cardinal to female-headed cocoa-farming households responding as well to the market incentives in export crop adoption as their male counterparts. They challenge policy makers to increase women's access to the key resources through land reforms which must have the objective of promoting increased acquisition of land by women.

In Chapter 11, 'Global integration, price transmission and household welfare in Ghana', Ackah, Osei and Botchie investigate the nature of price transmission from the world markets to the Ghanaian market for three main food crops, namely, rice, maize, and groundnuts, looking further into the welfare implications for households affected by price changes in the aforementioned food crops. The degree of openness determines the degree of price transmission from the world to a given economy, with the effect of world prices on domestic prices being significant and positive. The welfare simulations in the chapter demonstrate that a substantial number of households in Ghana are vulnerable to food price shocks and have likely suffered significant welfare losses from rising food prices. At the national level, the commodity that had the highest impact on poverty as a result of increases of its prices on the international market is rice. Although food price increases had differential effects on the population, for the vast majority of urban and female-headed households, the higher food prices brought severe hardship. Since the poor include both net consumers and net sellers of food commodities, a change in their price in either direction will inevitably hurt some of the poor and benefit some of the poor at the same time. It is therefore imperative for developing country governments and their development partners to be seen to be making efforts to improve smallholder productivity in the rural areas, even if they produce for home consumption mainly. Sufficient attention should be paid to maintaining or even improving the levels of social protection and poverty reduction expenditures.

This volume was carried out with the objective of improving our understanding of the poverty and distributional impact of trade policy reform in Ghana. Overall, the messages of this volume are clear in that trade liberalisation generated positive and negative effects for the Ghanaian population. It has improved Ghana's competitiveness in the domestic market and provided better opportunities for exporters in international markets. The country has seen tremendous economic growth through liberalisation though dearths of quality employment opportunities exist. This is partly explained by the fact that liberalisation has had a negative impact on wages in the Ghanaian manufacturing sector, particularly, for unskilled workers although simultaneously it has benefited workers in exporting firms. The benefit of liberalisation seems centred on exporting firms, skilled workers, households with higher incomes and male farmers involved in cocoa production while it hurts some of the poor and exhibits traces of female discrimination, particularly in access to land. To include the poor in the benefits of trade liberalisation, government should ensure the existence of policies that maintain or improve levels of social protection and poverty reduction expenditures. Gender discrimination should be reduced by improving women's access to land as this would help increase their participation in export markets, reduce poverty, and increase household income and food security. Overall, trade liberalisation need not be stopped because of the potential negative effects it has on the poor because the overall benefits through income growth in the economy compensate for these effects. Nevertheless, the findings presented in this volume can help policy makers design complementary pathways to enhance the benefits of trade liberalization for everyone.

References

Alderman, H. (1994), "Ghana: Adjustment's Star Pupil?" in Sahn (ed.), *Adjusting to Economic Failure in African Economies*, Ithaca and London: Cornell University Press.

Aryeetey, E. (2005), "Globalization, Employment and Poverty in Ghana", mimeo, Institute of Statistical, Social and Economic Research, University of Ghana.

Aryeetey, E. and McKay., A. (2007), "Ghana: The Challenge of Translating Sustained Growth into Poverty Reduction" in T. Besley and L. Cord, *Delivering on the Promise of Pro-Poor Growth; Insights and Lessons from Country Experiences*, Basingstoke and Washington D.C.Palgrave Macmillan and World Bank.

Bhagwati, J. (2004), *In Defense of Globalization*, Oxford University Press.

Bhagwati, J. and. Srinivasan T.N. (2002), "Trade and Poverty", *American Economic Review Papers and Proceedings*, vol. 92, no. 2, pp. 180-183.

Dollar, D. and Kraay, A. (2000), "Growth is Good for the Poor", *World Bank Policy Research Working Paper* no. 2587.

Dollar, D. and Kraay, A. (2001), "Trade, Growth, and Poverty", *World Bank Policy Research Working Paper* no. 2615.

Goldberg, P., Pavcnik, N. (2004), "Trade, inequality, and poverty: What do we know? Evidence from recent trade liberalization episodes in developing countries", *NBER Working Paper No. 10593*.

Harrison, A. (2005), "Globalization and Poverty", mimeo, University of California at Berkeley and NBER.

ISSER (various years). *The State of the Ghanaian Economy*, University of Ghana, Legon: Institute of Statistical, Social and Economic Research.

Jenkins, R. (2004), "Globalization, Production, Employment and Poverty: Debates and Evidence", *Journal of International Development*, vol. 16, pp. 1-12.

Krueger, A. (1983), *Trade and Employment in Developing Countries, vol. 3: Synthesis and Conclusions*, Chicago;University of Chicago Press.

McCulloch, N., Winters, A. and Cirera, X. (2001), *Trade Liberalisation and Poverty: A Handbook*. London: CEPR.

Ocran M.K.,Darko-Osei R. & Adjasi C.K.D.,(2005), "Trade liberalization and the dynamics of poverty: Empirical evidence from household surveys in Ghana", UNU-WIDER Conference on the Impact of Globalization on the poor in Africa, Johannesburg, 1-2 December 2005

Ravallion, M. (2004), *Competing concepts of inequality in the globalization debate.*, in: Collins, S., Graham, C. (eds.) *Brookings Trade Forum* 2004. Brookings Institution, Washington, DC.

Rodríguez, F. and Rodrik, D. (2001), "Trade Policy and Economic Growth: A Skeptics Guide to the Cross-National Evidence", in B. Bernanke and K. Rogoff (eds.), *Macroeconomics Annual 2000*, pp. 261-324, Cambridge, : MIT Press for NBER.

Sachs, J.D. and Warner, A.M. (1995), "Economic Reform and the Process of Global Integration," *Brookings Papers on Economic Activity*, vol. 1, pp. 1-118.

Winters, L.A., McCulloch, N. and McKay, A. (2004), "Trade Liberalization and Poverty: The Evidence So Far", *Journal of Economic Literature*, vol. 42, no. 1, pp. 72-11.

An Overview of Trade Policies and Developments in Ghana

Albert Laryea and Sarah Akuoni

1. Introduction

Prior to gaining independence from British colonial rule in 1957, Ghana, a small country whose main exports were primary products, operated a liberal payments regime. This was followed after independence by the pursuit of an import substitution industrialisation policy, as the then president, Dr. Kwame Nkrumah, embarked on an ambitious industrialisation plan. However, difficulties with the strategy emerged by the 1960s and 1970s as the balance of payments was put under severe strain. This resulted in the introduction of quantity and exchange rate controls in an attempt to sustain the external sector. These measures did not solve the problem and the resulting economic decline experienced in the Ghanaian economy as a whole finally compelled the government to embark on a World Bank/IMF prescribed economic recovery programme from the early to mid -1980s. These reforms, which were aimed at removing distortions in the economy, included trade and exchange rate liberalisation. Subsequently, further steps were taken to promote the export sector with a particular emphasis on the development of non-traditional exports.

Currently, Ghana pursues an export-led industrialisation strategy, which aims at improving the competitiveness of Ghanaian exports by providing a supportive liberalised environment in which exporters can successfully compete both in the domestic and international market. This is indicated in Ghana's most recent development plan, the Growth and Poverty Reduction Strategy (GPRS II).

It is clear that in the five decades of Ghana's existence, her trade policy has evolved from a fairly liberal one in the 1950s through a significantly controlled regime in the 1970s after which the economy underwent major trade and economic reforms in the 1980s to give rise to the liberalised trade policy currently in existence. This policy is largely guided by developments which have taken place in the arena of international trade under the General Agreement on Trade and Tariffs (GATT) and World Trade Organisation (WTO), trade agreements between Ghana and major trading partners as well as the country's own economic development policy. Ghana's trade policy has also been influenced, especially in the 1980s and 1990s by the Bretton Woods institutions.

This chapter provides an overview of Ghana's trade policy over the five decades since independence. The main objective is to relate trade policy to performance in the external sector.

The ways in which the external sector has changed will also be examined. Particular attention will be paid to the trade reforms that started in 1983 and their aftermath. In the process, policies over the years will be compared and more successful ones in terms of performance will be highlighted to serve as a guide for future policy. The rest of the chapter is structured as follows: the next section provides a historical overview from independence to the onset of the economic reforms in 1983. This is followed by Section 3 which reviews trade policy during and after the reforms and touches on tariff and quota reforms, reforms in the exchange rate, related reforms in trade policy, sector-specific reforms and recent developments in Ghana's trade policy. In Section 4, developments in Ghana's relations with multilateral partners and institutions are discussed. Section 5 presents some evidence of developments in exports, imports and direction of trade. The chapter concludes with Section 6.

2. Ghana's Trade Policies Between 1957 and 1983

During the 1950s there was debate regarding relevant trade policies for developing countries (Todaro, 1992). This debate was largely between free market ideology and trade protectionism. While the proponents of free market supported an outward-oriented, export-led trade regime, trade protectionists advocated inward-oriented, import-substitution trade policies.

Ghana's general economic policies after independence required massive government involvement in the economy with relevant and sector-specific controls and restrictions. The perceived dearth of entrepreneurial talent and low savings in the private sector led to the establishment of numerous state enterprises in the agricultural, manufacturing and services sectors. On the external front Nkrumah embarked on an import-substitution strategy which required further controls. For this policy to work it was necessary to have an overvalued exchange rate to enable inputs to come in cheaply and to put restrictions on final goods imports to protect domestic industry.

Ghana's leadership followed trade protectionism ideology, in part because of some consensus on the part of development economists that there needed to be massive government involvement in the economy. This was informed by the usual market failure argument but many development economists of the 1950s felt that what was involved here was a much broader concept than the Marshallian-type external economies. Marshallian-type marginal economics was felt to be too static to be relevant to the essentially dynamic question of development (Killick, 1978).

Consequently the government's general trade policy was characterized by exchange controls, tariffs and quantitative controls. The motivation, following the protectionism ideology, was to encourage indigenous manufacturing that was relevant to Ghana's resource endowment. It was believed at the time that greater self-reliance could be achieved only if the movement of goods, people and information was restricted and multinational enterprises were kept out in order to allow domestic infant industries to grow (Streeten, 1973).

Between 1950 and 1961 Ghana's payments regime was a liberal one with virtually no restrictions. Whatever minimal restrictions that existed were related to trade with nations outside the sterling area. This period saw the accumulation of reserves following the commodity boom associated with the Korean War and the gradual drawing down of the reserves. However, there was a turnaround in the 1960s when the government started industrialization with the import-substitution strategy contained in the Seven-Year Development Plan. Nkrumah launched an ambitious programme of infrastructure building – the most prominent of which were the artificial harbour at Tema, the Accra-Tema motorway and the Akosombo hydro-electric dam. Such projects required a lot of resources which came partly from domestic sources and partly from foreign borrowing.

In the middle of 1960s, there were widespread falls in primary product prices, especially cocoa, which impacted the economy of Ghana significantly. This and other reasons led to the failure of the import substitution approach to industrialization. Many of the enterprises set up performed poorly, especially after Nkrumah's overthrow, and thus drained the state of resources as many had to be bailed out continually (Killick, 1978). The policy also required an exchange rate that was low enough to let in imported inputs accompanied by restrictions to discourage final goods imports. In the process however exports were penalized.

The problem largely persisted after the 1966 coup. The payment system remained unsustainable and the civilian government of Dr. K. A. Busia was left with only two options – seeking debt relief and/or a massive devaluation. Very little debt relief was forthcoming and the government devalued the currency by an enormous 44 percent This devaluation led to a big jump in prices of imported goods and thus the general price level. It did not go down well especially in urban areas and the government was toppled by a military coup in January 1972. There was a revaluation of the currency that resulted in a smaller overall devaluation of about 20 percent.

The period between 1970 and 1983 has been described as one in which there was little macro management. What happened to the budget and to monetary variables was the result of decisions taken on political rather than economic grounds by a regime that showed little understanding of their macro consequences (Aryeetey and Harrigan, 2000). The poor economic conditions triggered coups in 1979 and 1981.[1]

3. Ghana's Trade Policies After 1983

In an attempt to prop up the Ghanaian economy, which was in crisis at the time, the then military leader Jerry Rawlings, with the support and guidance of the World Bank and IMF,

---

[1]   For more detailed accounts of trade policy before 1983 see Killick, 1978; Leith, 1974; Jebuni *et al* 1994.

embarked on Economic Recovery and Structural Adjustment programme (ERP and SAP). Key among the policies contained in those programmes was trade liberalization. Trade policy under SAP included tariff adjustments, import liberalization, liberalization of foreign exchange, deregulation of domestic market prices and controls and institutional reforms that particularly affected revenue generating bodies such as the Customs, Excise and Preventive Service (CEPS). The main objectives of these reforms were to restore incentives for the production of exports and increase the overall availability of foreign exchange, and to improve foreign exchange allocation and channel it into selected, high-priority areas (Republic of Ghana, 1983). The following sub-sections concentrate on reforms that eased restrictions and liberalised prices, involving reforms of tariffs, quotas and the exchange rate.

3.1 Tariff Reform and Quota reforms

With the advent of the Economic Recovery Programme (ERP) in 1983, Ghana's trade regime shifted towards more liberal, market-oriented and outward-oriented policies. Significant trade liberalization began with the adjustment of tariff rates in 1983. Rates were adjusted downwards from 35 percent, 60 percent and 100 percent to 10 percent, 20 percent, 25 percent and 30 percent. Tariffs were further simplified and lowered to 0 percent, 25 percent and 30 percent the following year to create a uniform pattern of protection although some import controls remained in place. Further reductions occurred in 1986 when the higher rates were lowered to 20-25 percent. In addition, the authorities reduced the number of restricted imports.

In 1986 there was a re-definition of import license categories with the introduction of a new exchange rate system. Import licenses were divided into three categories. The first category, the 'A' license, allowed the holder to bid for foreign exchange at the foreign exchange auction but restrictions were placed on the type of goods that could be imported using the license. The second category, the 'S' license, prevented the holder from bidding at the auction and the third type of license was issued to government organizations for the importation of essential goods and services. In 1987 there was a substantial increase in the number of goods that could be imported under the 'A' license. With the process of reforming the exchange rate system to a market-determined rate largely completed in 1988, the import licensing scheme which was considered redundant was abolished and was replaced with a special tariff on imports.

The structural adjustment programme was implemented in 1987 as the second phase of the economic reforms. From 1987 to 1991 there were major changes to the tariff structure. The tariff on luxury goods was lowered in 1988 but this was replaced with a super sales tax in 1990 which ranged from 50 percent to 500 percent. Imported fruits such as bananas, plantain, pineapples and guavas were subject to a tax of 500 percent while vegetables such as onions, potatoes and beans were subject to a tax of 100 percent. However this was reduced to the range of 10 to 100 percent in 1991.

Further liberalization occurred with the lowering of the import tax rate on raw materials and capital goods by 5 percentage points in 1990. The sales tax on imported basic consumer goods was also reduced between 1989 and 1994. However, protective duty rates were introduced for specified goods in 1990 and in 1994 to help some import-substituting industries such as those producing vegetable oil and soap, which were being subjected to intense competition. In 1994 import duties on all goods which were imported under exemption were raised to 10 percent and goods classified as standard saw an increase from 20 percent to 25 percent (Table 1).

Thus by 1994, Ghana had a relatively simple tariff structure, comprising three major rate categories:

(i)   A low rate of 0 percent (with some items raised to 5 percent) reserved primarily for primary products, capital goods, and some basic consumer goods;

(ii)   A moderate rate of 10 percent applied primarily to raw materials and intermediate inputs, as well as some consumer goods; and

(iii)   A higher rate of 25 percent, mainly on final consumer goods. In addition, there were a number of programmes under which imports could be exempted from duties and manufacturers could apply for permission to import raw materials and intermediate inputs at concessionary duty rates.

Table 1: Import duties structure in 1993 and 1994.

	1993 (%)	1994 (%)
Zero-rated	0	0
Exempted	0	10
Concession	10	10
Standard	20	25
Luxury	25	25

Source: Budget Statement 1994

Table 2: Sales tax (on imports) structure in 1993 – 1995 (%)

	1993	1994	1995
Zero-rated	0	0	0
Exempted	0	0	0
Concession	7.5	15	17.5
Standard	17.5	15	17.5
Luxury	35	35	17.5

Source: Ibid

In 1995, as part of efforts to increase government tax revenue a 10 percent import duty was imposed on selected zero-rated and exempted goods regarded as non-essential. However all import duties except those on vehicles remained the same. The import sales tax was also revised in 1995 (Table 2). In 1994, a number of tariff rationalization measures were proposed. Some imported items lost their zero-rated status while the rates for some other items were lowered. With regard to sales tax (on imports) the rate on goods classified as concessionary was raised from 7.5 percent to 15 percent while the rate for goods classified as standard was reduced from 17.5 percent to 15 percent (Table 2). In 1995 a uniform tax of 17.5 percent was placed on all taxable imported items.

The most radical tax reform in Ghana in the 1990s, which also impacted significantly on the country's external sector, was the replacement of the sales tax with the Value Added Tax (VAT) in 1998. The VAT was adopted for several reasons. First, it brought Ghana in line with the Economic Community of West African States (ECOWAS) protocol that made it mandatory for members to adopt the VAT system by the end of 1999 (Osei, 2000). Secondly, this system of taxation was thought to be more efficient, less burdensome in terms of its incidence, and its overall impact more equitable than the sales tax (GOG, 1994).

Table 3: Structure of MFN tariffs, 2007

	2007	U.R.
1. Bound tariff lines (% of all tariff lines)	14.7	n.a.
2. Duty-free tariff lines (% of all tariff lines)	11.9	0.0
3. Non-*ad valorem* tariffs (% of all tariff lines)	0.2	0.0
4. Tariff quotas (% of all tariff lines)	0.0	0.0
5. Non-*ad valorem* tariffs with no AVEs (% of all tariff lines)	0.2	0.0
6. Simple average tariff rate	12.7	92.3
Agricultural products (WTO definition)[a]	17.5	96.8
Non-agricultural products (WTO definition)[b]	12.0	37.8

	2007	U.R.
Agriculture, hunting, forestry and fishing (ISIC 1)	15.7	96.5
Mining and quarrying (ISIC 2)	11.4	n.a.
Manufacturing (ISIC 3)	12.6	90.4
7 Domestic tariff "spikes" (% of all tariff lines)[c]	0.0	0.0
8. International tariff "peaks" (% of all tariff lines)[d]	41.9	100.0
9. Overall standard deviation of applied rates	6.9	19.3
10. "Nuisance" applied rates (% of all tariff lines)[e]	0.0	0.0

n.a.   Not applicable.
a   WTO Agreement on Agriculture definitions.
b   Excluding petroleum.
c   Domestic tariff spikes are defined as those exceeding three times the overall simple average applied rate (indicator 6).
d   International tariff peaks are defined as those exceeding 15 percent.
e   Nuisance rates are those greater than zero, but less than or equal to 2 percent.
Source: :WTO Secretariat calculations, based on data provided by the Ghanaian authorities.

Initially the VAT rate was 10 percent but was subsequently increased to 12.5percent in 2000. Since then a 12.5 percent value added tax (VAT) has been tacked on the duty-inclusive value of all imports, with a few selected exemptions. In 2000, Ghana imposed an additional 0.5 percent ECOWAS levy on all goods originating from non- ECOWAS countries.

With respect to the WTO Ghana increased its coverage of bindings during the Uruguay Round from zero to 14.7 percent of tariff lines (Table 3). Some 12 percent of tariff lines are duty-free. In agriculture all tariffs were bound mainly at the ceiling rate of 99 percent. Lower bound rates of 40 percent and 50 percent were set on a few agricultural products to apply from 1995. Very few industrial tariffs – 1percent of tariff lines were bound at ceiling rates of between 30 percent and 45 percent. Bindings were limited primarily to agricultural inputs such as fertilizer as well as tools and equipment. Applied rates are, however, much lower, as shown in Table 3. The reason for the big difference is to give the government some leeway in raising tariffs when, for instance, severe balance of payments problems arise without contravening the rules of the WTO.

Ghana's simple average tariff with all the changes made in the 1990s fell to 13 percent in January 2000 from a high of 17 percent in 1992. This did not last long though as in April of the same year a 'special import tax' of 20 percent was re-introduced covering some 7 percent of tariff lines. This raised the tariff on many consumer goods to 40 percent - well above the previous rate of 25 percent and consequently raised the average tariff to 14.7 percent.The cumulative frequency of Ghana's most favoured nation(MFN) tariffs (as shown in Chart 1) indicates that 90 percent of tariff lines are at or below 20 percent. In 2002 Ghana abolished its 20 percent 'special import tax' in an effort to bring its tariff structure into harmony with ECOWAS and WTO provisions.

In February 2003, the government imposed higher tariffs on imported rice and poultry but this was never implemented as development partners objected. The National Health Insurance Law was passed in September 2003 and, to partly finance it, the VAT was increased from 12.5 percent to 15 percent.

Currently Ghana's tariff structure comprises four bands of 0 percent, 5 percent, 10 percent and 20 percent. Finished/consumer goods attract the highest rate of 20 percent while raw materials and intermediate goods are either zero-rated or attract a tariff of 10 percent. This applies to all goods except for some petroleum products which face specific tariffs. The average applied tariff is now 12.7 percent, down from 14.7 percent in 2000 (Table 3).

Breakdown of tariff rates, 2007

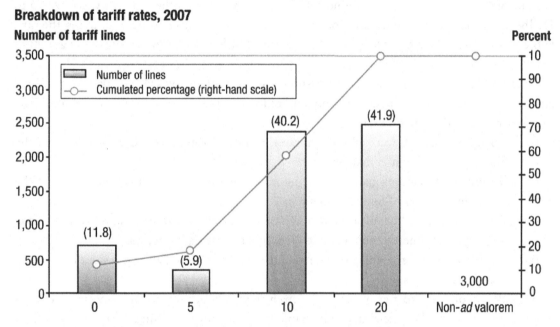

Note: The figures in the brackets correspond to the percentage of total lines

Source: WTO Secretariat calculations, based on data provided by the Ghanaian authorities.

3.2 The Exchange Rate After 1983

The exchange rate was a very visible symbol of the large distortions in the Ghanaian economy and tackling this particular problem was thus a central part of the whole liberalisation process. To pursue this goal the government had four main objectives: firstly, to realign the official exchange rate, secondly, to achieve a convergence of official and parallel rates, thirdly, to absorb the parallel market into the legal market and fourthly, to allow demand and supply to determine the rate and allocation of foreign exchange (Dordunoo, 1994).

A straightforward devaluation was perceived by some to be politically damaging given that the Busia government had been overthrown in 1972 mainly for devaluing the currency and the governments that followed had consequently taken devaluation off the list of available policy options for several years. Thus the whole process was done gradually and in phases.

The first phase in 1983, retained the official rate of ¢2.75 to $1 but instituted a system of bonuses and surcharges for exports and imports . Thus, exporters were given bonuses that varied according to what was being exported while importers were surcharged according to what they imported. The effect was to institute a multiple exchange rate regime. In effect traditional exports and imports of crude oil, essential raw materials, basic foodstuffs and capital goods were subject to a rate of ¢23.375 to $1. The rate for non-traditional exports and other imports was ¢29.975 to $1. The official rate was changed six months later to ¢30 to $1 thus effectively unifying the rate. Subsequently there were fairly large devaluations until in January 1986 the rate stood at ¢90 to $1.

The second phase involved a series of measures aimed at moving towards a market -determined rate. First, a retail foreign exchange auction market for selected transactions was introduced. The basic objectives of the foreign exchange auction were:

(i)   To minimize and eventually eliminate the use of administrative mechanisms in the allocation of foreign exchange;

(ii)   To provide foreign exchange financing in a timely manner at prices which reflect the prevailing scarcity of foreign exchange;

(iii)   To promote trade liberalization through easing and finally eliminating controls on trade and payments, thereby enhancing the volume of external trade; and

(iv)   To bring foreign exchange held outside the banks into the banking system by offering competitive prices.

Secondly, an official two-tier system was introduced whereby imports and exports of selected goods were subject to the official fixed rate while the remaining two-thirds of Ghana's external transactions were subject to the auction rate. This two-tier system was unified in February 1987 at ¢150 to $1 with all transactions being settled at the weekly auction rate. The auction was initially characterised by increased instability but this stabilised after a few weeks.

The third phase of the reform process began in February 1988 when the parallel market was legalised with the granting of licenses to individuals to operate foreign exchange bureaux. The main aim of allowing the operations of such bureaux was to attract additional foreign exchange to official channels. Other aims were to facilitate the acquisition of small amounts of foreign exchange on a daily basis and to bring about convergence between parallel and auction rates (Oduro and Harrigan, 2000). Thus the rate was now wholly a market-determined rate. Subsequently a wholesale market auction introduced in 1990 to be replaced by an inter-bank market in 1992. With these changes the gap between the inter-bank rate and the bureaux rate was largely eliminated.

One remarkable thing about the substantial devaluations was the absence of what is known as 'contractionary devaluation'. This is a scenario in which devaluation can lead to contraction in output because of mainly supply-side factors such as the increase in the prices of imported inputs and wage demands which accompany the resultant increase in prices. Some reasons have been given for this. They include the fact that prices were already being determined by the black market rate which made the impact of the devaluation almost negligible. Other factors include the inflows of foreign exchange from donors and the fact that fiscal policy emphasized expenditure control within the context of revenue generation (Oduro and Harrigan, 2000).

Subsequently, the broad policy objective was to maintain the flexible exchange rate regimes that had been established. Having an exchange rate that was freely determined by market forces and thus neither undervalued nor overvalued is considered to be consistent with the outward oriented policies initiated in the 1980s.

The year 2006 saw the passing of the Foreign Exchange Act 723 in December. Until then the foreign exchange market was operated in accordance with the Exchange Control Act, 1961, Act 71 and subsequent amendments to that Act. Through the issue of Notices and Regulations by Bank of Ghana (under the authority of the 1961 Act), the Exchange Control Act was operationally amended to a very large extent, thereby substantially liberalising current account transactions. Capital account liberalization has, however, not been achieved. The new Foreign Exchange Act 2006, Act 723 removed all exchange controls and authorized dealer banks and agencies can undertake foreign exchange transactions without recourse to the central bank.

3.3 Other Trade-Related Reforms

These are general reforms such as the creation of special institutions, programmes and projects to buttress the reforms.

During the 1990s the Ghana Export Promotion Council (GEPC) was made more of a promotional agency than a regulatory one. In line with this, a Product Development Division was created within the council to help identify new products and producers, organize exporters into production associations and provide information to entrepreneurs in the field. Education programmes were also organised for exporters and export facilitators throughout the period. Solo exhibitions in selected ECOWAS countries were organised to promote exports into the sub-region.

In 1993, two programmes were established under the Ministry of Trade and Industry to enhance the supply capabilities of exporters by assisting them with incentives. These are the USAID-sponsored Trade and Investment Programme (TIP), and the Private Enterprise and Export Development (PEED) initiative sponsored by the World Bank. The TIP was a US$80 Million programme which lasted for five years. Its objective was to help eliminate the various obstacles to export expansion in order to achieve accelerated export growth. The programme's emphasis was on creating an enabling environment for the promotion of exports and improving on the low capacity of firms to export by providing institutional support for exporters. The TIP put in place Trade and Investment Management Unit which comprised all ministries and other organizations whose activities relate to export development. Accomplishments included the removal of foreign exchange control measures that required non-traditional exporters to surrender most of their foreign exchange earnings to the monetary authorities and the removal of restrictions on what could be exported.

At the end of TIP in 1999, USAID followed up with the Trade and Investment Reform Programme, (TIRP.) Under TIRP, all restrictions on non-traditional exports were removed, paving the way for a tremendous increase in the value and volume of non-traditional exports. This was followed by the Trade and Investment Programme for a Competitive Export Economy; (TIPCEE 2004-2009) also aimed at creating an enabling environment for further growth in non-traditional exports. TIPCEE had as one of its major objectives, the building of capacity for exporters in business development. It also aimed to provide technical assistance to smallholder farmer groups in the horticultural sector and businesses involved in agro-processing for export.

To address the problem of inadequate financial services for exporters, the PEED scheme, a US $51m credit facility was introduced. It aimed at addressing the financial problems of exporters of non-traditional goods, and was designed to provide finance in foreign exchange or in cedis for Ghanaian non-traditional exporters. Two methods of financing exports were offered under the PEED scheme. These are the Export Refinance Scheme, and the Export Credit Guarantee Scheme. Export refinance meant that, the Bank of Ghana would refinance short-term export credits made by banks to non-traditional exporters. For the repayment to be made in respect of loans provided under the refinancing scheme, the Bank of Ghana was to set aside US$4 million under the Export Credit Guarantee Scheme to guarantee up to 65 percent of loans made by banks to non-traditional exporters. Other incentives provided included the waiver of duty for exporters who used imported inputs.

In addition to the programmes outlined above, a Business Assistance Fund (BAF) was launched as a short-term measure to support distressed but potentially viable Ghanaian non-traditional exporting enterprises. This guarantee scheme was followed in 2000 by the Export Development and Investment Fund (EDIF) with the aim of boosting the financing available from the banking sector to exporters. The industries targeted for support were textiles/garments, wood and wood processing, food and food processing and packaging. Money was to come from 10 percent of divestiture proceeds and a levy on dutiable values of all non-petroleum products imported for commercial purposes. EDIF provides concessionary financing at the rate of 12.5 percent for exporters. It also helps with export insurance, re-financing and credit guarantees through designated financial institutions.

Other interventions were made to improve the efficiency of institutions offering trade-related services. These were the Customs, Excise and Preventive Service (CEPS), Ghana Ports and Harbour Authority, Ghana Investment Promotion Centre, Ghana Immigration Service and the Ghana Free Zones Board. This support was part of the Ghana Trade and Investment Gateway project which was launched in 1999 to further buttress the initiatives adopted to attract investment into the country The project was to help modernise the equipment and raise the human capacity base of the institutions listed above for the prompt handling and the provision of offsite infrastructure for the export-processing zone enclave.

The objective of the Gateway project was to attract a critical mass of export-oriented firms to kick-start export-led growth as well as facilitate trade. This involves the creation of an enabling environment to facilitate the increased level of private investment, reduce the cost of doing business as well as provide the necessary infrastructural services and the provision of off-site infrastructure for on-site facilities.

In the area of customs valuation, Ghana in 2000 adopted the WTO Valuation Agreement concurrently with the Destination Inspection Scheme (DIS). This is as a result of the implementation of the Gateway project. Prior to this, Ghana had over the previous 28 years been operating the Pre-Shipment Inspection (PSI) scheme. The PSI scheme was long and cumbersome and required a 100 percent physical inspection of imports. Thus, on the average, goods took between 4-6 weeks before being cleared.

Furthermore, in May 2002, the WTO and Ghana's Customs Excise and Preventive Service (CEPS) signed an agreement on customs valuation and trade facilitation to simplify customs procedures and facilitate swift clearance of goods. This was to establish a transparent environment for the conduct of international trade and underlined the importance of a commercial system that is standardized and fair. Under the initial valuation system, the 'Commissioner of Valuation' has the final judgment on any queries regarding the declared value of goods but this was removed under the new agreement.

3.4 Sectoral Trade Reforms

This involves reforms that specifically targeted particular sectors. While traditionally sectors are divided into agriculture, industry and services in Ghana's case-specific policies tended to target broad categories such as traditional and non-traditional exports. By ensuring that the exchange rate was now a market-determined rate, the bias against exports was largely eliminated. Right from the beginning of the reform process policies were adopted to promote exports.

3.4.1 Traditional Exports

According to the Export and Import Act, 1994 Act 503 traditional exports consist of the following: cocoa beans, lumber and logs, unprocessed gold and other minerals and electricity. Lately, yams have been added to this category. Apart from the general liberalisation, policies were adopted to target this category. The main objective of policy was to increase foreign exchange earning from the cocoa sector mainly through the provision of incentives to cocoa farmers. Other objectives included the maintenance of Ghana's distinctive position as the supplier of the finest and most consistent quality cocoa and in addition retain the traditional premium obtained by Ghana's cocoa on world markets.

Measures taken included the privatisation of inputs distribution and the provision of credit to purchase inputs following the removal of input subsidies. The most important measure though was the increase in the producer price paid to farmers. By the start of the reforms the percentage of the world price received by farmers had fallen to as low as 25 percent. It was even in single digits if assessed at parallel market rates (Sarris and Shams, 1991).

This percentage was thus gradually increased to about 46 percent. All of these incentives boosted exports. The output of cocoa doubled between 1983 and 1989 even though the world price fell by over 50 percent during the period. In these difficult circumstances, the steady improvement thus stalled but since the late 1990s there has been a steady increase and the aim of policy is to increase in the producer price to 70 percent. Currently, it is 68 percent. Since 2001 the government has also intensified the mass spraying of cocoa farms. The operations of Ghana Cocoa Board (COCOBOD) were also streamlined in order to reduce overhead costs and to intensify research on diseases and pest controls.

Gold production has increased since the ERP began because of the more favourable investment climate created which allowed investment in the sector to expand. The broad policy objectives for the mining sector have been
- incentives to increase and sustain investment in the sector;
- avoidance of degradation of the environment; and
- ensuring that people in the sector benefit from exploitation of the mineral resources.

For timber a new forest and wildlife policy was adopted in 1994 through which the government initiated a series of control measures including a ban on the export of logs, the designation of resource areas and the concept of "annual allowable cut". A Timber Resource Management Act was also passed in 1998 to improve the allocation system of logging permits and to control illegal chainsaw operators. The Act also provided for a more efficient and transparent allocation process based on a new contract scheme – the Timber Utilization Contract (TUCs). Under the system, firms bid for contracts to log particular sections of the forest. Each contract has duration of 40 years and is renewable as long as the contractor manages its designated logging area according to specified criteria. Implementation, however, suffers from malpractices (UNCTAD, 2003). Other policy initiatives include encouraging the use of lesser known species and the placement of levies on exports to support reforestation.

3.4.2 Non-Traditional Exports

This category consists of all items exported other than those classified as traditional. Prominent among them are horticultural products such as pineapples, processed agricultural products, furniture and processed aluminium products. One of the principal aims of the reform programme was the diversification of exports and right from the beginning, non-traditional exports were targeted. Duty-free imports of machinery were allowed and income tax rebates were given to exporters. A foreign exchange retention scheme for non-traditional exports was liberalised and the proportion that could be retained was increased from 20 percent to 35 percent in 1987. As a further boost to non-traditional exports, agricultural pricing and marketing arrangements on all products except for cocoa were removed in 1990 and export procedures were made less cumbersome. At present, non-traditional exporters pay a company tax rate of 8 percent instead of 35 percent. Further incentives followed. Import tax rebates were introduced in 1991 and the surrender requirements for non-traditional exports were abolished. At the moment, surrender requirements exist for only gold and cocoa. During the first six years of the reforms there was a big increase in the number of non-traditional exporting enterprises.

3.5 Recent Developments in Ghana's Trade Policy

The General Agreement on Trade in Services (GATS) process has started and Ghana has made some commitments. Compared to many other developing countries Ghana has relatively few restrictions. Ghana made specific commitments in five areas under the GATS. These were construction, education, tourism and travel-related services, maritime transport and financial services. This implies that Ghana is committed to liberalising these areas subject to specific limitations contained in the schedule. For most sectors listed in the schedule there are no limitations on foreign participation, consumption abroad, cross-border supply or commercial presence.

In February 2004 a new trade policy document was adopted. This policy was set within the context of Ghana's strategic vision of achieving middle-income status by 2012 and becoming a leading agro-industrial country in Africa. The policy provides clear and transparent guidelines for the implementation of government's domestic and international trade agenda. It is also designed to ensure a consistent and stable policy environment within which the private sector and consumers can operate effectively and with certainty.

This policy emphasized two parallel strategies: an export-led industrialization strategy and a domestic market-led industrialization based on import competition. These new strategies are supported through the promotion of increased competitiveness of local producers in domestic and international market based on fair and equal competition and by introducing an import and domestic trade regime which promotes and protects consumer interests.

Underlying the broad policy was the targeting of seven thematic areas for close attention. These were:

- International Trade: relating to multilateral trade issues;
- Import-Export Regime: dealing with tariff and non-tariff measures.;
- Trade Facilitation: covering customs clearance and related issues;.
- Enhancing Production Capacity: addressing bottleneck issues such as investment finance, production inputs, infrastructure and access to land;
- Domestic Trade and Distribution: dealing with domestic trade;
- Consumer Protection and Fair Trade: dealing with issues of health and safety of consumers;
- Intellectual Property Rights.
- It is hoped that this comprehensive approach will enable the country to take advantage of opportunities offered by trade.

A strategic plan-- the Trade Sector Support Programme (TSSP) was launched in 2006 to implement the policy prescriptions in the Ghana National Trade Policy. Essentially this consists of a series of projects aimed at improving the legal and regulatory environment for business and consumers.

4. Developments in Relations with Multilateral Institutions and Partners

4.1 ACP-EU Relations

Ghana as a member of the African, Caribbean Pacific and (ACP) group of states has been part of the relationship since its inception in 1975. The reason for this relationship was the desire of some members of the then European Economic Community (EEC) to maintain some influence in their former colonies. It was also to maintain economic ties that gave them access to raw materials and provide a market for their finished goods. The former colonies on their part hoped to get aid to develop their economies and to enhance their exports by gaining duty-free access to the EEC market. Four Lome Agreements were subsequently signed and the fifth and latest ACP/EU accord is the Cotonou Agreement.

There were some fundamental components to the agreements —specifically, the trade part which ensured the removal of tariff barriers to the entry of ACP exports to the EU market. This agreement was non-reciprocal in the sense that the ACP countries could impose restrictions on EU goods entering their markets. A second component of the agreement was development aid which over the years resulted in quite substantial inflows to ACP countries. Lately a third component, the political dimension, has become increasingly important. This involves political dialogue over the arms trade, excessive military expenditure, drugs and organized crime, democratic principles and the rule of law and good governance.

By the time the Cotonou Agreement was signed, there was general agreement that ACP countries for various reasons had not been able to take advantage of opportunities offered by the duty-free access to EU markets. Some of the reasons included lack of adequate information to prospective exporters, complicated rules of origin provisions, and inadequate trade infrastructure. At the same time some provisions of the Agreement violated WTO principles such as non-reciprocity. Thus a waiver had to be granted to the EU-ACP but other developing countries outside the ACP were no longer willing to grant this waiver.

A timetable for the completion of WTO consistent trade agreements was subsequently endorsed by WTO members at its 2001 ministerial conference in Doha, Qatar. At this meeting the EU was granted a waiver of its WTO commitment with respect to the Cotonou Agreement through 2007. At the end of the period unilateral preferences were to be replaced by reciprocal Economic Partnership Agreements (EPAs) between the EU and individual ACP countries or groups of countries. If Ghana had to sign as a member of a bloc it had to be as a member of ECOWAS.

ECOWAS was formed in 1975 with the express aim of gradually removing barriers to eventually create a customs union. The countries, however, could not lower barriers as envisaged and to move things along a trade liberalization scheme was introduced in 1990. Matters did not improve and in 1993 the ECOWAS Treaty was revised. The objective then was to establish a Free Trade Area by removing all barriers on all goods traded between member states by 1 January 2000. A Common External Tariff (CET) was to be established by 1 January 2004 to finalise the establishment of a customs union. However these have been delayed. Meanwhile a bloc within ECOWAS, the West African Economic and Monetary Union (WAEMU) was formed among members of the CFA zone. This bloc managed to create a CET. It was then expected that non-WAEMU countries were to gradually align their tariffs with the WAEMU CET. Negotiations on this are on-going and all the ingredients needed for ECOWAS to sign an EPA as a bloc are not yet present.

Thus Ghana faced the prospect of an end to unrestricted access to the EU market. One option open was to agree on an interim EPA pending the creation of a fullyi-fledged customs union and the signing of a full EPA. Ghana is yet to sign this agreement although it is being largely implemented.

4.1.1 The Interim EPA

It was necessary to reach agreement on the interim EPA to avoid disruption of trade that would have occurred with the expiry of the waiver granted by the WTO. Of the 77 countries in the

ACP 36 had signed either interim or full EPAs by the time Ghana reached its agreement. Another 31 were least developed countries (LDCs) which, under WTO rules could continue to enjoy non-reciprocal agreements with the EU under the Everything But Arms (EBA) initiative. Within ECOWAS only Ghana, Cote D'Ivoire and Nigeria were non-LDCs. Cote d'Ivoire reached agreement just before Ghana did, leaving only Nigeria which exercised the option of adopting GSP+.

Ghana signed the interim EPA with the EU on 12 December 2007. The main features of the agreement included:

- Duty-free and quota-free access into the EU for all imports as of 1 January 2008 with a transition period until 2010 for rice and 2015 for sugar.
- Ghana's commitment to liberalise 80 percent of imports from the EU representing 81percent of tariff lines over the next 15 years.
- A chapter on trade defence with bilateral safeguards allowing each party to reintroduce duties or quotas if imports of the other party disturb or threaten to disturb their economy.
- A chapter on Technical Barriers to Trade (TBT) and Sanitary and Phyto-Sanitary (SPS) measures to help Ghanaian exporters to meet EU import standards.
- A chapter aiming to facilitate trade through measures such as more efficient customs procedures and better co-operation between administrators.

In this regard Ghana, excluded a number of agricultural goods and non-agricultural processed goods. The exclusion list included chicken and other meats, tomatoes, onions, sugar, tobacco, beer and worn cloth.

Other features included a detailed dispute settlement mechanism to support the effective implementation of the agreement, and new improved rules of origin. There was also an agreement on development co-operation which included the reinforcing and upgrading of the capacity of the productive sectors, co-operation over fiscal adjustment, improvement of the business environment and implementation of trade rules.

5 Developments in Exports, Imports and Capital Flows

This section considers some of the developments which have accompanied the changes in trade policy from the early 1980s.

The reforms undertaken opened up the trade sector, with both exports and imports increasing. However, we can see that imports have been outstripping exports with the gap growing wider in recent years. (Table 4).

The initial growth in imports that took place in the earlier phase of the reforms (i.e. between 1983 and 1986) was a response to the gradual removal of import restrictions and tariffs. It will be recalled that tariffs were adjusted gradually between 1983 and 1986 from 35 percent, 60 percent and 100 percent to 0 percent, 20 percent and 25 percent respectively. By 1988 the exchange rate reforms aimed at the adoption of a market-determined rate had been completed. Consequently the import licensing scheme was dropped. Within 10 years of the reforms imports had grown by more than 200 percent in value.

Exports on the other hand expanded by a little over 100 percent. Indeed the exchange rate adjustment resulted in a considerable depreciation of the real effective exchange rate from 1984. This allowed the government to increase prices paid to farmers, resulting in an increase in their incomes. They consequently responded by increasing production. Part of the increase in exports has been explained by the diversion of cocoa from unofficial to official sources (Jebuni et al, 1994).

According to Jebuni. (1994) the trade deficit during most of the period from1983 to 1989 may be explained by the decline in the terms of trade and not necessarily because of a failure of export sector performance. It is further explained to a large extent by high levels of external support. In fact, inflows of long and short-term capital doubled between 1983 and 1984 and doubled again between 1985 and 1986. These allowed the balance of payments to be in surplus. The trade deficits have continued over the years even though the terms of trade have generally improved, so there may be some other reasons for this. Some other studies have identified export supply bottlenecks such as high transport costs and inadequate credit as the reason for this state of affairs.

Table 4: Exports and Imports in Current Dollars

Year	Goods			Services	
	Credit	Debit	Balance	Credit	Debit
1982					
1983	439.1	-449.7	-60.6	32.8	-134.4
1984	565.9	-533	32.9	32.9	-162.9
1985	632.4	-668.7	-36.3	38	-167.5
1986	773.4	-712.5	60.9	39.7	-227.6
1987	826.8	-951.5	-124.7	72.4	-237.5
1988	881	-993.4	-112.4	71.4	-255
1989	807.2	-1002.2	-195	75.5	-270.7
1990	890.6	-1198.9	-308.3	79.3	-295.4
1991	997.6	-1318.7	-321.1	95.1	-318.8
1992	986.4	-1456.7	-470.3	110.3	-371.3
1993	1063.6	-1728	-664.4	144.7	-445.3
1994	1237.7	-1579.9	-342.2	147.5	-420.8

Year	Goods			Services	
1995	1431.2	-1687.8	-256.6	150.6	-432.7
1996	1570.1	-1937	-366.9	156.8	-456.4
1997	1489.9	-2128.2	-638.3	164.9	-505
1998	2090.8	-2896.5	-805.7	438.6	-673.6
1999	2005.5	-3228.1	-1226.6	467.8	-665.9
2000	1898.4	-2741.3	-842.9	504.3	-597.3
2001	1867.11	-2968.5	-1101.4		
2002	2015.19	-2707	-691.8		
2003	2562.39	-3232.8	-670.4		
2004	2704.46	-4297.3	-1592.8	702.29	-1058.47
2005	2802.21	-5347.3	-2545.1	1106.5	-1273.1
2006	3726.68	-6753.7	-3027	1398.7	-1532.8
2007	4194.71	-8073.6	-3878.9	1861.9	-2021.7
2008	5275.33	-10260.98	-4985.7	1820.9	-2210.96

Source: Bank of Ghana and World Bank African Development Indicators

Table 5 shows the trends and values of non-traditional exports since 1980. A major aim of the trade reforms was to diversify the export base. This implies an expansion in non-traditional exports. Apart from the 1981 figure which looks out of place, the trend is very clear. Modest improvements started in the early 1990s and there were more dramatic improvements starting from the mid-1990s.

Table 5: Proportion of Non-traditional Exports

YEAR	NTE (US$M)	Total Exports	Proportion
1980	11.4	1132.9	0.010
1981	338	978.87	0.345
1982	136.7	792.91	0.172
1983	163.8	1157.8	0.141
1984	32	535.55	0.060
1985	71.5	610.07	0.117
1986	23.8	859.67	0.028
1987	28	780.62	0.036
1988	42.4	826.31	0.051
1989	34.7	1018.5	0.034

YEAR	NTE (US$M)	Total Exports	Proportion
1990	62.3	898.8	0.069
1991	62.6	997.7	0.063
1992	68.4	986.3	0.069
1993	71.7	1050.9	0.068
1994	119.3	1237.7	0.096
1995	159.7	1431.2	0.112
1996	276.2	1570.1	0.176
1997	329.1	1489.9	0.221
1998	401.7	2090.8	0.192
1999	404.4	2005.5	0.202
2000	400.7	1936.3	0.207
2001	459.6	1867.1	0.246
2002	504.3	2015.2	0.250
2003	588.9	2562.4	0.230
2004	705.4	2704.5	0.261
2005	777.6	2802.2	0.277
2006	892.9	3726.7	0.240
2007	1164.5	4194.7	0.278
2008	1340.9	5275.3	0.254

Source: Ghana Statistical Service and Ghana Export Promotion Council

The figures show that in 2008 non-traditional exports constituted over 25 percent of exports which is quite impressive. Earlier work carried out by Jebuni *et al.*(1992) identified three trends in the data on NTEs. Firstly, there had been growth in the value of exports and the number of firms involved in the sector. Secondly, the composition had been towards processed and semi-processed products and thirdly there had been increased earnings by firms. Tables 5 and 6 indicate that these trends have largely continued into the new millennium.

Using both firm-level survey data and more general data from available statistics, Jebuni (1992) showed that the most important factor responsible for the increase in NTEs has been the real depreciation of the exchange rate. Another prominent factor identified is import availability. An important issue is the sustainability of firms' exporting activities. Only a minority of the firms could be described as producers of exports. A suggestion made in the study was the need to maintain the enabling environment to sustain the increasing number of producers for exports. This environment has been maintained and that accounts for the continuation of the trends since the study.

Table 6: Evolution of Non-Traditional Exports (figures are in current dollars)

	1988	1989	1990	1991	1992	1993	1994	1995	1996	1997	1998	1999	2000	2001
Value (Total)	42.3	34.7	62.3	62.6	68.4	71.7	119.3	159.7	276.2	329.1	401.7	404.4	400.7	459.6
Agric.	27.1	21.1	28.9	33.0	22.1	26.1	39.2	27.4	50.3	57.4	77.8	84.5	74.5	82.0
Processed	15.2	13.3	33.1	28.6	44.9	43.0	77.8	130.2	223.0	266.9	317.5	313.3	321.1	362.7
Handicrafts	0.07	0.2	0.45	0.88	1.47	2.58	2.33	2.07	2.92	4.72	6.39	6.66	5.0	14.9

	2002	2003	2004	2005	2006	2007	2008	2009
Value (Total)	504.3	588.9	705.4	776.6	892.9	1164.5	1340.9	1216
Agric.	85.7	138.1	159.9	151.9	203.4	197.3	187.6	150.9
Processed	407.2	446.6	540.4	604.8	685.0	963.4	1150.0	1063.3
Handicrafts	11.3	4.2	5.2	20.9	4.5	3.8	3.3	2.4

Source: Ghana Export Promotion Council

Table 7: Capital Account (millions of current dollars)

	1983	1985	1990	1995	2000	2001	2002	2003	2004	2005	2006	2007	2008
Capital Account	102.0	62.40	284.0	459.1	369.29	392.23	-38.62	340.36	201.57	834.49	1,053.44	2,346.91	2,666.04
Official Account	27.70	32.10	190.4	135.5	139.70	84.61	-115.18	85.77	52.45	141.14	212.64	1,168.6	486.62
Private Capital	13.40	5.80	52.8	261.2	176.80	137.31	105.66	199.91	331.98	559.29	817.84	1,061.48	2,307.20
Short-term Capital	60.90	24.50	-59.2	62.4	52.79	170.31	-29.10	54.67	-182.86	134.05	22.96	158.7	-401.64

Source: Bank of Ghana

While capital flows have increased substantially, their overall growth has been less than that of the flows experienced in merchandise trade. There has, however, been some substantial growth in private capital flows in the last few years (Table 5)

6 Conclusion

Ghana's trade policy since independence has seen a lot of changes from a regime that required a lot of government involvement using non-price instruments such as controls and restrictions to promote the policy of import substitution to one that is increasingly more market oriented and thus more outward oriented. Developments over the years indicate that clear conclusions can be drawn from the experience. Comparatively, better results were achieved with the more outward -oriented policies and these policies have been sustained over the last 25 years. Increasingly, Ghana has become more integrated into the world economy. This presents both challenges and opportunities. There is increasing competition for domestic producers, better deals for consumers and opportunities for exporters. Ghana will therefore have no choice but to position itself to get the maximum benefit from these trends.

References

Aryeetey, E. and Harrigan J. (2000) 'Macroeconomic and Sectoral Developments since 1970' in Aryeetey, Harrigan E. , J and Nissanke, M. (eds.) *Economic Reforms in Ghana,* Africa World Press.

Aryeetey, E. and Fosu, A. (2008) 'Ghana's Post-Independence Economic Growth 1960-2000' in Aryeetey, E and Kanbur, R. (eds) *The Economy of Ghana: Analytical Perspectives on Stability, Growth and Poverty* , James Currey and Woeli Publishing Services.

Dordunoo, C. (1994) *The Foreign Exchange Market and the Dutch Auction System in Ghana.* Research Paper No. 24, Nairobi: African Economic Research Consortium.

Jebuni, C.D, Oduro, A, Asante Y, Tsikata G.K (1992) *Diversifying Exports: The supply response of Non-Traditional Exports to Ghana's Economic Recovery Programme* Overseas Development Institute and University of Ghana

Jebuni C. D, Oduro, A, Tutu, K. A. ((1994) *Trade, Payments Liberalization and Economic Performance in Ghana* AERC Research Paper 27, Nairobi:African Economic Research Consortium

Killick, T. (1978) *Development Economics in Action* London: Heinemann.

Leith, J. C. (1974) *Foreign Trade Regimes and Economic Development: Ghana.* New York: National Bureau of Economic Research.

Oduro, A and Harrigan, J. (2000) "Exchange Rate Policy and the Balance of Payments 1972-96" in Aryeetey, E, Harrigan, J and Nissanke, M. (eds) *Economic Reforms in Ghana,* Trenton:Africa World Press

Osei P. (2000) "Political Liberalisation and the Implementation of Value Added Tax in Ghana.' The Journal of Modern African Studies, vol. 28, no. 2.

Sarris and Shams (1991) *Ghana under Structural Adjustment: The Impact on Agriculture and the Rural Poor* New York University Press..

Streeten P.(1973) "Trade Strategies for Development – Some Themes for the Seventies" in *World Development* 1 pp 1-10

Trends in Growth, Employment and Poverty in Ghana

Charles Ackah and William Baah–Boateng

1. Introduction

In the five decades since its independence from British rule in 1957, Ghana has gone through different cycles of growth, marked mostly by poor economic performance and military *coup d'etats* through to the 1980s. National economic policies during this period were often devoid of market principles, and characterized by frequent price and income controls. At best, the economy muddled through, with low productivity, high and volatile prices, an overvalued currency and high interest rates. In such an unfavorable investment climate, would-be investors and government officials found it more profitable to engage in rent-seeking and other corrupt behaviours, rather than growth-enhancing activities.

The return of multi-party democracy and constitutional rule in the early 1990s began an economic and political stabilization process never seen before in the post-colonial era. Together with high commodity prices (especially gold and cocoa) and a set of prudent market-oriented policies, stabilisation has boosted investor confidence and created an enabling environment for the private sector to grow. Ghanaians in the diaspora have also gained more confidence in the growth prospects of their native country, as demonstrated by large amounts of money they remit into Ghana for private investment.

Ghana's remarkable growth performance since 1984 made some analysts describe it as a frontrunner in the economic growth process (Leechor, 1994). Ghana undertook a major economic reform in the early 1980s after decades of domestic economic mismanagement and unfavourable external economic conditions which plunged the country into severe economic recession. The outcome of the reform was a strong recovery of the economy to record impressive growth for almost three decades. However, the fact that the majority of the country's workforce is engaged in vulnerable employment with a high level of informality in the labour market and over a quarter of all households are estimated to be poor, raises concern about the quality of growth. Ghana is often showcased as the economic success in Africa by the Bretton Woods, but many Ghanaians continue to show little appreciation for the country's growth achievement in view of high rates of vulnerable employment and working poverty.

Indeed, the poverty reduction impact of economic growth can be effectively realised through productive employment generation. Economic growth is a necessary rather than sufficient condition for poverty reduction if it fails to generate the needed productive jobs for the growing labour force. Many studies have pointed to the pattern of growth and the labour intensity of growth as important for effective poverty reduction[2]. But the decline in the employment elasticity of growth in Ghana in the 1990s and beyond raises concern about the quality of growth. Despite the importance of employment as the link between growth and poverty reduction, it was only in 2008 that employment targets and indicators were incorporated in the Millennium Development Goals (MDG). The focus of this chapter is to carry out a trend analysis of growth, employment and poverty over the last two decades, and assess Ghana's performance in creating productive and decent employment with the aim eradicating extreme poverty and hunger.

2. Growth and Poverty Linkage: The Role of Employment

Poverty reduction has become the most important goal of development efforts, as evidenced by many Poverty Reduction Strategy Papers (PRSPs) and the Millennium Development Goals (MDGs) set by the United Nations which include halving world poverty by 2015. Indeed, achieving this crucial goal requires either: a) the acceleration of growth; provided this does not benefit the rich disproportionately and thereby increase inequality; or b) a redistribution of income, provided that this does not retard growth simultaneously; or, more likely, c) some combination of these two strategies (Bourguinon, 2002).

A number of theoretical models provide many compelling reasons why economic growth stimulates poverty reduction. There is a very strong claim that globalization leads to faster economic growth and that the poor share (to some extent) in the benefits of growth (Jenkins, 2004). Implicitly, faster growth leads to increased incomes for the poor through some form of "trickle down" which ensures that the general benefits of growth are not typically offset by simultaneous worsening in income distribution (see Bruno, Squire and Ravallion, 1998), cited in McKay et al (2002). However, it is also possible to construct theoretical models in which the poor are actually bypassed by growth or even become increasingly marginalized (Bhagwati and Srinivasan, 2002). Thus, the issue of the impact of economic growth on poverty remains a matter of empirical testing.

Employment as a vehicle through which growth can impact on poverty has in recent times been acknowledged in many policy fora. As noted by Islam (2004), the premise of earlier theories of development that the benefits of economic growth would automatically trickle down to the poor was first questioned by many including Ademan and Moris (1973). It followed on Kuznets (1955) hypothesis of an inverted U shape of the relationship between economic growth and income

---

2   See for example World Bank, 1990; McKay, 1997; Goudie and Ladd, 1999

inequality. From the late 1980s, many studies on growth recognised the pattern of growth and labour intensity as critical for effective poverty reduction (Goudie and Ladd, 1999). Baah-Boateng (2008) identified weak integration of employment strategies in the Ghana Poverty Reduction Strategy (GPRS I) as a major flaw in the design and implementation of the medium-term strategy.

Quite clearly, there seem to be no disagreement that economic growth is a necessary condition for poverty reduction but falls short of being a sufficient condition. The source and pattern of growth that reflects the creation of productive employment and improvement in incomes of workers is critical for the realisation of effective poverty reduction. Indeed, the poverty reduction effect of growth depends on the employment outcome of growth and wage and income effect of employment which in turn depends on the kind of economic activity the poor are engaged in. The employment outcome of growth for poverty reduction does not only imply the number of jobs that could be generated from growth but, also, more importantly, the type of jobs. Growth-employment linkage at the macro level could be drawn from Okun's law[3] which suggests that any given dip in growth is accompanied by loss of jobs. According to Okun (1962), growth-employment elasticity varies between 0.35 and 0.4 and this brings to the fore, the importance of labour intensity of growth as the principal link in the growth-poverty nexus. Using cross country data, Islam (2004) demonstrates the link between poverty reduction and the employment intensity of growth, confirming earlier studies[4].

The poverty reducing effect of employment also depends on a number of factors including promotion of wage employment, increase in real wage and increase in productivity in self-employment culminating in the reduction in vulnerable employment. Higher growth recorded in many developing countries has not effectively translated into significant reduction in poverty because of the high incidence of informal employment associated with low productivity and limited expansion of wage employment. In sub-Saharan Africa, wage employment accounted for 25 percent of total employment in 2008 compared with 45 percent in East Asia, and 64 percent in Latin America and the Caribbean (ILO, 2008). In Ghana, informal sector constitutes over 80 percent of total employment with less than 20 percent engaged in wage employment in spite of the average 5 percent growth of GDP experienced since 1984.

In effect, growth-poverty nexus that emphasises employment intensity of growth measured by gross output elasticity of employment without looking out for the type of job has been questioned. Sundaram and Tendulkar (2002) contend that output growth is just one of several determinants of employment growth and that principal among them is the rate of change in the 'real' wage rate. Thus, economic growth that fails to increase wage employment and promote the expansion of productive self-employment would not be associated with effective poverty reduction.

---

3   Implies a reduction of 1 percent in unemployment raises output by 3%

4   See for example World Bank, 1990,, Squire, 1993

3. Ghana's Growth Performance

The dismal growth trend that characterised the Ghanaian economy ended in 1983 with the introduction of economic reforms supported by the Bretton Woods institutions. The country recovered strongly from low and negative growth in the late 1970s and early 1980s to record 8.6 percent in 1984. This remarkably favourable growth has continued until now with little variance. Ghana's growth performance was quite remarkable during the first six years of the reforms, with annual average growth of 5.7 percent. The decade that followed witnessed a slower growth rate with an annual average growth of about 4.4 percent between 1990 and 1999. The economy picked up again to record a 5.3 percent annual average growth rate the over the 10-year period between 2000 and 2009.

Figure 1: Ghana's Economic Growth Performance, 1980–2010

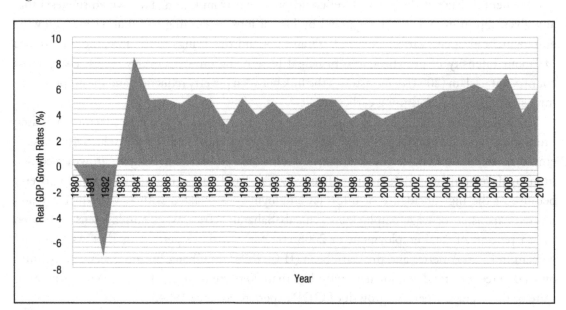

Source: *Ghana Statistical Service*

The impressive post-1983 growth rate was largely driven by the industrial sector which recorded annual average growth of 9.3 percent between 1984 and 1990. This emanated from the remarkable growth performance of the manufacturing sub-sector which was largely attributed to improved capacity utilisation on account of the minimisation of foreign exchange constraints that resulted from the foreign exchange reforms. The liberalisation of the foreign exchange market created the opportunity for industrial enterprises to easily access foreign exchange for importation of needed raw materials, spare parts and equipment for industrial production.

The worst performing sector has been agriculture with less than 3 percent growth rate during the period. The sector however picked up gradually in the second half of the 1990s but could not match the strong growth performance of services and industry. Consequently, the sector's contribution to GDP has consistently shrunk from about 41 percent in the early 1990s to 36 percent in 2010 as against an increase in the share of service from 31 percent to 36 percent The composition of industry has however remained relatively stagnant around 28 percent over the last two decades. The sector's growth performance since the beginning of the 1990s has been driven by mining and construction with the dominant manufacturing struggling to survive.

Table 1: Sectoral Growth Performance and Composition of GDP, 1985-2010 (%)

Year	Agriculture	Industry	Manufacturing	Services
1985-89	2.2 (47.1)	9.3 (26.6)	10.2 (11.2)	7.4 (26.3)
1990-94	1.1 (42.2)	4.4 (27.8)	2.7 (10.7)	4.1 (30.0)
1995-99	4.4 (40.5)	4.4 (27.8)	3.8 (10.1)	4.7 (31.7)
2000-04	4.7 (39.7)	4.2 (27.4)	4.3 (10.0)	5.0 (32.8)
2005-09	4.4 (38.1)	7.3 (27.9)	3.1 (9.0)	7.9 (34.0)
2010	4.8 (35.6)	7.0 (28.3)	4.0 (8.3)	6.1 (36.1)

Based on 1993 constant prices; original figures for 1985–1992 adjusted to 1993
Sectoral composition of GDP in parenthesis
Source: *Computed from Quarterly Digest of Statistics, GSS*

Ghana's growth pattern since the introduction of economic reform suggests little structural change as depicted in Table 1. There has been a shift from agricultural dominance to services with little change in the share of industry in GDP. Agriculture has witnessed a consistent decline in its share from about 48 percent in the second half of 1980s to 35.6 percent in 2010 against a surge in services share from 26.3 percent to 36.1 percent over the same period. Industry contribution to GDP has seen marginal improvement from 26.6 percent to 28.3 percent over the past twenty five years. Manufacturing, which has a relatively high labour absorption rate, has however seen its contribution to GDP drop from 11 percent to only 8 percent reflecting its dismal growth performance over the past two decades. Lack of consistent supply of power, high cost of credit, and competition from external sources are some of the challenges confronting manufacturing. The mining and construction subsectors have been the main drivers of industrial growth with the gradual collapse of hitherto dominant manufacturing subsector. With the discovery and commercial production of oil, the composition of national output and export earnings is expected to change. This undoubtedly has adverse implications for employment, poverty and inequality if steps are not taken to prevent potential neglect of the productive sectors of agriculture and manufacturing.

The dominance of the services sector has largely been driven by wholesale, retail, restaurants and hotels which are considered to be low-order sub-sectors. As shown in Figure 2, the share of these activities in GDP has consistently increased from 6.0 percent in 1991 to 8.8 percent in 2010 compared with less than 2 percentage-point gain in the contribution of other services to national output over the same period. This is consistent with faster growth of the trade sub-sector relative to other services. The trade sub-sector recorded an average annual growth rate of 7.4 percent as against 5.5 percent of other sub-sectors in the services sector between 1991 and 2010. The dominance of the services sector has become much more pronounced with the rebasing of national accounts from a 1993 base year to 2006. The rebasing exercise raised the share of servicesin GDP to 51.1 percent compared with 30.2 percent for agriculture and 18.6 percent for industry. The share of trade and related activities also appreciated on the new base to about 11.5 percent compared with 8.8 percent under the old series in 2010. The share of remaining sub-sectors also increased in the new series. The increasing importance of trade and related activities in the overall national economy could be linked to the external trade liberalisation that accompanied the economic reforms introduced in 1983 and the increasing incidence of globalisation.

Figure 2: Growth Rate of Trade Sector and its Share in National Output

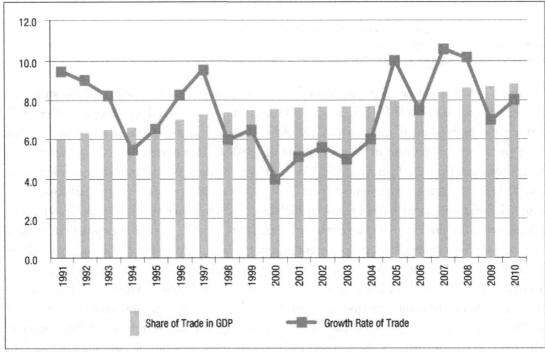

Source: *Computed by Authors*

4. Employment in Ghana

Employment is the outcome of interaction between demand and supply of labour. The supply of labour in aggregate terms is generally determined by the growth and skills of the labour force. On the one hand, labour demand is mainly influenced by the growth of the economy and on the other, source of growth. The favourable growth performance in response to economic reforms appears to have failed to translate into adequate and good quality employment growth in Ghana and this has implications for unemployment and poverty. This is largely explained by the slow growth of manufacturing and agriculture which are noted as the high labour absorption sectors. Indeed, mining, finance and telecommunication considered to be the driving force behind the favourable economic growth of recent times, are estimated to have low labour absorption capacity.

Generally, over the past 25 years employment growth has not kept pace with economic growth and this is reflected in a consistent decline in employment elasticity of growth from 0.64 in 1992-96 to 0.4 in 2004-08 (ILO, 2008). Indeed, a 4.8 percent annual average economic growth between 1984 and 2000 could only translate into 2.0 percent annual average employment growth compared with over 2.5 percent annual average expansion of the labour force and 3.2 percent annual average growth of the adult population (Table 2). In effect, the Ghanaian economy's ability to create jobs during this period suffered, with a drastic drop in employment-to-population from about four-fifths to about two-thirds. Consequently, unemployment rates rose from 2.3 percent to 10.1 percent over the period.

Table 2: **Annual Average Growth of Employment and Labour Force (%)**

Year	Employment	Labour force	Adult Population 15 years +
1960-70	2.04	5.25	1.99
1970-84	4.00	1.48	2.88
1984-00	1.99	2.51	3.15
1991-99	3.94	3.90	3.80
1999-06	2.69	1.99	4.07

Source: *Computed by Authors from Population Censuses and GLSS*

The 1990s, however, saw an improvement in the labour absorption rate, with strong annual employment growth of 3.9 percent against 4.6 percent annual average GDP growth between 1991 and 1999. This was reflected in a marginal surge in the employment-to-population ratio from 73.2 percent to 73.9 percent during the period indicating an improvement in the economy's employment generation ability. The improved job creation effort could not be sustained beyond the 1990s as the employment-to-population ratio dropped again by 7 percentage points between 1999 and 2006. In effect, annual GDP growth of 5percent was able to create annual employment growth of only 2.7 percent.

Agriculture remains the main source of employment for the growing workforce in Ghana even though its share in total employment has shrunk by 8 percentage points between 1984 and 2000. During the same period the contribution of industry and services increased by 2.5 and 5.5 percentage points respectively. Between 1991 and 2006, agriculture lost 7 percentage points of its employment share in favour of industry and services which gained 5.5 and 1.5 percentage points respectively. The declining share of agriculture in employment in favour of industry and services has not been as drastic as the drop in the contribution of agriculture to GDP. Indeed, agriculture remains the main source of livelihood for Ghanaian workers, accounting for about 55 percent of total employment in 2006 compared with 31 percent in services and 14 percent in industry. Manufacturing remains the key source of industrial sector employment, accounting for over 80 percent of total industrial sector employment or 11percent of total employment despite its poor performance in terms of national output.

Table 3: Employment Trend, 1991 - 2006

Indicators	1984	1991/92	1998/99	2000	2005/06
Employment 15+ (in millions)	5.42	5.74	7.59	7.43	9.14
Employment by Economic Sector (%)					
Agriculture	61.1	62.2	55.7	53.1	54.9
Industry	12.9	10.0	11.7	15.5	14.2
Manufacturing	0.9	8.2	8.3	10.7	11.4
Service	25.0	27.8	32.6	31.5	30.9
Trade	14.6	15.3	15.4	17.3	18.0
Employment Type/Status (%)					
Wage Employment	16.2	16.6	14.2	15.8	17.5
Self-employed	69.7	81.6	67.7	73.5	59.5
Other	14.1	1.8	18.1	10.7	20.4

Source: *Computed by Authors from GLSS*

Within the services sector, trade and related activities accounted for over half of employment or 18 percent of total employment in 2006. Employment in trade and related activities has improved considerably since 1984, as reflected in the consistent growth of the sector's share in total employment. As reported in Table 3, the contribution of trade and related activities to total employment increased from 14.6 percent in 1984 to 17.3 percent in 2000 based on population census. Using the Ghana Living Standards Survey (GLSS) dataset, the share of trade in total employment rose from 15.3 percent in 1991/92 to 18.0 percent in 2005/06. Generally, trade employment is dominated by own account work or self-employment. For instance, in 2005/06, own account work constituted for almost three quarters of total employment in trade and related activities (see Figure 3). Wage employment constituted about 13 percent while 5 percent comprised of employers or self-employed with employees.

Figure 3: Distribution of Trade Employment by Status (%), 2006

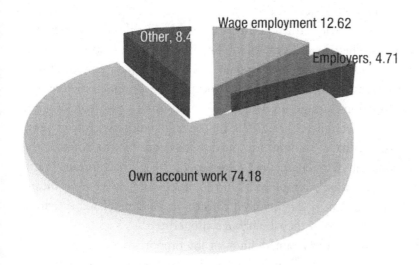

Source: *Computed from GLSS5, Ghana Statistical Service*

Generally, overall wage employment has remained consistently low since 1984, accounting for less than one fifth of total employment. The proportion of wage employment declined marginally by 0.4 percentage point between 1984 and 2000 but improved from 16.6 percent to 17.5 percent between 1991 and 2006. Self-employment is considered to be a vulnerable type of employment and constitutes the major employment type. In 2006, about 60 percent of Ghanaian adult workers were self-employed with over half of them engaged in agriculture (see Table 3). Only 8 percent of self-employed people have employees with over 90 percent engaged as own account workers with very low earnings. In effect, the impressive growth performance in Ghana has not translated into the generation of gainful and decent employment which comes from the formal sector. The reduction in public sector employment through retrenchment and privatisation coupled with slow growth of the private sector could be blamed for the lower proportion of wage employment.

Employment and the MDGs

On the basis of the recognition that decent and productive work for all is central to addressing poverty and hunger, a new target and four new indicators were added to the Millennium Development Goals (MDGs) in 2008. The new target MDG1b is to "achieve full and productive employment and decent work for all including women and young people". The four indicators used in monitoring the employment target are; growth rate of labour productivity;, employment-to-population ratio, working poverty rate; and vulnerable employment rate. The other employment indicator relates to gender empowerment and is measured by the share of women in wage employment in the non-agricultural sector.

The rate of growth of productivity provides the basis for assessing the likelihood of a country's economic environment creating productive and decent employment that will help in reducing poverty and hunger. It is measured by the annual change in GDP per person employed of a country. Indeed, productivity increases often influence the social and economic environment positively, leading to poverty reduction through investment, sectoral shifts, trade, technological progress and increases in social protection (ILO, 2009). The second indicator, employment-to-population ratio, measures the ability of a country to provide jobs and it is measured as the proportion of a country's working-age population that is employed. A high ratio means that a large proportion of a country's population is employed. On the other hand, a low ratio means that a large proportion of the population is not involved directly in market-related activities, because they are either unemployed or out of the labour force altogether.

The third indicator is the working poverty rate, defined as the proportion of working poor in total employment. It provides a measure of quality of employment and poverty reduction implications of job creation. It is measured by the number of employed persons living in a household with incomes below the poverty line as a percentage of total employment. The rate is an indication of the lack of decent work i.e. whether a person's work is decent and productive enough to earn sufficient income to move him/her and household members out of poverty. The fourth indicator is the vulnerable employment rate and it measures the proportion of employed people working in precarious circumstances as indicated by the employment status. It is computed as the proportion of own-account and contributing family workers in total employment and gives an indication of quality of employment in the country.

Ghana's performance in the MDGs in the area of employment has largely been disappointing. The increased growth of labour productivity between 1991 and 2006 has not translated into the creation of decent and productive employment as measured by a reduction in the number of vulnerable jobs and working poor. As reported in Table 4, annual growth of labour productivity fell from 1.3 percent in 1991/92 to 0.5 percent in 1998/99, culminating in a decline in the country's ability to create jobs as measured by a drop in the employment-to-population ratio over the period. Consequently, the vulnerable employment rate rose marginally by 0.1 percentage point before dropping by 5 percentage points by 2005/06. At the same time, the working poverty rate surprisingly declined by 9 percentage points to 35 percent with the extreme working poverty rate dropping by about 6 percentage points.

Table 4: MDG Employment Indicators

Indicator	1991/92	1998/99	2005/06
Growth of Labour Productivity	1.34	0.48	3.75
Employment-to-population ratio	71.7	61.4	67.3
Vulnerable employment rate	82.8	82.9	77.4
Working poverty rate	44.1	35.1	25.6
Extreme working poverty rate	30.3	23.6	16.1
Share of women in non-agriculture wage employment	30.2	27.3	26.1

Source: *Computed by Authors from Ghana Living Standards Survey 3,4&5*

The country's progress towards the achievement of MDG1b was confirmed between 1998 and 2006 with a consistent rise in the growth of labour productivity, reaching almost 4 percent in 2005/06. Employment-to-population ratio also went up by about 6 percentage points while vulnerable employment rate dropped from about 83 percent to 77 percent, indicating some improvement in the creation of productive and decent employment. Nonetheless, the vulnerable employment rate remains high and this can be explained by the limited availability of formal sector employment and large number of uneducated workers. Baah-Boateng and Sparreboom (2011) estimate that about a third of employed adults have not had any formal education. The proportion of employed adults in households living below the upper poverty line further declined by 10 percentage points to 25.6 percent while those under lower poverty lines dropped from 23.6 percent to 16.1 percent over the period. The share of women in wage employment has however witnessed consistent decline from 30 percent in 1991/92 to 27 percent in 1998/99 and further down to 26 percent in 2005/06. This is against the backdrop of the improved educational attainment of women over the years (Baah-Boateng, 2009). This implies that there may be other obstacles to women's access to wage employment in Ghana.

5. Pattern of Poverty in Ghana

Ghana is one of the few countries in sub-Saharan Africa that has been able to almost halve poverty within a period of 15 years. The country witnessed a remarkable reduction in national poverty incidence from 51.7 percent in 1991/92 to 39.5 percent in 1998/99 and further down to 28.5 percent in 2005/06 (see Figure 4). At the same time, the incidence of extreme poverty consistently dropped by about 10 percentage points from 36.5 percent between 1991/92 and 1998/99 and further down to 18.2 percent in 2005/06. Poverty in Ghana is fundamentally a rural phenomenon with about 39.2 percent of rural households estimated to be poor in 2005/06 compared with 10.8 percent of households in urban areas. Within rural areas poverty is said to be most endemic in the rural savannah and lowest in rural coastal areas. Poverty incidence in rural Ghana declined substantially by 14 percentage points in the 1990s as against a decline of about 10 percentage points between 1998/99 and 2005/06 to 39 percent.

Figure 4: Poverty Incidence by Locality, 1991 – 2006 (%)

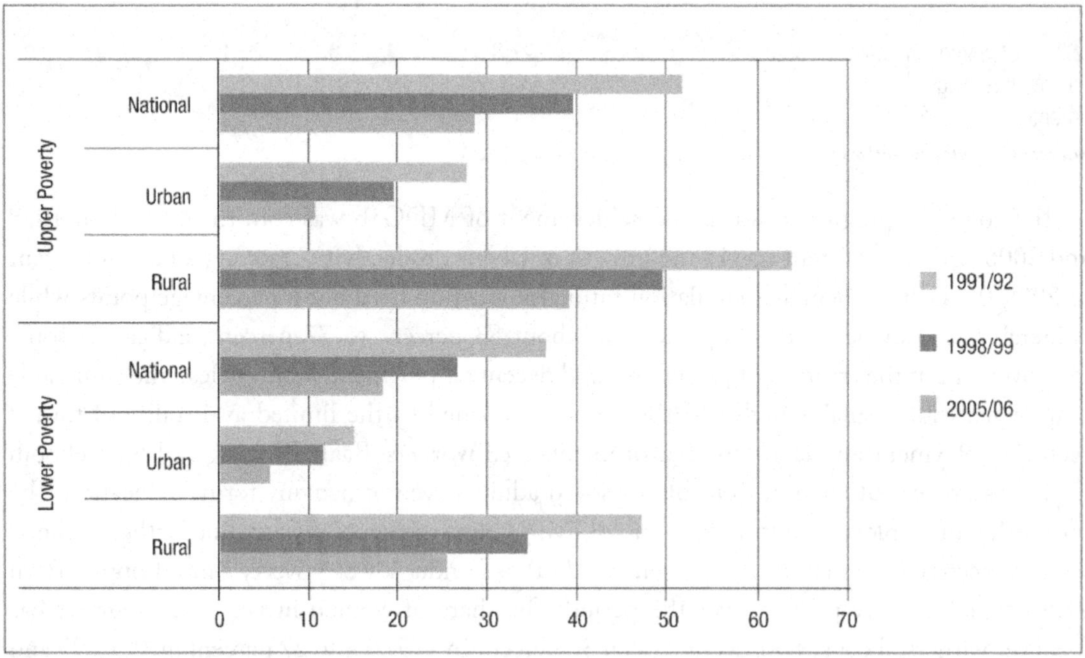

Source: *Ghana Statistical Service (2007)*

Poverty in urban areas is observed to be relatively low and was estimated at 10.8 percent in 2005/06. The urban coastal area, excluding Accra, has the lowest poverty incidence while urban savannah has the highest poverty incidence in urban areas. Surprisingly, Accra, which is generally noted to have had the lowest poverty incidence in the 1990s, saw poverty incidence surge between 1998/99 and 2005/06. Urban poverty has seen consistent decline since 1991/92 with only the urban forest recording declining poverty in line with the overall urban poverty trend. Poverty incidence in the urban coastal and urban savannah areas surged in the 1990s before dropping afterwards.

Incidence of Poverty by Economic Activity

One important dimension of the incidence of poverty is the main economic activity in which the household is engaged. Poverty incidence in Ghana used to be highest among food crop and export farmers confirming the general assertion that poverty is a rural phenomenon. In 2005/06, about 46percent of food crop farmers and 24percent of export farmers were found to be living below the upper poverty line. Poverty incidence is also estimated to be high among non-farm self-employed. Unsurprisingly, the lowest poverty incidence is reported among formal sector employees where higher income opportunities exist with low-risk vulnerability in employment. The incidence of poverty has consistently declined in all economic activities since 1991 with workers in the formal sector and export farmers experiencing the most drastic decline. This culminated in a consistent decline in the contribution of the formal sector and export farming to national poverty between 1991 and 2006. The decline in poverty incidence is however moderate among food crop farmers and this accounted for a surge of the contribution of this economic activity to national poverty by over 11 percentage points over the 15 years.

The drastic decline in poverty incidence among formal sector workers, particularly, those in the public sector, could be linked to the government's social policy of protecting workers at the lower echelon of the job ladder through a minimum wage. Although, the minimum wage determined by the National Tripartite Committee (NTC) had no legal backing until the passage of the Labour Act in 2003, (Act 651), formal sector workers have nonetheless benefited from the implicit government policy of keeping the minimum wage above the poverty threshold. In contrast, workers in the informal economy, particularly food crop farmers and non-farm self-employed, hardly benefit from minimum wage provisions.

Table 5: Poverty Incidence by Economic Activity, 1991-2006 based on Upper Poverty Line (370.8 Ghana cedis).

Economic Activity	Incidence			Contribution to Poverty		
	1991/92	1998/99	2005/06	1991/92	1998/99	2005/06
Public Sector Employment	34.7	22.7	7.8	9.1	6.2	1.9
Private Formal Employment	30.3	11.3	10.1	2.3	1.4	2.5
Private Informal Employment	38.6	25.2	17.1	2.3	1.9	4.0
Export Farming	64.0	38.7	24.0	7.8	6.9	6.2
Food Crop Farming	68.1	59.4	45.5	57.3	58.1	68.5
Non-Farm Self-employment	38.4	28.6	17.0	20.5	24.5	15.6
Non-working	18.8	20.4	13.3	0.7	1.1	1.3
Trade and related activities*	29.7	19.6	10.6	9.3	8.3	7.5

* Computed at the individual level by Authors
Source: Ghana Statistical Service (2007)

The substantial decline in poverty incidence among export farmers is also linked to the technical support and other export promotion packages the government continues to provide . (Baah-Boateng, 2008). Over the years, farmers in the cocoa sector have benefited from guaranteed prices and other forms of support such as cocoa mass spraying and these have created stable and increased income among farmers in this sector. On the other hand, no such comparable schemes are available for food crop farmers, making them more likely to continue with low productivity and low incomes.

Poverty among workers in the trade sector is estimated to be relatively low and declining over a period of 15 years. This is due to more jobs created in the sector and its contribution to economic growth. The sector witnessed a decline in poverty incidence of about 10 percentage points in the 1990s and about a 9 percentage point decline subsequently between 1998/99 and 2005/06. As a result, the contribution of the sector to national poverty also dropped from 9.3 percent to 7.5 percent between 1991 and 2006.

Poverty-Reducing Impact of Growth

The issue of pro-poor growth is quite critical in analysing the quality of growth. Ravallion and Chen (2003) define pro-poor growth as growth that reduces poverty. There is a strong link between overall economic growth and the speed of poverty reduction and greater poverty reduction arises when policies facilitate the participation of the poor in growth (World Bank, 2005). The extent to which the poor in Ghana have benefited from the remarkable growth performance of the economy depends on how pro-poor growth is perceived and measured. The Ghana Statistical Service (2007) used the growth incidence curve[5] to assess whether Ghana's growth has been pro-poor and it concluded that Ghana's growth over the 15-year period from 1991 has not been pro-poor if pro-poor growth is seen as that which is faster for the poor than richer households. However, if pro-poor growth is seen as that which raises the welfare levels of all households measured per percentile, then Ghana has indeed experienced pro-poor growth. In a nutshell, the drastic decline in national poverty incidence by about 23.2 percentage points over the 15-year period suggests that to a considerable extent the poor have benefited from the impressive growth performance of the economy.

6. Conclusion

Ghana's growth performance since the introduction of economic reforms in 1983 has been quite remarkable but the structure of the economy still remains fragile, with the gradual collapse of productive employment-friendly manufacturing and stagnant agriculture. The start of oil production in commercial quantities is expected to facilitate the acceleration of growth but may worsen the plight of agriculture and manufacturing if steps are not taken to halt the apparent continuity of policy neglect. The favourable growth performance has failed to translate into the generation of quality employment. The labour market is still dominated by agriculture and vulnerable employment, with about a quarter of employed people estimated to be working poor. The disconnect between growth and employment is explained by the favourable growth of low labour absorption sectors of mining, telecommunications and finance while employment-friendly sectors such as agriculture and manufacturing continue to struggle. Nonetheless, the Ghanaian economy has recorded a consistent decline in poverty incidence since 1991, with formal sector workers and export farmers being the greatest beneficiaries. Poverty remains endemic among food crop farmers who continue to face exclusion from minimum wage policies and government support schemes for farmers. In all, Ghana appears to have experienced pro-poor growth if the phenomenon is taken to mean growth that inures to the benefit of all households.

---

5   This approach is credited to Ravallion (2004)

References

Adelman, I., and C.T. Morris (1973) "Economic Growth and Social Equity in Developing Countries", Stanford University Press, Stanford

Aryeetey E and Fosu K A (2002), "Economic Growth in Ghana: 1960-2000", AERC Growth Project.

Baah-Boateng W and Sparreboom Theo (2011) "Ghana: MDG Employment Indicators" Sparreboom (ed.) Towards Decent Work: Monitoring MDG1B employment Indicators in Sun-Saharan Africa, published by ILO, Geneva Switzerland, forthcoming

Baah-Boateng W. (2009) "Gender Perspective of Labour Market Discrimination in Ghana" *Unpublished PhD Thesis*, Department of Economics, University of Ghana

Baah-Boateng, W. (2008) "Employment Generation for Poverty Alleviation", in Amoako-Tuffour and Bartholomew Armah (ed.) "Poverty Reduction Strategies in Action: Perspectives and Lessons from Ghana", Lexington Books Lanham MD USA.

Bhagwati, J. and. Srinivasan, T.N. (2002), "Trade and Poverty", American Economic Review Papers and Proceedings, vol. 92, no. 2, pp. 180-183.

Bourguignon, François (2002), "The Distributional Effects of Growth: Case Studies vs. Cross-Country Regressions, Working Paper No 2002 -233, Delta, Paris.

Ghana Statistical Service (2007) "Pattern and Trends of Poverty in Ghana 1991-2006", Ghana Statistical Service, Accra

Goudie, A., and Paul Ladd (1999): "Economic Growth, Poverty and Inequality". *Journal of International Development*, Vol. 11

Goudie, A., and Paul Ladd (1999): "Economic Growth, Poverty and Inequality". *Journal of International Development*, Vol. 11

ILO (2009) "Guide to the new Millennium Development Goals Employment Indicators", International Labour Office, Geneva

ILO (2008) "Key Indicators of the Labour Market, International Labour Organisation", International Labour Office, Geneva

Islam R. (2004), "The Nexus of Economic Growth, Employment and Poverty Reduction: An Empirical Analysis" International Labour Office, Geneva, January

Kuznets, S. (1955): "Economic Growth and Income Inequality". American Economic Review, Vol. *45*

Leechor C., (1994) "Fragile Still: The Structure of Ghana's Economy 1960-94" in Husain and Rashid Faruque (Eds.) Adjustment in Africa: Lessons from Case Studies, Washington D.C World Bank

Lipton, M. and M. Ravallion (1995): "Poverty and Policy", in Handbook of Development Economics, Vol. IIIB. North-Holland, Amsterdam

McKay, Andrew (1997): "Poverty Reduction through Economic Growth: Some Issues". Journal of International Development, Vol. 9, No. 4.

McKay A.; Winters L. Alan, and Kedir A. M. (2000) "A review of empirical evidence on trade, trade policy and poverty", report prepared for the Department of International Development, London, July, 2000.

Ravallion, M (2004) "Pro-poor Growth: A Primer", Policy Research Working Paper No. 3242, The World Bank

Ravallion M and Shaohua Chen (2003) "Measuring Pro-Poor Growth" Economic Letters, 78 (1), 93-99

Squire, L (1993): "Fighting Poverty". American Economic Review, May 1993 (Papers and Proceedings of the Hundred and Fifth Annual Meeting of the American Economic Association

Sundaram, K. and S.D. Tendulkar (2002): "The Working Poor in India: Employment-Poverty Linkages and Employment Policy Options". Issues in Employment and Poverty Discussion Paper 4, ILO, Geneva

World Bank (2005) "Pro-Poor Growth in the 1990s: Lessons and Insights from 14 Countries", The World Bank

World Bank (1990): World Development Report: Poverty, Oxford University Press, New York.

Wage and Employment Effects of Trade Liberalization: The Case of Ghanaian Manufacturing

Charles Ackah, Ernest Aryeetey and Kwadwo Opoku

1. Introduction

The persistence of poverty in many developing countries, especially in sub-Saharan Africa, in the face of increased globalisation and rapid trade liberalization over the past three decades has inspired a serious controversy on the impact of globalisation, in general, and trade liberalisation, in particular, as well as on economic growth and poverty. Proponents of liberalization argue, on the basis of the Stolper-Samuelson theorem of international trade theory, that the poor (unskilled labourers) will be the chief beneficiaries of trade liberalisation in developing countries. The standard argument is that trade liberalisation would lead to a reallocation of resources to areas of comparative advantage, typically towards the production of labour-intensive goods. Thus, depending on the structure of the prevailing labour market, the resulting increase in demand for labour should classically translate into some combination of an increase in employment and/or wages. In other words, since developing countries are more likely to have a comparative advantage in producing unskilled labour-intensive goods, one would expect trade reforms in these countries to be inherently pro-poor (see Krueger 1983; Srinivasan and Bhagwati 2002; Bhagwati 2004; Harrison 2005).

While the logic of this argument is fairly compelling and generally supported by the experiences of the newly industrialized economies of East Asia[6], the experience of many developing countries, particularly in SSA, has been disappointing and in many cases, poverty has increased following trade liberalisation (see Easterly, 2001). Not surprisingly, labour market consequences of trade liberalisation still remain controversial. The evidence so far shows that trade creates or expands some activities and destroys or diminishes others. For developing countries, it is widely feared that trade implies increasing job losses and downward pressure on wages, often resulting in demands for protection. In recent times, the interest in the labour market response of trade liberalisation in developing countries has been intense, particularly due to the extensive trade reforms implemented in a large number of these countries since the early 1980s and the increasing trend of regional and multilateral free trade agreements in which developing countries are involved.

While a vast literature exists that studies the labour market outcomes of trade liberalisation, it appears most of the papers are focused on Latin America, with very little empirical evidence produced in Africa so far. In Latin America, while there is no consensus yet, the message

---

6   There is still some debate over the extent to which East Asian countries actually 'opened up' their economies (i.e. some sectors are said to have been protected during the so-called period of liberalization).

that emerges from the majority of papers suggests that tariff liberalisation has increased the economy-wide wage and created disparity in labour earnings between skilled and unskilled workers.[7] In the case of Africa in general, and Ghana in particular, despite the general concerns expressed by many, relatively little empirical evidence has been produced on the matter. Indeed, in Ghana, the debate over the internal distributional consequences and labour market outcomes of trade reforms has heightened in the policy community, particularly as Ghana pursues regional economic integration in ECOWAS, which is expected to implement a Common External Tariff (CET) among member countries, and as the country becomes a signatory to the Economic Partnership Agreement (EPA) with the European Union. The underlying anxieties appear to be anchored on purely anecdotal evidence of the apparently dismal performance of the Ghanaian manufacturing sector coinciding with the period of liberalization, and certainly not informed by empirical work on the labour market outcomes of the reforms in Ghana.

This chapter aims to improve our understanding of the labour market impact of trade policy reforms in Ghana and in particular, if the outcome has been pro-poor. By so doing, it is our hope that we can make some contribution to the existing empirical evidence on the matter of trade liberalization and labour market outcomes in developing countries. Indeed, Ghana lends itself as a valuable case study, as it is regarded by many as 'adjustment's star pupil' (Alderman, 1994). To preview our results, we find strong evidence that the growth of employment in the manufacturing sector in Ghana was significantly negatively impacted by the trade policy reforms of the 1990s and early 2000s, as high job losses were found in sectors with the largest tariff cuts. The evidence suggests that trade protection creates more employment for he unskilled labour than skilled labour in the manufacturing sector. Moreover, we find that trade liberalization in the manufacturing sector led to a fall in the average wage paid by manufacturing firms in Ghana, suggesting that workers employed in industries that were more exposed to liberalization experienced lower wages. We also find that greater openness is likely to be associated with significantly lower wages in firms which employ workers with low levels of education (the unskilled) contrary to the predictions of Heckscher-Ohlin and Stolper-Samuelson theory, suggesting high trade protection that shields manufacturing firms from outside competition protects the wages of unskilled workers.

Furthermore, the study confirms that the impacts of trade liberalization on the wage bill of manufacturing firms significantly depend on the export status of firms. We discover that, following trade liberalization, workers in export firms found in low tariff sectors enjoy relatively higher wages than those in low-tariff-non-exporting firms. Thus, for firms with similar characteristics in a given sector (and thus facing similar tariffs) but with different export status (exporters and

---

7   For a review of the recent empirical findings on trade and wage inequality in developing countries, see Goldberg and Pavcnik (2004); Attanasio *et al.* (2004); Hanson and Harrison (1999); Galiani and Sanguinetti (2003); and on trade and employment, see Hoekman and Winters (2005).

non-exporters), a tariff reduction in that sector will have different effects on their respective workers wage bill. Workers in export firms stand to lose less than workers employed in non-exporting firms.

The remainder of the chapter is organized as follows. In Section 2, we provide a brief background on trade reforms and labour market developments in Ghana. Section 3 presents the theoretical and empirical literature related to trade reforms and labour market outcomes. Section 4 describes the empirical methodology and the data used in the econometric estimations. In Section 5, we present and discuss the econometric results. Finally, Section 6 concludes the chapter by briefly outlining some general policy implications deriving from the empirical findings.

2. Trade policy reforms and labour market developments in Ghana

In this section, we provide a brief historical overview of trade policy reforms as well as developments in the Ghanaian labour market over the last three decades when the economy was liberalised and opened to external economies.

Trade policy reforms

Ghana was one of the first countries in SSA to initiate a programme of economic stabilisation and market reform under the banner of the Economic Recovery Programme (ERP) it was launched in 1983 and supervised by the IMF and the World Bank, to rectify the economic imbalances and distortions that contributed to the stagnation and decline of the economy in the 1970s and early 1980s. As discussed in Aryeetey *et al.* (2000), the main focus of Ghana's economic reforms has been in the area of trade and exchange rate liberalisation.

Like the vast majority of SSA countries, Ghana has had restrictive and distortionary trade policies from independence until the 1980s (at least), typically motivated by some desire to protect domestic producers. Following independence from British colonial rule in 1957, Ghana embarked on a process of import-substituting industrialization for the next two decades. The economy had been characterized by a quantity-controlled and fixed exchange rate regime subject to infrequent devaluations, and controlled import quantities through foreign exchange allocations. The fixed exchange rate regime was characterized by a highly overvalued official exchange rate, an active parallel market in foreign exchange, capital controls and allocation of foreign exchange based on import licenses.

Ghana has undertaken a significant and discernible trade liberalisation, one that has been associated with substantial structural adjustment to the economy. Over the course of the early 1980s and throughout the 1990s, Ghana has liberalized its trade regime quite substantially, though the liberalization process has been gradual and uneven. External trade policy has evolved from a regime of controls to a liberal one with emphasis on export diversification. With the inception of the ERP, the new trade policy has the long-term objective of replacing the quantitative restrictions with price instruments and the liberalization of trade in an environment of more liberal, market-oriented and outward-oriented policies. Trade reforms under the ERP included tariff adjustments, import liberalization, liberalization of foreign exchange, deregulation of domestic market prices and controls and institutional reforms that particularly affected revenue-generating bodies such as the Customs, Excise and Preventive Service (CEPS). Conscious efforts were made to dismantle the import licensing regime via reductions in the number of products listed under the banned or restricted category.

Ghana was already open by the early 1990s, and has become continuously more open since then. The stabilisation and adjustment policies were generally maintained in the 1990s. The state continued to undertake extensive economic reforms and trade policies aimed at transforming the economy from a largely state-controlled one to a market economy in the 1990s. In the 1990s, extensive reforms aimed at reversing previous inward-looking policies were pursued. This included major structural reforms in both the real and financial sectors of the economy, and trade and investment liberalization has been an integral part of them. Trade reforms in the 1990s included specific export promotion measures aimed at improving the relative incentives to producers of exportables. These policies were pursued with the aim of creating an enabling environment for the achievement of middle-income status by the year 2020 underlined in Ghana's Vision 2020 development strategy. The growing openness of the economy, has resulted in both imports and exports increasing as a proportion of GDP, but with the latter consistently exceeding the former, and to an increasing extent over time.

Tariffs remain Ghana's main trade policy instrument after elimination of quota and other quantitative restrictions during the implementation of the ERP. By the end of the 1990s, the tariff rate had been notably cut, the tariff structure had been considerably simplified and few non-tariff-barriers were applied. By January 2000, Ghana's tariff structure showed an average rate of 13 percent having reduced from a high rate of 17 percent in 1992. However, the special import tax rate of 20 percent which was imposed on some 7 percent of tariff lines raised the tariff on many consumer goods to 40 percent - well above the previous rate of 25 percent. This policy action defeated the aim of the trade policy reform, which had been undertaken since the structural adjustment programme, to rationalize the incentive system and improve the competitiveness of the domestic manufacturing sector. Thus, by the end of 2000, Ghana had a relatively simple tariff structure, comprising four bands; 0 percent, 5 percent, 10 percent and 20 percent. The average applied tariff was 14.7 percent, having increased from 13 percent in January 2000, with sectoral averages of 20.2 percent and 13.8 percent on agriculture and manufacturing respectively (WTO Trade Policy Review, 2001). In an effort to bring Ghana's tariff structure into harmony with ECOWAS and WTO provisions, the 20 percent special import tax imposed on selected "non-essential" imports in 2000 was eliminated in 2002.

Labour market developments

The labour market in Ghana has experienced dramatic changes over the past three decades due to globalisation and the economic reform programme that led to the reduction in the direct role of government in the productive economic activities (Baah-Boateng and Turkson, 2005). One of the most interesting issues that have come out of Ghana's reform efforts of the last three decades has been the rather slow growth of formal employment. This has often been linked to the slow growth in investment and the absence of employment- generating investment. In fact, in the public sector, which forms a major part of the formal sector, the redeployment exercise introduced in 1987 as part of the ERP and Structural Adjustment Programme (SAP) contributed substantially to the loss of public sector employment between 1985 and 1991.

Although Ghana has been categorized as a relatively successful adjuster, trade liberalization has had a negative impact on the manufacturing sector. Manufacturing value-added did rise rapidly after 1983, when imported inputs were made available to industries that were suffering from substantial excess capacity. However, as liberalization spread to other imports and excess capacity was used up, the exposure to world competition led to a steady deceleration of manufacturing growth. For instance the rate of growth of manufacturing value added fell from 5.1 per cent in 1988 to 1.1 per cent in 1992. Indeed, between 1981 and 2001, manufacturing value added per capita grew annually by less than 0.9 per cent, from US\$37 to US\$44 (ISSER, 2004). Employment in manufacturing declined from a peak of about 78,000 in 1987 to 28,000 in 1993. Indeed, between 1992 and 2003, the proportion of the working population aged 15 years and above that was employed declined from 8.2 per cent to 6.4 per cent.

The performance of the manufacturing subsector can be viewed as consisting of two periods: the import substitution industrialization era soon after independence (1960-1982); and the era of the structural adjustment and economic recovery programme (1983-2000).

Import Substitution Industrialization/Pre-ERP Era (1960-1982)

Under an import substitution industrialisation (ISI) strategy, the manufacturing sector between the early 1960s and the early 1970s saw tremendous changes with the state taking an important and growing role in the process. An aspect of the nationalism of the early post-independence period was the perception that Ghana had an opportunity to chart its own path to development. An integral part of the development agenda was the Import Substitution Industrialization (ISI) strategy that was then being practiced in Latin America.

The expectation was that ISI would facilitate the transformation of the Ghanaian economic structure from a predominantly agricultural economy to a modern industrialized economy. The share of industry in GDP was expected to rise, generate opportunities for employment, and raise levels of productivity and incomes as well as the standard of living of the majority of the population. By restructuring the predominantly primary structure of production to a value -added structure of production, the industrial sector, especially manufacturing, was expected to create a more diversified export sector in which exports of manufactured products would play an increasingly important role in external trade.

The logic behind the ISI strategy was to seek economic independence through the domestic production of imported goods as well as to improve the deteriorating terms of trade that characterized trade between African countries and the rest of the world. The expectation of the Ghanaian government just after independence was that in broad terms, the ISI strategy was going to ensure structural transformation and export diversification. In line with the ISI strategy, massive capital investments were undertaken by the government. The rationale was to provide sufficient investment in order to get Ghana on a high growth path and to break the political and economic concentration of power in the hands of foreigners.

Thus, with the view that industrialization was a key factor in modernization and development, industrial strategy over the period 1960 to 1982 was characterized by (i) strong emphasis on import substitution through high levels of effective protection, (ii) reliance on administrative controls rather than market mechanisms to determine incentives and resource allocation and (iii) reliance on large-scale public sector investment as the leading edge in industrial development.

The emphasis of policy on these areas was due to the belief that the country wanted to reduce economic dependence and that if market mechanisms were allowed to determine prices and allocate resources, they would not meet the objectives of national development. Thus high levels of protection were given to manufacturers of import substitutes. The protection took the form of high tariff and quantitative restrictions on imported products. By the late 1960s effective protection for nearly half of the manufacturing industries in the country had exceeded 100 percent (Asante and Addo, 1997).

The manufacturing sector responded positively to these policy initiatives by recording some significant gains until the late 1970s and early 1980s when the performance of the sector started experiencing economic downturn. The import substitution and direct control policies stimulated rapid growth of manufacturing output and employment with an annual average output growth of 13 percent and annual average employment growth of 8 percent (Asante and Addo 1997). In 1977, the manufacturing sub-sectors contribution to GDP had increased to 14 percent. The increasing role of the state in industrial development saw state-owned manufacturing enterprises and joint public/private firms accounting for about 49 percent of value-added in manufacturing with private firms accounting for the remaining 51 percent.

With respect to capacity utilization, though evidence from estimates obtained by the Ghana Statistical Service on medium and large manufacturing establishments indicates that average capacity utilization which stood at 52 percent in 1971 had declined to around 40 percent between 1972 and 1978, some individual product groups such as textiles, garments, non-metallic minerals, and pharmaceuticals had significantly better performances than others.

However, between 1978 and 1982, the manufacturing sub-sector experienced a significant decline in output and contribution to overall industrial sector and GDP growth. Total manufacturing output as a percentage of GDP declined continuously from its peak of about 14percent in 1977 to 7.4 percent in 1982. The manufacturing sector growth rate declined at an annual average rate of -2.5 percent over this period. Between 1981 and 1982 alone, manufacturing output declined by about 32.1 percent.

Table 1: Share of Industry and Manufacturing in GDP 1970 to 1983(%)

Subsector	1970	1971	1972	1973	1974	1975	1976
Industry	19.3	18.6	17.2	19.9	18.6	21.0	21.2
Manufacturing	12.7	11.3	10.5	12.7	11.2	13.9	13.8
	1977	1978	1979	1980	1981	1982	1983
Industry	21.5	18.4	15.1	14.8	15.2	12.6	11.3
Manufacturing	13.9	12.4	10.7	10.5	10.9	7.4	6.9

Source: Quarterly Digest of Statistics, GSS

An unfavourable international economic environment, a distorted domestic incentive and policy framework as well as mismanagement were the main factors that contributed to the abysmal performance of the manufacturing sector in the 1970s and early 1980s. The global recession that was experienced during that period resulted in terms of trade shocks that created balance of payments problems for the economy. This resulted in the non-availability of foreign exchange required to import the needed inputs (i.e. raw materials, equipment, spare parts, etc.) for efficient and effective utilization of the installed capacity of many import-substitution industries. This was so because the structure of production under the ISI strategy was heavily dependent on imported raw materials and spare parts. What Ghana failed to do was to produce the capital goods that were necessary to support the import substitution industries. For instance, between 1977 and 1982, the average contribution of capital goods to manufacturing was only 3 percent as against the average percentage contribution of 46.3 percent by consumer goods. By 1983 the share of capital goods in manufacturing had declined to 0.9 percent.

At the same time, an increasingly overvalued cedi (resulting from price and distributive controls) and import restrictions discouraged efforts at export promotion by providing massive protection to import-substitution industries. The price and distributive controls which favored trade and discouraged agricultural production undermined the support that the agricultural sector was offering to the resource-based processing of manufactured exports. For instance, there was a drastic decline in the production of rubber, sugar, tobacco, etc. as a result of production rigidities (poor transportation infrastructure and shortages of inputs) within the agricultural sector.

The Era of Structural Adjustment and the Economic Recovery Programme (1983-2000)

The reform effort in Ghana which begun in 1983 sought to arrest and reverse the economic turmoil of the mid-1970s and early 1980s. The reform effort, which focused on stabilization and liberalization was principally aimed at introducing a market-based economy and at promoting the private sector as the "engine" of sustained economic growth by removing all forms of protection and minimizing the involvement of the state in the allocation of resources.

Industrial strategy over this period shifted from an import-substitution and over-protected strategy to an outward-oriented and less protected or liberalized strategy. The liberalized strategy emphasized two main areas: first, the development of a more internationally competitive industrial sector with an emphasis on local resource-based industries with the capacity for increased exports and efficient import substitution, and secondly, the introduction of measures that would attract entrepreneurs and investors, into all major sub-sectors with special emphasis on the development of appropriate technologies in small- and medium-scale manufacturing industries (Asante and Addo, 1997).

In order to achieve these two broad industrial goals, the ERP had specific objectives for the industrial sector. These were to increase production of manufactured goods through greater use of existing capacity; to remove production bottlenecks in efficient industries through selective rehabilitation; to encourage the development of local resources to feed industries and promote the development of agro-based and other resource-based industries; to strengthen existing institutions providing assistance to the industrial sector; and to develop economically viable linkages among local industries and between key economic sectors (Asante and Addo, 1997).

Among the most significant and successful measures adopted were exchange rate liberalization, fiscal discipline and restructuring of the tax and tariff system, tightening of monetary policy, foreign trade and financial sector reforms, privatization of state-owned enterprises, investment expansion, price deregulation, and labour market reforms.

The manufacturing sector initially responded positively to the various policy measures adopted under the reforms after several years of continuous decline. Indeed, one of the initial benefits of liberalization that accrued to Ghana's manufacturing sector was the improved utilization of installed capacity. This was a direct result of foreign exchange reforms that were pursued as part of the adjustment process. Exchange rate liberalization in Ghana initially eased foreign exchange pressures that had built up the early 1960s to the late 1970s. The reduced pressure made available and accessible the foreign exchange required to import the needed inputs (i.e. raw materials, equipment, spare parts, etc.) for efficient and effective utilization of the installed capacity of many import substitution industries.

As a result of increased imports of machinery, raw materials, as well as essential spare parts and the replacement of obsolete machinery and plants, capacity utilization increased steadily from 18 percent in 1984 to about 40 percent in 1989 and 46 percent in 1993 even though by 1987 production from the manufacturing sector was still 35 percent and 26 percent lower than in 1975 and 1980 respectively. Before this remarkable improvement, the sub-sector's capacity utilization had declined continuously from 40 percent in 1978 to 18 percent in 1984. Some sub-sectors, mainly the local resource-based manufacturing firms showed remarkable increases in capacity utilization of over 50 percent, with tobacco and beverages recording 76.3 percent, metals 80 percent, wood processing 65 percent, non-metallic minerals 72.8 percent and food processing 52.3 percent, On the other hand, other manufacturing industries such as textiles, garments and electrical products which depended heavily on imported inputs did not perform well because of stiff competition from imports.

In terms of output, the manufacturing sector during the early years of reforms responded positively by growing at an annual average rate of 14.5 percent between 1984 and 1987 while contribution to GDP averaged 8.5 percent over the same period. This was against the background of growth of -36.2 percent and -11.2 percent recorded in 1982 and 1983 respectively. In 1988, the growth rate of the industrial sector and the manufacturing sub-sector started slowing down. The strong correlation in growth rates (Figure 1) can be explained by the fact that industrial growth under ERP was manufacture-led. For instance, between 1988 and 1995, annual industrial and manufacturing growth declined to 4.4 percent and 2.6 percent respectively from the 12.2 percent and 14.5 percent recorded between 1984 and 1987. The manufacturing subsector's dominance in the industrial sector continued as its share in real industrial output stood at 65.2 percent over the period 1984-87, lower than the average for the decade preceding the ERP but higher than the average for the period 1988-2000. The decline in the rate of growth of both the industrial sector and the manufacturing sub-sector was due to the pace of trade, exchange rate and financial sector liberalization and the fact that new investment in the industrial sector went to the non-manufacturing sectors such as mining and electricity.

In the late 1990s, the performance of the manufacturing sub-sector was mixed, with an annual average growth rate of 4.5 percent from 1995 to 2000. While in some years the growth rate increased, in other years it declined. For instance, in 1996, the manufacturing sub-sector grew by 4.7 percent and this increased to 6.4 percent the following year. However, it fell to 3.2 percent in 1998 and then increased to 4.9 percent in 1999 and then to 3.8 percent in 2000. During the latter part of the 1990s, the decline in the manufacturing sub-sector's growth rate was attributed to the increase in crude oil prices, high domestic interest rates, significant depreciation in the value of the cedi and the domestic energy crisis that hit the economy in 1998. In addition, manufacturing industries in the textile and garments sub-sectors experienced substantial declines in output as a result of the intense competition that they were exposed to from cheaper imports.

Figure 1: Growth in industrial and manufacturing sub-sector, 1983-2000 (%)

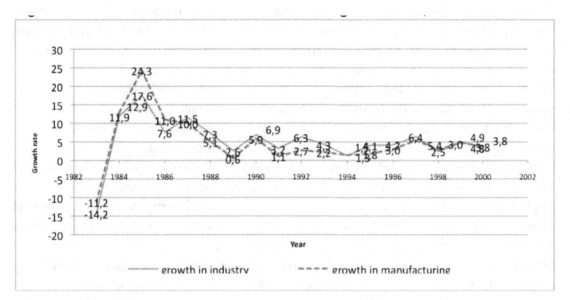

Source: Quarterly Digest of Statistics, GSS

3. Literature review

The literature on the labour market effects of trade liberalization has been dominated by the Heckscher-Ohlin model and its extensions. The standard argument with regard to trade and poverty is based on the Stolper-Samuelson theorem, which suggests that international trade will lead to a rise in the relative returns of the abundant factor;- unskilled labour in the case of developing countries. Thus, according to this theory, the poor (unskilled labour) will be the largest beneficiaries of trade liberalisation. In other words, we would expect trade reforms in developing countries to be inherently pro-poor, since these countries are more likely to have a comparative advantage in producing goods which use unskilled labour relatively more intensively[8]. The claim is that specialization within developing countries in the production of labour-intensive products will lead to an increase in employment in the labour-intensive sector. Also, as this sector utilizes, for the most part, unskilled labour, the relative demand for unskilled workers should increase, and therefore, the wage gap between unskilled and skilled workers should decrease. In other words, wage inequality should decline.

---

8   For an empirical example, see Hertel *et al.* (2003) who estimate that global trade liberalization leads in the long run (i.e. when labour and capital are mobile across sectors) to a decline in poverty for all strata of the population largely because of increased demand for unskilled labour.

Recently, these sharp predictions of the Stolper-Samuelson theorem have been challenged. According to the new theories, trade liberalization could reduce the wages of unskilled labour even in a labour abundant country, thereby widening the gap between the rich and the poor. Many observers find the Stolper-Samuelson theorem quite restrictive, in that the theorem does not offer definitive conclusions if one or more assumptions are relaxed (see Davis, 1996). Davis and Mishra (2004 cited in Harrison, 2005), argue that the popular expectation that trade openness should increase the incomes of the poor in low-income countries is based on a very narrow interpretation of the standard Heckscher-Ohlin model. Davis and Mishra show that in a world of many factors and many goods, a poor country might no longer have a comparative advantage in producing unskilled-labour intensive goods. Similarly, if a poor country has large supplies of non-labour factors of production (land or mineral resources), trade liberalization may not benefit the labour-intensive sectors. The empirical literature has shown that the predictions of the traditional trade models do not hold for developing countries. For example, liberalization may promote exports but also induce import substitution of goods produced in the previously protected sectors, increasing unemployment and informal labour. Moreover, in many developing countries, there is evidence of a rise in wage inequality following trade liberalization.

The specific sector and the Ricardo-Viner models have become the natural alternative to the Heckscher–Ohlin model and the associated Stolper–Samuelson theorem. According to these models, workers may gain from trade reforms depending on which sectors (import-competing or exporting) they are attached to. The models focus on the short- to medium-run and assume imperfect factor mobility, with one factor mobile across sectors while the other is taken to be sector-specific. With these assumptions, the models predict a positive association between protection and returns to factors of production (e.g. wages). Protection reduces imports, and reduced imports increase labour demand, which in turn increases wages. When the price of a good falls following trade liberalization, the model predicts that the factor specific to the sector that experienced price reduction loses, while the other specific factor gains in real terms. In other words, if trade liberalization occurred, workers affiliated to the industries that experience large tariff reductions would see a decline in their wages relative to the economy-wide average wage, while workers attached to relatively protected industries would gain, relatively.

Edwards (1998), investigates labour market adjustment to trade liberalization for a small, two-factor (capital (K) and labour (L) economy that produces three goods (exportables (X), importables (M) and non-tradeables (N)), in the context of a specific-factors model. This specific factor model typically allows for short-run capital-specificity (i.e. the capital is immobile between sectors in the short run), labour mobility between sectors and inelastic aggregate factor supply (Mussa, 1978). Production functions of these commodities are assumed to have conventional properties with the following ranking of factor intensities; $(K/L)_M > (K/L)_N < (K/L)_X$. The model further assumes incomplete specialisation and fixed supplies of inputs. The model is used to investigate the adjustment of employment and wages to trade liberalisaton in both the short run and the long run. The main findings of Edwards are summarised in Table 2.

Table 2: Sectoral Employment and Wage Changes Following Trade Liberalisation

	Short-run	Long-run
Employment Change		
Exportables	↑	↑
Importables	↓	↓
Non-tradeables	?	?
Wage Change		
Exportables	↓	↑
Importables	↓	↑
Non-tradeables	↓	↑

Source: Adapted from Milner and Wright (1998:511) Table 1.
Note: ↑ and ↓ denotes increase and decrease respectively with ? denoting ambiguity. Wages are defined in relative terms, i.e. relative to the numeraire, the price of non-tradeables.

Long-run effects

In this model of a small economy with three goods operating in a freely liberalised environment, the long -run effects of the fall in the relative price of importables following liberalization are in line with those predicted by the Stolper-Samuelson theorem. Thus, if exportables are relatively labour-intensive, tariff reduction increases demand for the economy's abundant factor, driving wages higher (and the return to capital lower). With respect to adjustment of employment in the tradeables sector, the within-tradeables shift in production and employment is unambiguously towards exportables and away from importables, given the rise in the relative price of exportables. Thus, in the long run the model, just like the Heckscher-Ohlin model, predicts employment to increase in the labour-intensive exportable sector. For the non-tradeable sector, while trade liberalisation unambiguously increases wages of workers as determined by export prices, its effect on employment is, however, ambiguously determined. On the one hand, production of non-tradeables can be expected to be higher, given the assumed pattern of factor intensities as demand grows (due to switching from tradeables and any positive income effects of tariff reduction) but on the other hand, production of non-tradeables (as is the case in all sectors) will be more capital-intensive following the rise in wages.

Short-run

In the short run, given the sector specificity of capital, the direct link between the price of tradeables and factor rewards is broken. Hence, prices of non-tradeables will be determined by both demand and supply factors. If capital is immobile across sectors as assumed in this model, a reduction of the price of importables resulting from trade liberalisation generates changes in the price of non-tradeables, which depends on the pattern of substitution and on the extent of income effect. Thus, if non-tradeables are a gross substitute in consumption and production with tradeables, and the substitution effect of a tariff change dominates the income effect, then the price of non-tradeables will fall relative to exportables but will rise relative to that of importables following liberalisation. Hence, the output and employment implications of these adjustments is that employment will increase in the exportables sectors, while their adjustments in the non-tradeables sector are ambiguous as they depend on the pattern of substitution between tradeables and non-tradeables. In the importable sector, however, the fall in the relative price of importables combined with capital specificity reduces production, labour intensity and employment.

4. Empirical methodology

In this study, we use regression techniques to examine the impact of trade liberalisation or increased trade on employment in the manufacturing sector of Ghana. Following Milner and Wright (1998), we adopt a fairly simple static profit-maximizing model of firm behaviour and assume a Cobb-Douglas production function of the form:

$$Q_i = A^\gamma K_i^\alpha L_i^\beta \qquad (1)$$

where:

Q = real output

K = capital stock

L = units of labour utilised

A = total factor productivity

and where α and β represent the factor share coefficients, γ allows for factors changing the efficiency of the production process. A profit-maximising firm will employ labour and capital at such levels that the marginal revenue product of labour equals the wage (w) and the marginal revenue product of capital equals the user cost (c). Solving this system simultaneously to eliminate capital from the expression for firm output allows us to obtain the following expression:

$$Q_i = A^\gamma \left(\frac{\alpha L_i}{\beta} \cdot \frac{w}{c} \right)^\alpha L_i^\beta \qquad (2)$$

Taking logarithms and rearranging equation (2) allows us to derive the firm's derived demand for labour as:

$$\ln L_i = \theta_0 + \theta_1 \ln\left(\frac{w}{c}\right) + \theta_2 \ln Q_i \qquad (3)$$

where:

$$\theta_0 = -(\gamma \ln A + \alpha \ln \alpha - \alpha \ln \beta)/(\alpha + \beta)$$
$$\theta_1 = -\alpha/(\alpha + \beta)$$
$$\theta_2 = 1/(\alpha + \beta).$$

Our main goal is to estimate the effects of trade liberalization on firm-level employment and wages, while controlling for other sources of variation in employment and wages across firms. The estimating equations with the introduction of our measure of trade policy (tariff) are as following:[9]

$$\ln L_{ijt} = \theta_1 \ln W_{ijt} + \theta_2 \ln Q_{ijt} + \theta_3 \ln T_{jt} + \theta_4 X_{ijt} + \tau_t + \lambda_j + \delta_{ij} + \varepsilon_{ijt} \qquad (4)$$

$$\ln W_{ijt} = \beta_1 \ln L_{ijt} + \beta_2 \ln Q_{ijt} + \beta_3 \ln T_{jt} + \beta_4 X_{ijt} + \beta_5 \ln W_{ijt-1} + \tau_t + \lambda_j + \delta_{ij} + \varepsilon_{ijt} \qquad (5)$$

where:

L_{ijt} = total employment in firm i in sector j during time t,

W_{ijt} = average real wage in firm i in sector j during time t,

Q_{ijt} = real output in firm i in sector j during time t,

T_{jt} = tariff in sector j during time t,

X_{ijt} = other exogenous variables,

τ_t = time effect common to all firms,

λ_j = sector-level fixed effect,

δ_j = firm-level fixed effect,

ε_{ijt} = unobserved error term.

Data Description

In this subsection we describe the data and the main features of the variables that are relevant for the subsequent econometric analysis. The data for this study were drawn from two main sources. That is a dataset that combines micro-level data on firms and worker characteristics in the manufacturing sector with data on import tariffs obtained from the UN COMTRADE database. The World Bank Regional Project on Enterprise Development (RPED) survey is a

---

9   Following Milner and Wright (1998), we assume perfect capital markets. By this assumption, the user cost of capital can only vary over time, so that in estimation its variation can be captured by time dummies.

comprehensive panel dataset from surveys of the Ghanaian manufacturing sector conducted in seven rounds between 1991 and 2002. The data was collected by a team from the Centre for the Study of African Economies (CSAE), University of Oxford, University of Ghana, Legon, and the Ghana Statistical Service. The first sample of firms was drawn randomly from the Census of Manufacturing Activities conducted in 1987. The firms were categorized based on sector and location. They were also categorized by location: Accra, Cape Coast, Kumasi and Takoradi, all of which constitute major industrial centres in Ghana. The coverage of this dataset is quite extensive as most of the major manufacturing sub-sectors at the time under investigation are represented. When firms exited from the sample, they were replaced with firms of the same size category, sector, and location, so that approximately (but not exactly) 200 firms were sampled in each year. The dataset has the advantage of containing a large number of firms over a long period of time and information on many firm characteristics. We have a panel of nine (3-digit ISIC level of aggregation) manufacturing industries for the 10 years from 1993 to 2002. We use data on *ad-valorem* import tariffs to measure changes in Ghanaian trade policy. We construct a database of annual tariff data for 1993 to 2002 to calculate average sector-level tariffs.

Since we have information both cross-sectionally and through time, the modelling of employment and wages adopts panel estimation techniques. To obtain consistent estimates, equations (4) and (5) are differenced so as to eliminate the fixed effects, and dynamic labour demand and wage equations are implemented. The one used in this chapter is the Generalized Method of Moments (GMM) technique proposed by Arellano and Bond (1991). This estimator relies on first-differencing to eliminate unobserved individual-specific effects, and then uses lagged values of endogenous or predetermined variables as instruments for subsequent first-differences. However, eliminating the fixed effects introduces a correlation between the lagged dependent variable and the new error term. To address the endogeneity problem, Arellano and Bond recommend using the lagged values of the explanatory variables in levels as instruments under the assumptions that there is no serial correlation in the error term ε_{it} and the right-hand side variables. Thus, the GMM estimation procedure simultaneously addresses the problems of correlation and endogeneity. The consistency of the GMM estimator depends on the validity of the assumption that the error term does not exhibit serial correlation and on the validity of the instruments. By construction, the test for the null hypothesis of no first-order serial correlation should be rejected under the identifying assumption that the error is not serially correlated; but the test for the null hypothesis of no second-order serial correlation, should not be rejected. We use two diagnostic tests proposed by Arellano and Bond (1991) and Blundell and Bond (1998), the Sargan test of over-identifying restrictions, and whether the differenced residuals are second-order serially correlated.

Table 3: Composition of the Sample

Sector	Number of Firms	Percent
Bakery	240	8.4
Garment	550	19.2
Textile	100	3.5
Wood	230	8.0
Furniture	540	18.9
Metal	540	18.9
Machine	90	3.1
Chemicals	170	5.9
Food	400	14.0
Location of firms		
Accra	1,680	58.7
Kumasi	880	30.8
Takoradi	180	6.3
Cape Coast	120	4.2
Total	2,860	100

Source: Authors' calculation from RPED data

Table 4: Summary Statistics

Variable	1993 Mean	Standard Dev.	2002 Mean	Standard Dev.
Real Monthly Wages	2.29	1.63	3.61	1.95
Firm Age	15.27	11.38	24.44	11.81
Exports	0.13	0.33	0.19	0.39
Employment	50.54	88.66	65.39	155.81
Real Output	21,295	78,230	31,677	107,905
Foreign Direct Investment	0.17	0.37	0.17	0.37
Education of Workers	10.15	2.37	9.38	2.79
Age of Workers	29.55	7.09	35.83	7.83
Tenure of Firm Workers	4.71	3.27	11.06	4.63
Tariff	19.0%	0.04	17.0%	0.03

Source: Authors' calculation from RPED data

5. Estimation results

Trade and Employment

The estimated employment equations are given in Table 5. The estimated coefficients are generally highly significant, fairly reasonable, and are in line with theoretical predictions. Increases in a firm's output increase the demand for labour, whereas increases in average wage rates cause a fall in employment, *ceteris paribus*. It may also be seen that employment exhibits strong persistence as the growth of a firm's employment depends significantly on its lagged value. The implication of the estimated coefficient is that firms that pay higher wages employ few workers. Specifically, a 10 percent increase in the wage rate is estimated to be associated with employment growth of 0.86 percent. It can also be observed from the estimated coefficient of the lag of employment that employment exhibits persistence as the change of employment depends significantly on its lagged value. Turning to the effects of trade liberalization, the results of the regression found in columns 2 and 3 of Table 5 indicate that protection has a significant positive effect on employment.[10] Thus, trade protection is found to protect jobs in the manufacturing sector in Ghana. This finding is evidence that trade liberalization or greater import penetration, *ceteris paribus*, will lower the level of labour demand in manufacturing. Specifically, the results suggest that a 10 percentage point decrease in tariffs reduces labour demand by 0.3 percentage points. The results therefore suggest that trade liberalization, by exposing manufacturing firms to external competition, may have had adverse effects on manufacturing employment in Ghana. This might be interpreted as evidence of a disciplinary effect, with greater competition from imports inducing greater efficiency and reducing labour demand. Following the Edward model, these findings suggest that either the adverse employment effect of trade liberalization in the import-competing sector far exceeds the favourable employment effect in the exportable sector or trade liberalization has harmful employment effects on both importable and exportable sectors.

---

10   We treat tariffs as endogenous in all regressions and use tariffs dated $t-2$ as instruments.

Table 5: Trade Policy and Manufacturing Employment: Dynamic Regressions (GMM)

DEPENDENT VARIABLE IS THE LOGARITHM OF EMPLOYMENT			
Variables	1	2	3
$\Delta \ln Employment_{t-1}$	0.875***	0.869***	0.868***
	(0.0106)	(0.0092)	(0.0076)
$\Delta \ln Wages$	-0.086***	-0.086***	-0.088***
	(0.0107)	(0.0088)	(0.0067)
$\Delta \ln Wages_{t-1}$	0.082***	0.084***	0.086***
	(0.0093)	(0.0082)	(0.0065)
$\Delta \ln Wages_{t-2}$	-0.021***	-0.021***	-0.022***
	(0.0047)	(0.0043)	(0.0040)
$\Delta \ln Output$	0.045***	0.042***	0.046***
	(0.0070)	(0.0065)	(0.0058)
$\Delta \ln Output_{t-1}$	0.025***	0.033***	0.019***
	(0.0072)	(0.0055)	(0.0047)
$\Delta \ln Tariff$		0.031***	0.040***
		(0.0087)	(0.0096)
Foreign -owned firm			0.025
			(0.0118)
Exporting firm			0.102***
			(0.0093)
Sector dummy	Yes	Yes	Yes
Year dummy	Yes	Yes	Yes
Constant	-0.727***	-0.755***	-0.562***
	(0.072)	(0.063)	(0.0661)
Sargan test (p-value)	0.36	0.40	0.40
Second order	0.241	0.245	0.190
Observations	1051	1051	1025
Number of firms	194	194	187

Note: Standard errors in parentheses, *, **, and *** denote significant at 10%; 5%; and 1% respectively.

Trade and Wages

Four specifications are examined. The first specification estimates a standard wage equation, modelling the effects of employment and output on wages. The remaining specifications investigate the effects of introducing tariffs and other explanatory variables directly into our wage equation. In specifications 3 and 4, the trade variable is interacted with the average level of education of workers and export dummy to show the differential effects of trade liberalization on workers characterized by different levels of education and belonging to firms of different export orientations.

The results of all the regressions indicate a positive and significant impact of trade liberalization on workers' wages at the firm level. The positive and significant relationship between tariff and wages is observed to be robust to different specifications, despite the differences in the magnitude of the estimated tariff coefficients. According to these results, a reduction (rise) in tariff is associated with a decrease (increase) in the real hourly wage of workers, implying that trade liberalization (protection) is bad (good) for workers in the manufacturing sector. In other words, wages would be lower for workers who were previously employed in protected sectors which were subsequently exposed to import competition during the era of trade liberalization in Ghana. The finding seems to suggest that tariffs may protect wages of workers employed in relatively protected manufacturing sectors.

In model 3 in column 3, we present the estimates of the differential impact of the trade reforms on skilled or education level of workers. Thus, tariff is interacted with the skill level in order to examine how the effect of trade liberalization on workers may vary by education. The interaction term is meant to capture the non-linearity in the impact of trade policy on wages, in order to ascertain whether the impact of greater openness is borne disproportionately by different skill groups. The significant coefficient of the interaction term indicates the existence of such [skill] contingency relationships between trade liberalization and wages, suggesting contingency bias results of the models discussed previously.

Table 6: Trade Liberalization and Firm Wage: Dynamic Regressions (GMM)

DEPENDENT VARIABLE IS THE LOGARITHM OF REAL WAGE				
EXPLANATORY VARIABLES	1	2	3	4
$\Delta \ln Wages_{t-1}$	0.679***	0.675***	0.574***	0.573***
	(0.0052)	(0.0044)	(0.0046)	(0.0049)
$\Delta \ln Employment$	-0.145***	-0.149***	-0.0777***	-0.0890***
	(0.0269)	(0.0254)	(0.0232)	(0.0236)
$\Delta \ln Employment_{t-1}$	0.195***	0.202***	0.112***	0.120***

DEPENDENT VARIABLE IS THE LOGARITHM OF REAL WAGE				
EXPLANATORY VARIABLES	**1**	**2**	**3**	**4**
	(0.0256)	(0.0225)	(0.0225)	(0.0217)
$\Delta \ln Employment_{t-2}$	-0.0249***	-0.0247***	-0.0670***	-0.0669***
	(0.0087)	(0.0084)	(0.0091)	(0.0083)
$\Delta \ln Output$	-0.0501***	-0.0097	-0.0196*	-0.0032
	(0.0134)	(0.0106)	(0.0101)	(0.0095)
$\Delta \ln Output_{t-1}$	0.0890***	0.0528***	0.0372***	0.0176*
	(0.0059)	(0.0047)	(0.0094)	(0.0096)
$\Delta \ln Tariff$		0.105***	0.384***	0.095***
		(0.0146)	(0.0910)	(0.0156)
$\Delta \ln Tariff * Skill$			-0.158***	
			(0.0384)	
$\Delta \ln Tariff * Exporter$				-0.108***
				(0.0309)
Average education of workers			0.0135*	0.0501***
			(0.0081)	(0.0025)
Average age of workers			0.0282***	0.0262***
			(0.0017)	(0.0015)
Average tenure of workers			0.0059**	0.0093***
			(0.0026)	(0.0023)
Foreign-owned firm			0.0216	0.0333
			(0.0233)	(0.0231)
Exporting firm			0.0207	-0.163***
			(0.0156)	(0.0625)
Sector dummies	Yes	Yes	Yes	Yes
Year dummies	Yes	Yes	Yes	Yes
Constant	0.900***	1.023***	0.840***	0.701***
	(0.133)	(0.128)	(0.149)	(0.137)
Sargan test (p-value)	0.51	0.60	0.35	0.49
Second order	0.019	0.020	0.045	0.035

DEPENDENT VARIABLE IS THE LOGARITHM OF REAL WAGE				
EXPLANATORY VARIABLES	1	2	3	4
Observations	1074	1074	1050	1070
Number of firms	200	200	199	200

Note: Standard errors in parentheses, *, **, and *** denote significant at 10%; 5%, and 1% respectively.

This result implies that, *ceteris paribus*, trade liberalization would disproportionately reduce the earnings of unskilled workers in the manufacturing sector in Ghana. Skilled workers, on the other hand, lose less, following trade liberalization. We can therefore infer that unskilled workers in highly protected sectors enjoy relatively higher wages than they otherwise would. Hence, trade liberalization will worsen their plight disproportionately, increasing the skill wage gap and inequality, contrary to the predictions of the Heckscher-Ohlin and Stolper-Samuelson.

Finally in column 4, we investigate the effects of introducing an interaction between tariff and the export status of a firm to allow wage responses to vary between workers employed in exporting and non-exporting firms. We are assuming that the wage responses to trade liberalization may depend on the mode of globalization of the firm in which a worker is employed (see Amiti and Davis, 2008). The coefficient on the interactive term gives the differential effect between exporters and other firms. The results of this estimation, reported in the last column of Table 5, indicate a positive and statistically significant coefficient on tariff, suggesting that, in general, a cut in tariffs reduces wages. In effect, it shows that trade liberalization reduces the average wage bill of the manufacturing industry. The coefficient on the interactive term is negative and statistically significant, suggesting that greater openness is likely to be associated with significantly higher wages to workers employed in exporting firms. This means that workers in export firms found in low-tariff sectors enjoy relatively high wages than those in low-tariff non-exporting firms.

Hence, further trade liberalization will increase their wages disproportionately, *ceteris paribus*. A decline in tariffs reduces the wages of workers at firms that sell only in the domestic market, but raises the wages of workers at firms that export. The net effect of trade liberalization on workers employed in exporting firms also reinforces the relative beneficial effect of trade liberalization. The negative result of the sum of the two coefficients implies that trade liberalization first benefits workers in exporting firms relative to those employed in non-exporting firms (indicated by the negative sign of the interactive term), and finally enhances their overall wages. In other words, while a positive wage effect of trade liberalization is ascertained for workers in exporting firms, workers in non-exporting firms experience lower wages when trade is liberalized in Ghana. Thus, for firms with similar characteristics in a given sector (and thus facing similar tariffs) but with different export status (exporters and non-exporters), a tariff reduction in that sector will have different effects on their respective wage bill. While workers in exporting firms stand to gain from trade liberalization, workers employed in non-exporting firms suffer in terms of decline in wages.

We find interesting results on other control variables which are deemed important for firm wage determination, hence the need to discuss their effect on manufacturing wages in Ghana as shown in models 3 and 4 in Table 3. Persistence of wage determination as indicated by the significance of the lag of real wage suggests that previous wage levels affect current wage determination in Ghana. Education is found to be positively correlated with manufacturing wages, implying that firms which hire workers with high-level education tend to pay high wages. Age of workers tends to affect the wage that firms pay to these employees. Firms with relatively old employees pay high wages. Firm internationalization (foreign ownership and exporting) is found to be good for manufacturing workers in Ghana-firms which participate in international market by exporting and those with foreign ownership are found to pay high wages to their employees.

6. Conclusion and policy implications

While economic theory has long advocated openness to trade as an important element of sound economic policy, empirical evidence of the actual effects of trade liberalisation on the labour market, in general, and employment in particular, has been difficult to measure. Recently, discussions of the effects of regional integration and arguments for a more liberalized trade regime in developing countries and the effects on wages, employment and poverty have rekindled the debate.

This chapter seeks to test empirically a model of employment response to trade liberalization using data from Ghana 1993-2002, a period in which the country's market, and thus the environment faced by firms, underwent different episodes of tariff changes and trade reforms. A dataset of about 2,860 firms-- roughly 285 firms for each year covered by the survey – is used to estimate the firm employment effect of trade policy after controlling for differences in sector, regional and worker characteristics. The modified Edwards specific-factor model of labour response utilized in this chapter predicts that there may be differentials between firms that employ skilled and unskilled. In order to determine these differential responses, we estimated dynamic models of employment and wages using panel data estimation technique with skill level and tariff interaction in addition to tariff as explanatory variables.

Our results indicated that increased competition from foreign firms led to a fall in employment in the manufacturing industry in Ghana. In other words, while firms in sectors with high tariff semployed many workers, firms operating in lower tariff sectors employed few workers. Thus, while trade protection, by shielding local firms against foreign competitors, is able to create more jobs, trade liberalization significantly decreases employment and job creation. One implication is that opening up to trade by dismantling tariffs may increase unemployment in the manufacturing sector in Ghana. Thus, the Economic Partnership Agreement that is seeking about 90 percent dismantling of tariff may adversely affect output and employment in the already relatively small manufacturing sector in Ghana. Moreover, though trade liberalization hurts workers employment opportunities, we observe that unskilled workers suffer disproportionately. We find that a fall in trade protection decreased growth of employment creation in firms that employed relatively unskilled labour when compared to firms that employed skilled workers thus opposing the prediction of the Heckscher-Ohlin theory, which posits an employment expanding effect of trade liberalization for unskilled workers in a developing country. Also, the evidence that tariff reductions, and for that matter, trade liberalization, have adverse effects on both wages and employment implies that, if competition is good, then the rent accrued from tariff dismantling is only enjoyed by capital owners of manufacturing firms but not transferred for workers' benefit.

This study used firm-level data and tariff data to investigate the effect of trade liberalization on wages paid by firms to their employees. The study specifically examined the effects of trade policy on wages in Ghanaian manufacturing over 10 years using data sets that combined micro firm-level and average employee characteristics with data on tariffs. It is one of the first direct microeconomic studies of the relationship between trade policy and workers' welfare. Industry average tariffs for nine industries in the tradeable goods sector were calculated and matched to the firm-level data from 1993 to 2002. We examined whether trade liberalization has wage differential impacts on the level of workers' education as well as the export status of the firm.

Our major finding is that there is enough evidence that trade liberalization has a negative and significant impact on manufacturing workers' wages at the firm level, implying that manufacturing workers benefited from trade protection in Ghana. Thus, workers in manufacturing firms get their share of the rent accrued to the manufacturing sector from being shielded from external competitors. Hence, we find that greater openness has decreased manufacturing wages, as predicted by the Stolper-Samuelson theorem. We also find that greater openness is likely to be associated with significantly lower wages in firms which employ workers with low levels of education (the unskilled).

We also find that trade liberalization worsened the wages paid to unskilled workers in manufacturing firms, disproportionately contrary to the predictions of Heckscher-Ohlin and Stolper-Samuelson theory, suggesting that high trade protection that shields manufacturing firms from outside competition protects the wages of unskilled workers. Furthermore, the study confirmed that the impacts of trade liberalization on the wage bill of manufacturing firms significantly depend on the export status of firms. It was discovered that following trade liberalization, workers in export firms found in low tariff sectors enjoy relatively high wages than those in low-tariff non-exporting firms. Thus, for firms with similar characteristics in a given sector (facing similar tariffs) but with different export status (exporters and non-exporters), a tariff reduction in that sector will have different effects on their respective wage bill. Workers in export firms stand to lose less than workers employed in non-exporting firms.

References

Alderman, H. (1994), "Ghana: Adjustment's Star Pupil?" in Sahn (ed.), *Adjusting to Economic Failure* in *African Economies*, Ithaca and London: Cornell University Press.

Amiti, Mary and Davis, D. R. (2008), "Trade, Firms, and Wages: Theory and Evidence", NBER Working Paper 14106.

Arrelano, M., and S. Bond (1991), "Some tests of specification in panel data: Monte Carlo Evidence and application to employment equations." *Review of Economic Studies* 58: 277-297.

Aryeetey, E., Harrigan, J. and Nissanke, M. (eds.) (2000), Economic Reforms in Ghana: The Miracle and the Mirage, Oxford: James Currey and Woeli Publishers.

Asante, Y and Addo, S.E (1997): "Industrial Development: Policies and Options" in *Policies and Options for Ghanaian Economic Development* ed. Nyanteng, V.K. Institute of Statistical, Social and Economic Research, University of Ghana, Legon.

Attanasio, O., Goldberg, P.K. and Pavcnik, N. (2004), "Trade Reforms and Wage Inequality in Colombia", *Journal of Development Economics*, vol. 74, no 2, pp. 331-366.

Baah-Boateng, W. and Turkson, F.B. 2005: "'Employment", in Aryeetey, E. (ed.): *Globalisation, Employment and Poverty Reduction: A Case Study of Ghana*, Accra: ISSER. pp. 104-139.

Bhagwati, J. (2004), *In Defense of Globalization*, Oxford University Press.

Bhagwati, J. and. Srinivasan, T.N. (2002), "Trade and Poverty", *American Economic Review* Papers and Proceedings, vol. 92, no. 2, pp. 180-183.

Blundell. R, and S. Bond (1998), "Initial conditions and moments restrictions in dynamic panel data models", *Journal of Econometrics* 87: 115-143

Davis, Don and Prachi Mishra (2004), "Stolper-Samuelson is Dead and Other Crimes of Both Theory and Data", in Ann Harrison, ed., *Globalization and Poverty*, University of Chicago Press for NBER.

Easterly, William (2001), T*he Elusive Quest for Growth*, Cambridge: MIT Press.

Edwards, S. (1988) "Terms of trade, tariffs and labour market adjustment in developing countries", *World Bank Economic Review*, vol. 2, pp. 165-85.

Galiani, S. and Sanguinetti, P. (2003), "The Impact of Trade Liberalization on Wage Inequality: Evidence from Argentina", *Journal of Development Economics*, 72, 497-513.

Ghana Statistical Service: *Quarterly Digest of Statistics*, Various Issues.

Goldberg, Pinelopi and Nina Pavcnik, (2004), "Trade, Inequality, and Poverty: What Do We Know? Evidence from Recent Trade Liberalization Episodes in Developing Countries." NBER Working Paper No. 10593.

Hanson, G. and A. Harrison (1999), "Trade and wage inequality in Mexico," *Industrial and Labor Relations Review* 52(2), 271-288.

Harrison, A. (2005), "Globalization and Poverty", mimeo, University of California at Berkeley and NBER.

Harrison, A. and Hanson, G. (1999), "Who gains from trade reform? Some remaining puzzles", *Journal of Development Economics*, 59, 125-154.

Hertel, T.W., D. Hummels, M. Ivanic, and R. Keeney (2003), "How Confident Can We Be in CGE-Based Assessments of Free Trade Agreements", GTAP Working Paper No. 26, Center for Global Trade Analysis, Purdue University, West Lafayette.

Hoekman and Winters (2005), "Trade and Employment:Stylized Facts and Research Findings", Development Research Group, World Bank

Krueger, A. O. (1983), "Trade and Employment in Less Developed Countries: The Questions" NBER Chapters, in: Trade and Employment in Developing Countries, 3: Synthesis and Conclusions, page 1-9 National Bureau of Economic Research, Inc.

Milner, C., and P. Wright (1998), "Modelling labour market adjustment to trade liberalization in an industrializing economy", *Economic Journal*, 108, March 1998, pp. 509-528.

World Trade Organization (2007), "Trade Policy Review Report by Ghana", WT/TPR/G/194.

The Effects of Trade Liberalization on the Return to Education in Ghana

Charles Ackah, Oliver Morrissey and Simon Appleton

1. Introduction

The persistence of poverty in many developing countries, especially in sub-Saharan Africa (SSA), in the face of increased globalisation and rapid trade liberalization during the past two decades has inspired considerable public debate on the impact of globalisation, in general, and trade liberalisation, in particular, on poverty. The standard arguments, based on the Stolper-Samuelson theorem of international trade theory, are that trade liberalisation would lead to a rise in the incomes of unskilled labour in developing countries. Thus, according to the associated Ricardian comparative advantage theory, the poor (unskilled labour) will be the largest beneficiary of trade liberalisation. In other words, since developing countries are more likely to have a comparative advantage in producing unskilled labour-intensive goods, one would expect trade reforms in these countries to be inherently pro-poor (see Krueger (1983); Srinivasan and Bhagwati (2002); Bhagwati (2004); Harrison (2005)). However, the experiences of many developing countries, particularly in SSA, have been disappointing and in many cases poverty has increased following trade liberalisation (see Easterly, 2001).[11] It is estimated that more than 1 billion people still live in extreme poverty (based on the US$1 per day poverty line), and half the world's population lives on less than US$2 a day. These statistics have stimulated a lot of concern about whether the poor gain from trade liberalisation, and in what circumstances it may by-pass or actually hurt them.

Not surprisingly, the impact of trade reforms on the welfare of the poor has become an important subject of ongoing interest to researchers and policy makers alike. However, there has been limited empirical research on how these reforms affect poverty at the household level (Winters, 2002; Winters *et al.*, 2004). The main objective of this chapter is to make a contribution to this scanty literature through an empirical investigation of the poverty effect of trade protection, based on Ghanaian household data. This objective is motivated by the paucity of research in this area for Ghana. Very little evidence in Ghana concentrates on trade effects and few studies are based on household data. Despite general concerns expressed in many quarters, relatively little is known about the actual impacts of trade policy reforms on the welfare of the poor. While there

---

11   Compared to other regions, Africa, and especially SSA, has exhibited poor economic performance over at least the past two decades. While some countries have been exceptions to the trend and performed very well, the regional performance is cause for concern.

has been some work on poverty measurement and descriptive analysis of the characteristics of the poor, to our knowledge, there is no accessible multivariate econometric analysis using policy variables, such as tariffs, to examine the impact of trade policy on household poverty (whether measured in terms of wages or income) in Ghana. The scarcity of studies on this important topic is primarily due to the lack of representative household panel data sets on one hand, and the non-availability of trade policy data coupled with the problem of identification of the poverty effects of trade policy at the household level, on the other hand.[12]

This chapter takes a step towards filling this gap. Specifically, this is one of the first studies to use repeated cross-section data (RCS) from the Ghana Living Standards Survey (GLSS) data against the background of trade reforms of the 1990s to gauge some of the poverty effects of trade policy in Ghana. By so doing, we have moved beyond the limits of cross-sectional analysis into the realm of panel data that has long been acknowledged as required to address issues of endogeneity and heterogeneity. While the relationship between trade policy and poverty at the household level is not by any means clear and analysis, as a result, is complex, we demonstrate that even with limited data, it is still possible to assess some of the poverty effects of trade policy and therefore contribute to a more informed policy debate. Our analyses include static and dynamic, linear and non-linear levels and first-difference models to indicate that a lower industry tariff tends to be associated with lower welfare being earned by households affiliated to the industry, controlling for household-specific characteristics, geographic variables and industry fixed-effects. We find that this positive effect of protection is disproportionately greater for low skilled labour households, suggesting an erosion of welfare of unskilled labour households would result from trade liberalization.

The remainder of the chapter is organized as follows. The next section briefly reviews some relevant theoretical literature on international trade. Section 3 discusses the dataset and variable selection. Section 4 follows with a description of the empirical strategy. In Section 5, we summarize and assess the econometric results. Section 6 provides additional robustness checks while Section 7 concludes.

2. Trade and Labour Income: A Theoretical Consideration

This section provides a brief review of the main theories on the labour market impact of international trade. Specifically, we discuss what theory predicts about the impact of trade on labour income (wages) in developing countries. The standard argument with regard to trade and poverty is based on the Stolper-Samuelson theorem, which suggests that international trade will lead to a rise in the relative returns of the abundant factor; unskilled labour in the case

---

12   Coulombe and McKay (2003) cite the non-availability of panel data as one of the major limitations of using the Ghanaian Living Standards Survey in an analysis of the determinants of changes in poverty and inequality.

of developing countries. Thus, according to this theory, the poor (unskilled labour) will be the largest beneficiary of trade liberalisation. In other words, since developing countries are more likely to have a comparative advantage in producing goods that use unskilled labour relatively more intensively, we would expect trade reforms in these countries to be inherently pro-poor (see Krueger (1983); Srinivasan and Bhagwati (2002); Bhagwati (2004); Harrison (2005)).[13] These expected gains are conditional on a number of assumptions - including free mobility of labour, given technology and perfect competition[14]. However, the assumptions underpinning the theorem are inherently too restrictive to provide a practical interpretation of the complexity of the relationship between trade reform and poverty. Moreover, adjustment to trade may result in additional short- and medium-term costs and challenges for the poor (see Ackah and Morrissey, 2005:5-7 for a discussion of the benefits and costs of trade policy reforms).

Recently, these sharp predictions of the Stolper-Samuelson theorem have been challenged. According to the new theories, trade liberalization could reduce the wages of unskilled labour even in a labour-abundant country, thereby widening the gap between the rich and the poor. Many observers find the Stolper Samuelson theorem quite restrictive, in that the theorem does not offer definitive conclusions if one or more assumptions are relaxed (see Davis, 1996). Davis and Mishra (2004, cited in Harrison, 2005) argue that the popular expectation that trade-liberalisation should increase the incomes of the poor in low income countries is based on a very narrow interpretation of the standard Heckscher-Ohlin model. Davis and Mishra show that in a world of many factors and many goods, a poor country might no longer have a comparative advantage in producing unskilled intensive goods. Similarly, if a poor country has large supplies of non-labour factors of production (like land or mineral resources); trade liberalization may not benefit the labour-intensive sectors.

The specific sector and the Ricardo-Viner models have become the natural alternative to the Heckscher–Ohlin model and the associated Stolper–Samuelson theorem. According to these models, workers may gain from trade reforms depending on which sectors (import-competing or exporting) they are attached to. The models focus on the short to medium run and assume imperfect factor mobility, with one factor mobile across sectors while the other is taken to be sector-specific. With these assumptions, the models predict a positive association between protection and returns to factors of production (e.g. wages). Protection reduces imports and reduced imports increase labour demand, which in turn increases wages. When the price of a good falls following trade liberalisation the model predicts that the factor specific to the sector

---

13   For an empirical example, see Hertel *et al.* (2003) who estimate that global trade liberalization leads in the long run (i.e. when labour and capital are mobile across sectors) to a decline in poverty for all strata of the population largely because of increased demand for unskilled labour.

14   This is an assumption that is unlikely to hold in developing countries like Ghana, especially in the short run, where labour markets are characterized by significant labour rigidities.

that experienced price reduction loses while the other specific factor gains in real terms. In other words, if trade liberalisation occurred, households affiliated to the industries that experience large tariff reductions would see a decline in their incomes relative to the economy-wide average income, while households attached to relatively protected industries would gain, relatively.[15]

Given the apparent ambiguity in the theoretical literature discussed above, the relationship between trade liberalization and poverty appears an empirical matter. Empirically, it is not simple to disentangle the effects on incomes of trade reform from other macroeconomic policies and technological changes occurring simultaneously.

Although many economists tend to agree, in general, that in the long run openness to trade is good for poverty reduction, in the short and medium run, significant adjustment costs have been acknowledged. In fact, in the short run, trade liberalization appears to increase poverty and inequality (McCulloch *et al.*, 2001).

3. Data and Descriptive Statistics

In this subsection we describe the data and the main features of the variables that are relevant for the subsequent econometric analysis. Two sources of data for Ghana are used to assess the impact of trade policy on household welfare during the 1990s. The primary data source is the Ghana Living Standard Surveys (GLSS) the recent two of which were conducted in 1991/92 and 1998/99[16]. The second data source is the most favoured nation (MFN) tariff data for years close to the two household surveys. Tariff, our preferred measure of trade policy covers the period 1993 and 2000[17]. We construct a database of annual tariff data for 1993 and 2000 at the two-digit ISIC level to calculate average industry-level tariffs. The result is a two-digit classification of 26 industries per year, of which 19 are in the traded-goods sector and 7 in the non-traded sector[18]. Our sample is restricted to households with heads aged between 18-64 inclusive, employed in

---

15 Given the underdeveloped labour markets in most developing countries, this model appears a plausible starting point for thinking about the relationship between trade protection and income poverty in Ghana (see Attanasio *et al.*, 2004). There are good reasons to believe that the assumption of perfect labour mobility across sectors is unlikely to hold, at least in the short run, in most developing countries including Ghana. Even the assumption of perfectly competitive markets can only be envisaged in the long run. While we do not propose, in this paper, to subject these theories to empirical testing, we hope that in the end we are able to find a theoretical basis for explaining the observed changes in household welfare (income) and inequality in Ghana *vis-à-vis* the trade reforms in the 1990s.

16 The main advantage of using these two surveys is that they employed almost identical questionnaires, which aids in analysing changes in poverty between the two survey years.

17 Ideally, we would have required tariff data for 1998/99. However, for some reason these data are not readily available. This imposes a limitation on this study. Nonetheless, it is reasonable to assume that the tariff data captured in 2000 fairly represent tariffs prevailing in 1998/99. Evidence from Figure A1 in the Appendix A suggests that tariffs remained stable during the latter part of the 1990s (from 1997) and we believe this pattern may have continued into 2000.

18 Following Topalova (2005:16) all households employed in non-tradable industries are assigned a tariff of zero.

any sector (tradable or non-tradable). The sample is selected conditional on working so that the effects of protection conditional on being in the labour force are examined. Non-working households are excluded[19]. Each of the selected households is mapped on to one of the 26 sectors according to the sector of main employment of the household head. These exclusion restrictions leave us with a sample of 3,350 and 4,484 households from GLSS 3 and GLSS 4 respectively.

Among the household-level variables, we start by considering the following categories of variables: a set of demographic variables, variables relating to educational attainment, household size. Linear and quadratic terms in the age of the head of the household are also included to capture possible life-cycle effects. We include agro-climatic zones in our model as dummy variables to control for the effects of agro-ecological zone characteristics on household welfare. Doing so allows us to gauge the effects of the other determinants on household welfare independent of the effect of agro-climatic conditions on the household. To ascertain whether there were any significant changes in household welfare between the two periods, we introduce a survey-year dummy, *GLSS 4*. Furthermore, we allow for sectoral heterogeneity by including a dummy for households located in urban sectors, *Urban*. Using the information on the highest qualification obtained, we define five education indicators: No education, Basic education, Secondary education, Post-secondary education and Tertiary education (university degree). For each cross-section, Table 1 reports summary statistics of our key variables.

Ghana embarked on a massive expansion in the provision of education during the 1990s which has resulted in the increased educational attainment during the period. The proportion of households with illiterate heads (no education) fell from 32.3 percent to 28 percent. There were substantial increases in the proportion of households whose heads have completed more than primary school education. The proportion of heads with secondary education increased from 5.7 percent to 6.6 percent while those with post-secondary education increased from 3.5 percent to 6.6 percent. The share of heads with basic education has remained stable at around 57 percent. The percentage of heads with tertiary education, however, declined marginally - the share of those with university degrees fell from 0.8 percent to 0.6 percent. Over the period we observe a decrease (from 15.9 percent to 11.4 percent) in the share of households employed in the public sector, consistent with the public sector retrenchment which began in the mid-1990s under SAP/ERP (see Aryeetey, 2005). Even though food-crop farming is the largest source of employment for a great majority of households, its share declined significantly from about 40 percent in 1991/92 to 37 percent in 1998/99. On the other hand, the share of export farming increased by a massive 51 percent between the two surveys, but only from 5 percent to 7 percent. Non-farm self-employment saw a 14 percent increase in its share to maintain its position as the second largest employer.

---

19   This was necessitated by the fact that the survey questionnaire only solicited information about industry of employment for working individuals and since our tariff data is at the industry level.

Table 1: Summary Statistics

Variable	1991/92 Mean	Std. Dev.	1998/99 Mean	Std. Dev.
Welfare (consumption expenditure)	1,457,110	1,293,483	1,668,206	1,483,357
Log Welfare	13.927	0.710	14.056	0.729
Age of Head	38.169	9.823	42.281	10.504
Age of Head squared	1553	767	1898	921
Female-headed household	0.304	0.460	0.308	0.462
Household Head has -				
No Education	0.323	0.468	0.280	0.449
Basic Education	0.574	0.495	0.578	0.494
Secondary Education	0.057	0.231	0.066	0.248
Post-secondary Education	0.035	0.183	0.066	0.248
Tertiary Education (University)	0.008	0.091	0.006	0.074
Log Value of Land	3.510	5.597	3.419	6.283
Economic Activity indicators				
Public Sector	0.159	0.366	0.114	0.318
Private Formal	0.053	0.224	0.060	0.237
Private Informal	0.040	0.197	0.035	0.185
Export Farmer	0.047	0.211	0.071	0.257
Food -Crop Farmer	0.396	0.489	0.371	0.483
Non-farm Self-employment	0.304	0.460	0.347	0.476
Observations	3,350		4,484	

Note: The reported figures are weighted using survey weights. Values (welfare and land) are in constant prices of Accra in January 1999.

Table 2 provides information on the incidence of poverty and contribution to national poverty by each occupation. In 1991/92, the incidence of poverty in food crop and export farming households were quite similar, 68 percent and 64 percent respectively. However, by 1998/99 poverty incidence decreased to 39 percent in export farming households, whilst food crop farmers recorded about 59 percent. In terms of poverty shares, food -crop farmers actually saw a marginal increase in their share of national poverty from 57.3 percent to 58.1 percent. Similarly, the non-farm self-employed experienced an increase in their contribution to national poverty despite a drop in the incidence of poverty.

Table 2: Poverty, by Economic Activity and Location, 1991/92 and 1998/99

Economic Activity	1991/92		1998/99	
	Poverty incidence	Contribution to national poverty	Poverty incidence	Contribution to national poverty
Public Sector Employment	0.35	9.1	0.23	6.2
Private Formal Employment	0.30	2.3	0.11	1.4
Private Informal Employment	0.39	2.3	0.25	1.9
Export Farmers	0.64	7.8	0.39	6.9
Food crop farmers	0.68	57.3	0.59	58.1
Non-Farm Self Employment	0.38	20.5	0.29	24.5
Non-working	0.19	0.7	0.20	1.1
Location				
Rural	0.63	82.2	49.50	83.7
Urban	0.27	17.8	19.40	16.3
All Ghana	0.52	100.0	0.40	100.0

Source: Authors' calculation from GLSS, 1991/92 and 1998/99

Spatially, poverty in Ghana is almost entirely a rural phenomenon. With a population share of just about 64 percent the rural sector contributes a disproportionate 82 percent to total poverty, while urban households account for only 18 percent. The story that emerges from Tables 4.1 and 4.2 suggests that those who appear to have benefited the most from the economic policies of the 1990s were the urban and export farming households.[20] The rural households and food crop farmers who form the bulk of the population appear to have benefited the least. What is clear is that policy reform has had a differential impact on different groups of households. Indeed, our conservative measure of inequality, defined as the standard deviation of the log welfare, increased slightly over this period (from 0.71 to 0.73). This is broadly consistent with inequality as measured by the Gini coefficient which suggests a modest increase from 0.37 in 1991/92 to 0.39 in 1998/99 (Aryeetey and McKay, 2004).[21]

---

20 In principle, economic reforms (of which trade liberalisation is one aspect) are expected remove anti-export biases and shift incentives towards the production of tradables. To the extent that trade liberalisation leads to a rise in returns to exporting activities, it is not surprising that export farming households in Ghana recorded the highest reductions in poverty incidence during the 1990s. Aryeetey (2005) has argued, however, that one of the reasons why the export farmers performed relatively better than their counterparts engaged in food crop farming is due to the fact that while agricultural subsidies were removed in the food sector as part of the liberalisation process, export farmers were benefiting from governmental support in terms of technical training and other export- promotion packages.

21 See also Teal (2001) who finds that inequality as measured by the standard deviation of log household expenditure per capita (in 1998 prices) increased from 0.76 to 0.77. This evidence is further corroborated by his Gini coefficient measure based on household expenditure per capita in 1998 prices, which indicates a rise from 0.42 in 1991/92 to 0.46 in 1998/99.

Table 3: Economic Activity Shares, by Skill Levels, 1991/92

	Skill			
Economic Activity	Unskilled	Semi-skilled	Skilled	All
Public Sector Employment	0.61	0.19	0.20	1.00
Private Formal Employment	0.82	0.14	0.05	1.00
Private Informal Employment	0.89	0.10	0.01	1.00
Export Farmers	0.98	0.01	0.01	1.00
Food Crop Farmers	0.99	0.01	0.00	1.00
Non-farm Self Employment	0.94	0.03	0.02	1.00

Source: Authors' calculation from GLSS, 1991/92 and 1998/99

Note: Unskilled households are households whose head has completed basic or no education, semi-skilled for heads who have completed secondary or post-secondary and skilled for households with university graduate heads.

Table 4: Share of Skill Levels, by Rural/Urban Location, 1991/92

	Location		
Skill	Rural	Urban	All
Unskilled	0.67	0.33	1.00
Semi-skilled	0.27	0.73	1.00
Skilled	0.45	0.55	1.00

Source: Authors' calculation from GLSS, 1991/92 and 1998/99

Note: Unskilled households are households whose head has completed basic or no education, semi-skilled for heads who have completed secondary or post-secondary and skilled for households with university graduate heads.

Table 3 takes issues further by looking at the skill composition of these occupational groups while Table 4 does the same for the rural and urban sectors. Skilled (or semi-skilled) households are largely wage earners in either the public sector (39 percent) or the private formal sector (19%). Even though the unskilled dominate all socio-economic groups, almost all agriculture households (about 99 percent of food crop farmers and 98 percent of export farmers) are disproportionately unskilled. Moreover, while the unskilled are predominantly rural (67percent) the semi-skilled (73 percent) and skilled (55 percent) are largely located in urban centres. The foregoing descriptive evidence is instructive. The main message is that policy reforms in the 1990s were possibly not pro-poor if indeed unskilled labour households benefited the least.[22] Of course the simple descriptive analysis adopted here is unable to attribute changes to any

---

22   Teal (2000a, b) presents further evidence that the 1990s witnessed a continuing fall in real wages for unskilled labour in Ghana.

particular policy. A reasonable hypothesis is that trade policy is accountable for the observed evolution of poverty and inequality.

An alternative claim which seems to be gaining support is to say that trade is actually not to blame but rather skill-biased technological change is the problem (see for example, Görg and Strobl (2002). (Görg and Strobl 2002) using firm-level data on manufacturing in Ghana, have shown that skill-biased technical change arising from increased purchase of foreign machinery after the trade reforms has resulted in increased demand for skilled workers. However, to the extent that skill-biased technological change is an endogenous product of trade liberalisation, the relative non-performance of unskilled rural and food-crop farming households could be attributed, at least partially or indirectly, to trade liberalisation. Moreover, Teal (1999, 2001), using both firm-level and household data respectively, finds no evidence of any underlying technical progress in explaining increased income inequality in the 1990s. In a related study, Teal (2000) provides evidence which suggests that high rates of inflation and low investment are the two major factors responsible for the substantial falls in the real wages of the unskilled in manufacturing between 1992 and 1998. Unfortunately, Teal did not consider the role of trade policy in his analysis. In this chapter we argue that trade policy is one of the factors contributing to the observed trends in poverty and income inequality in Ghana during the period in question. However, one needs to test this with econometric methods, which we take up in Section 4.4.

Table A1 and Figure A1 in the Appendix show the average tariff levels and changes across all the 19 traded sectors between 1993 and 2000. It is worth pointing out that whereas the average unweighted scheduled tariff across *all* industries declined from 17 percent in 1992 to 8.5 percent in 1999 (Figure A1 in the Appendix) the structure and pattern of tariff reductions was not uniform across sectors. Hence, our data reveal that for a sizeable number of manufacturing industries (usually, relatively skilled sectors) the average tariff actually increased during the 1990s. Most manufacturing sub-sectors continued to enjoy high levels of protection, with the average tariff for the industry increasing by 12.41 percent. The agriculture and allied industries enjoyed especially high levels of protection to begin with but these are also the sectors where tariff reductions were intensive. This suggests that Ghana protected relatively unskilled, labour-intensive sectors during the era of import- substitution industrialization which persisted into the early 1990s, notwithstanding the economic reforms of the 1980s. The rapid and substantive liberalization of trade in agriculture in the 1990s was not accompanied by similar reforms in manufacturing. What is unique about the 1990s was the sudden attempt to change the structure of protection from low-skilled agriculture and relatively low-skilled manufactures to relatively high-skilled sectors.

Since Ghana's trade reforms entailed larger tariff reductions (and hence the largest reductions in the price of their output) in relatively unskilled and relatively protected sectors, the logic of the

Stolper-Samuelson theorem would imply that unskilled labour households will lose, relatively[23]. If labour is really perfectly mobile, i.e., if we assume an absence of labour market rigidities (which is very unlikely for Ghana), as the theory assumes very strongly, we would expect an accompanying reallocation of labour across sectors. We would expect to see labour reallocation from the sectors with the largest tariff reductions (the contracting unskilled sectors) to the sectors with the smaller tariff reductions (the expanding skilled sectors). The theory further predicts that the share of unskilled labour in industrial employment should rise as firms move away from skilled labour with the rising relative return to skilled labour. However, both predictions are not borne out by the evidence in Table A2. First, we fail to observe any discernible shifts in employment between sectors (see right panel of Table A2). In fact, shares of industry in total employment remained relatively stable between 1991/92 and 1998/99.

4. Empirical Methodology

In this section, we discuss the econometric models estimated and some econometric issues encountered. Our main objective is to investigate the causal effect of trade policy on household welfare in Ghana during the 1990s. Of particular interest here is the potential contingency of the effect of trade policy on educational qualification or skill type of the household. We are also interested in systematically distinguishing the long-run impact of trade protection on household welfare from that of the short run. In the end, we hope to provide answers to the following questions: (1) Does trade protection affect every household equally independent of the skill type of the household? In other words, would the effect of trade liberalisation be felt equally across households (skilled and unskilled)?; and (2) Is the effect of trade protection constant or time-dependent? Put differently, is the long-run impact of protection similar or different from that of the short run?

In order to investigate such questions, longitudinal data with multiple observations on the same households over time would be ideal. Unfortunately, such data are seldom available in developing countries, Ghana being no exception. The analysis in this chapter therefore applies pseudo-panel econometric techniques to our repeated cross-sectional data. We consider what can be learnt from analyzing repeated cross-sections, as is predominant in studies interested in consumption and labour supply issues (see Browning, Deaton, and Irish (1985). We extend these approaches for the analysis of trade policy and poverty in Ghana. In this way, this study circumvents the absence of 'true' panel data for Ghana, while still exploiting some of the attractive features of panel data analysis such as the ability to control for household-specific effects and unobserved heterogeneity (Deaton, 1985). This method has rarely been used in poverty analysis.

---

23   There is compelling evidence that the relative incomes of skilled labour in Ghana rose over the period under study (see Görg and Strobl (2002) and Teal (2000)).

After matching each household with the relevant industry tariff information, we examine how the standard of living measure relates to trade protection. The approach is based on modelling the natural logarithm of per adult equivalent consumption expenditure of survey households, adjusted for variations in prices between localities and over time (*Welfare*, used here as proxy for income and by implication poverty). One of the key features of the recent policy reforms in Ghana has been the significant changes in the levels of import protection. In the case of Ghana, household incomes and consumption expenditures are likely to have been significantly affected by the cross-sector pattern of tariffs.

We formalize the determinants of household welfare (or income) as follows:

$$\ln w_{it} = \alpha + \beta_1 age_{it} + \beta_2 age_{it}^2 + \beta_3 hsize_{it} + \beta_4 educ_{it} + \beta_5 urban_{it}$$

$$+ \beta_6 ecoz_{it} + \beta_7 land_{it} + \delta_1 tariff_{jt} + f_i + \lambda_j + \gamma_t + \varepsilon_{it} \qquad (16)$$

where the dependent variable is as previously defined, *age* is the age of household head at the time of the survey, age^2 is squared age, *hsize* is the size of the household, *educ* is education of the household head, *urban* is a 0/1 dummy which is 1 for households in urban localities, *ez* is agro-climatic zone, *land* is the value of land owned by the household (instead of the actual land cultivated, in order to implicitly account for land quality), *tariff* is the average (MFN) tariff applied to imports of industry j's products in year t, f is the household fixed effects, λ is the fixed effects for the household's industry affiliation, γ is the year fixed effect and ε is the error term. Subscripts i and t index households and survey years respectively. Year fixed effects are included to absorb economy-wide shocks (such as technological change) that may affect welfare while industry dummies control for sector-specific effects.

Each of the explanatory variables is likely to explain some of the differences in household welfare. However, it must be recognized that other unmeasured or unobservable differences among households may also matter. Unmeasured or unobservable individual heterogeneity is a problem that faces all survey research. A pooled analysis of the data based on equation (16) will be seriously flawed, in part because such analysis cannot control for unobservables, and in part because it assumes that repeated observations on each household are independent. The presence of f and λ in the model implies that we need panel data to consistently estimate the parameters in the model.[24] So to address these issues, we employ the ideas espoused by Deaton (1985) by constructing a pseudo panel from our repeated cross-sectional data. Following the pseudo panel

---

24   Pooling individuals across years has obvious advantages but generates a number of estimation issues regarding individual heterogeneity. It is likely that observations over time for the same individual will be more similar than observations across different individuals. This might be due to persistence in or unmodeled characteristics of household living standards. This is particularly pertinent to our analysis because there are good reasons to think that unobserved factors may affect household welfare. So we allow f to vary across households to capture unmeasured or unobserved heterogeneity.

data literature, the first extension is to take cohort averages of all variables and estimate (16) based on the cohort means.

$$\ln \overline{w}_{ct} = \alpha + \beta_1 \overline{age}_{ct} + \beta_2 \overline{age}_{ct}^{\,2} + \beta_3 \overline{hsize}_{ct} + \beta_4 \overline{educ}_{ct} + \beta_5 \overline{urban}_{ct}$$
$$+\beta_6 \overline{ecoz}_{ct} + \beta_7 \overline{land} + \delta_1 \overline{tariff}_{ct} + \overline{f}_{ct} + \overline{\lambda}_{ct} + \overline{\gamma}_{ct} + \overline{\varepsilon}_{ct} \qquad (17)$$

Equation (17) can be estimated via random- or fixed-effects estimators. The random-effects estimator generates consistent parameter estimates if the individual effects are uncorrelated with the other explanatory variables. The fixed-effects estimator is also consistent under this assumption, but is less efficient. Under the alternative hypothesis that the individual effects are correlated with other explanatory variables, only the fixed-effects estimator is consistent. We will use both methods to estimate (17), and report diagnostics to evaluate the estimators. To examine whether the trade policy changes can be directly linked to changes in living standards we will also estimate a differenced model based on (17) as an alternative econometric specification.

The consumption (welfare) models (16) and (17) both assume preferences to be time separable. However, some recent studies have drawn our attention to a class of time non-separable preferences, exhibiting habit formation or persistence. The distinctive characteristic of these models is that current utility depends not only on current consumption, but also on a habit stock formed from past consumption (see Fuhrer, 2000; and Deaton, 1992)[25]. In effect, equation (17) may be misspecified (dynamically) if dynamics really matter. The best solution would obviously be to directly model the dynamics; unfortunately this is very difficult without panel data. But failing to deal with the dynamics can cause serious problems. To test this we employ an alternative dynamic econometric specification, introducing the lagged dependent variable as additional regressor[26]. Here, for the same reasons discussed earlier in Section 2.2, we follow Moffit's (1993) guidance to estimate the model using the underlying micro data.

$$\ln w_{it} = \alpha + \beta_1 age_{it} + \beta_2 age_{it}^{\,2} + \beta_3 hsize_{it} + \beta_4 educ_{it} + \beta_5 urban_{it}$$
$$+\beta_6 ecoz_{it} + \beta_7 land_{it} + \beta_8 \ln w_{it-1} + \delta_1 tariff_{jt} + \lambda_j + \gamma_t + \varepsilon_{it} \qquad (18)$$

Equation (18) imposes a uniform and linear restriction on the parameter δ_1; the effect of tariff on welfare. The implicit assumption of such an approach is that the welfare effect of tariffs is uniform for all households. However, in light of the discussions in section 4.2 such an approach will be badly misspecified. The above specification may suffer from an un-modelled contingency in the relationship between tariffs and welfare. In other words, the assumption that all households would derive the same benefits from trade liberalisation is unlikely; and it is not supported by

---

25   A dynamic specification could be justified on several grounds. First, households are likely to incur short-term costs resulting from trade liberalisation due to rigidities. It may also take time to adjust to any policy shocks such as switching jobs from industries where wages are declining to ones where wages are rising.

26   A significant coefficient on the lagged dependent variable is evidence that the previous models were mis-specified or under-specified.

the evidence in Section 4.2. Equation (19) is a variant of (18) except now the structure explicitly allows the effects of tariffs on households to differ. We hypothesize that differences can, at least partially, be attributed to skill differentials among households and return effects on education. The resulting estimating equation is of the form:

$$\ln w_{it} = \alpha + \beta_1 age_{it} + \beta_2 age_{it}^2 + \beta_3 hsize_{it} + \beta_4 educ_{it} + \beta_5 urban_{it} + \beta_6 ecoz_{it}$$
$$+ \beta_7 land_{it} + \beta_8 \ln w_{it-1} + \delta_1 tariff_{jt} + \delta_2 Tariff_{jt} * Skill_{it} + \lambda_j + \gamma_t + \varepsilon_{it} \qquad (19)$$

where *Skill* comprises three mutually exclusive educational dummies (unskilled, semi-skilled and skilled) denoting the skill category of the household. Unskilled labour comprises households whose head has at least primary education; semi-skilled labour includes households with secondary education; and skilled labour is represented by households with graduate heads. This identification strategy assumes that tariff reductions during the 1990s affected households differently according to their skill type. We are thus able to assess whether trade protection is beneficial for households regardless of the level of skill.

4.1 Construction of the Pseudo Panel Data

Following the seminal work of Deaton (1985), we can construct a pseudo-panel and track cohorts of households through our two cross-sections. While we continue to wait for panel data to become available, we follow Deaton's procedure to create a pseudo panel for the econometric analysis in this chapter. Cohorts can be defined in terms of a single characteristic or multiple characteristics. In our case, since we have only two cross-sections, if the cohorts contain a large number of households, the number of cohort-groups will be small and hence the cross-sectional dimension of the panel will not be large. Thus, we construct our pseudo-panel by grouping households into cohorts based on some common multiple characteristics varying by generation (age category of head), gender of head and household's region of domicile. Since we are interested in a panel of households with heads between the ages of 18 to 64 and we have two cross-sections that are seven years apart then for the first cross-section (1991/92) the sample only includes households whose heads are aged 18 to 57, while the second cross-section (1998/99) only includes households with heads aged 25 to 64 so that all are in the normal working span in both surveys. Note that we add seven years to the age limits as we move to the next cross-section; this allows the households to "age" over time. We used five-year bands in defining the generational cohorts, resulting in eight birth cohorts constructed for each region in each survey year. For example, the first age cohort studied here was aged 18-22 in 1991/92 and 25-29 in 1998/99 (see Table A4 in the Appendix for details). Households whose heads are of these ages and are found in the relevant cross-sections are pooled to form the pseudo cohorts. Although the actual households surveyed will differ in each survey year, they will be representative of the full cohort in the population.

5. Econometric Results

In this section we discuss the econometric results, focusing on estimates of equations (17) to (19). First, we estimated all equations, (16) - (18) without controlling for industry-specific effects. The results are reported in Tables B1 and B2 in the Appendix. The effects of tariffs on welfare are negative for all the specifications. It is possible that these results in Table B1 and B2 exaggerate the effect of tariffs on income; other factors such as industry effects are potentially important. To examine if tariff effects can be accounted for by industry of employment, we re-estimate all the regressions but this time we include industry dummies. Not surprisingly, the effect of tariffs gets reversed controlling for industry fixed effects[27]. This suggests that unobserved industry heterogeneity was responsible for the negative tariff effect in the previous regressions. Thus, the rest of the analysis and discussions in this chapter refer to the regressions with controls for industry heterogeneity[28].

We now turn to an in-depth discussion of the regression results. Our main findings are reported in Tables 5 and 6. For a start, Table 5 reports the simple impact of the degree of openness on welfare. The first column lists the results for the case where we apply conventional ordinary least squares (OLS), based on equation (16), to the pooled cross-sections. Columns 2 to 4, on the other hand, are based on the pseudo panel equation (17).

Table 5: Trade Protection and Household Income (Welfare): Evidence from Static Regressions

Dependent Variable: Welfare (Consumption per adult equivalent)				
	Cross-Sectional	Pseudo Panel		
	Pooled OLS	Random Effects	Fixed Effects	Differenced
	(1)	(2)	(3)	(4)
Agehead	-0.022***	-0.038***	-	-
	(0.005)	(0.011)		
Agehead2	0.001***	0.001***	-	-
	(0.001)	(0.001)		
Hsize	-0.109***	-0.085***	-0.096***	-0.096***
	(0.003)	(0.014)	(0.025)	(0.025)
Urban	0.268***	0.310***	0.332**	0.332**

27 Other authors have found similar results. Attanasio *et al.* (2004), for example, estimates a positive tariff effect on industry wage premia only after controlling for unobserved sectoral heterogeneity. In their experimentation without industry dummies the tariff-wage effect turned negative.

28 A Wald test of the hypothesis that the effects of the industry dummies are simultaneously equal to zero was rejected at the 0.1 level or better.

Dependent Variable: Welfare (Consumption per adult equivalent)			
	Cross-Sectional	**Pseudo Panel**	
	Pooled OLS	**Random Effects**	**Fixed Effects**	**Differenced**
	(1)	**(2)**	**(3)**	**(4)**
	(0.016)	(0.077)	(0.146)	(0.140)
Basic	0.135***	0.103	0.126	0.126
	(0.016)	(0.087)	(0.165)	(0.193)
Secondary	0.360***	0.434	-0.787	-0.787
	(0.029)	(0.293)	(0.562)	(0.723)
Post-secondary	0.344***	0.414	0.303	0.303
	(0.033)	(0.311)	(0.511)	(0.542)
Tertiary	0.768***	1.880**	1.956	1.956
	(0.085)	(0.892)	(1.391)	(1.845)
Land	0.006***	-0.009*	-0.013	-0.013
	(0.001)	(0.005)	(0.010)	(0.015)
Forest	0.017	0.110*	0.026	0.026
	(0.015)	(0.064)	(0.194)	(0.128)
Savannah	-0.187***	-0.227***	0.169	0.169
	(0.019)	(0.062)	(0.372)	(0.350)
Tariff	0.010**	0.056***	0.068**	0.068**
	(0.005)	(0.020)	(0.027)	(0.029)
GLSS	4 0.127***	0.154***	0.185***	-
	(0.015)	(0.047)	(0.058)	
Constant	14.798***	15.818***	14.948***	0.185***
	(0.135)	(0.897)	(1.498)	(0.050)
Industry Dummies	Yes	Yes	Yes	Yes
No. of Obs	7834	310	310	152
R-squared	0.42	0.74	0.35	0.32

Note: Robust standard errors in parentheses, * denotes significant at 10%; ** denotes significant at 5%, *** denotes significant at 1%.

Columns 2 and 3 report random-effects and fixed-effects results respectively. Even though the key message is the same across these two models, we employed the Hausman specification test and report the diagnostic results in Table A3 in the Appendix[29]. To examine whether the trade policy changes can be directly linked to changes in living standards we also estimate the first-difference model in column 4 based on (17). This specification could also mitigate the potential for any spurious correlation between tariffs and welfare. The effects of protection on welfare are positive and significant in all regressions in Table 5. In other words, holding other factors constant, the pseudo-panel econometric evidence presented here suggests that welfare is higher (poverty is lower) in households (or cohorts) employed in protected sectors (sheltered from competition). The coefficient on tariff implies that increasing protection in a particular sector raises consumption expenditure (or incomes) in that sector. The corollary that reducing tariffs in previously protected sectors lowers incomes (or welfare) in those sectors is equally supported by the first-difference model in column 4.

Although the regressions in Table 5 provide interesting results, we can be sceptical about their static nature and the unwarrantable linearity (homogeneity) restriction on the coefficient of tariff. Thus, Table 6 presents results based on the dynamic models (18) and (19). The specifications as in column 1 of Table 6 and its variant as in column 2 are dynamically specified (with the lag of the dependent variable, log welfare, as a regressor) and estimated using 2SLS applied to RCS data as reviewed in Section 4.1. Moreover, column 2 presents the estimates of the differential impact of the reforms on unskilled and skilled labour households. In column 2, based on equation (19), tariff is interacted with the skill dummy to show the differential effect of trade protection on households characterised by different levels of education[30].

As discussed already, the main problem we face in estimating (19) is that the true value of the lagged dependent variable (lagged welfare), is unobserved because the same individuals are not tracked over time. Following Moffit (1993), however, the regressions in Table 6 are estimated by regressing the dependent variable (welfare) on the time-invariant explanatory variables using the observations in the first cross-section (1991/92). We then obtain the predicted dependent variable from the OLS estimation. In the second stage the predicted dependent variable is substituted in the original model (19) as the lagged dependent variable and estimated by OLS using all observations in both cross-sections; on the assumption that the (predicted) lagged dependent variable is asymptotically uncorrelated with the error term[31].

---

29 The test statistic equals 21.16 (probability of 0.98). This clearly fails to reject the null, at the 0.05 level of significance, that the unobserved heterogeneity is uncorrelated with the regressors, i.e. it finds that the random effects estimates are not significantly different from the fixed effects estimates. The more efficient random effects specification is therefore the preferred one.

30 The assumption of homogeneity implies that the coefficient on the interactive term should equal zero. This restriction is obviously rejected as indicated by the significant coefficient on the interactive term. This suggests that the regressions in Table 5 may suffer from an unmodelled heterogeneity.

31 It is important to mention that we test for the sensitivity of our results to this assumption in the section devoted to robustness checks.

Table 6: Trade Protection and Household Income: Evidence from Dynamic Regressions

Dependent Variable: Welfare (Consumption per adult equivalent) (Consumption per adult equivalent)		
	(1)	(2)
Lagged Welfare	0.386**	0.386**
	(0.156)	(0.156)
Agehead	0.036**	0.035**
	(0.015)	(0.015)
Agehead2	-0.001**	-0.001**
	(0.001)	(0.001)
Hsize	-0.063***	-0.063***
	(0.018)	(0.018)
Urban	0.067	0.067
	(0.070)	(0.070)
Basic	0.066***	0.096***
	(0.023)	(0.028)
Secondary	0.186***	0.227***
	(0.065)	(0.069)
Post-sec	0.195***	0.237***
	(0.062)	(0.065)
Tertiary	0.391**	0.447***
	(0.156)	(0.158)
Land	0.004***	0.004***
	(0.001)	(0.001)
Forest	0.040*	0.039*
	(0.022)	(0.022)
Savannah	0.029	0.028
	(0.031)	(0.031)
Tariff	0.009*	0.012**
	(0.005)	(0.005)
Tariff x Skill		-0.002*
		(0.001)
GLSS 4	0.093***	0.093***
	(0.033)	(0.033)
Constant	8.057***	8.042***

Dependent Variable: Welfare	(Consumption per adult equivalent)	(Consumption per adult equivalent)
	(1)	(2)
	(2.473)	(2.473)
Industry Dummies	Yes	Yes
No. of Observations	7834	7834
R-squared	0.45	0.45

Note: Robust standard errors in parentheses, * denotes significant at 10%; ** denotes significant at 5%, *** denotes significant at 1%. Regressions include controls for cohort group (dummies) suppressed here for brevity.

Interestingly, we still find robust evidence regarding the effects of tariffs on poverty. In both regressions (Table 6) the average welfare responds positively to tariffs, so that tariff reductions would lead to a decline in welfare. In other words, welfare would be lower in households employed in protected sectors which were exposed to import competition. This finding supports the interpretation that incomes fell most in those industries where openness increased the most. Thus, we again find a positive and statistically significant correlation between trade protection and household welfare. Although the magnitude of the tariff coefficient changes, the positive and statistically significant relationship between tariffs and welfare is robust. The estimated effect of protection on welfare drops, however, from an average of about 0.064 in columns 2 to 4 of Table 5, to 0.009 and 0.012 in columns 1 and 2 respectively of Table 6. These results suggest, in the case of Ghana, that trade policy reforms had a significant effect (albeit marginally) on household welfare. Households whose heads work in industries with the largest tariff reductions (mainly the agriculture and allied sectors) would tend to experience a decline of their welfare (income) relative to the economy-wide average[32]. The evidence seems to suggest that tariffs may protect incomes of households employed in relatively protected sectors. This implies that some of the economic rents are shared with labour, so that liberalisation could reduce incomes and potentially increase poverty (in protected sectors). Whether inequality increased depends on whether the sectors with the largest tariff reductions were the ones in which the poor are mainly located. Anecdotal evidence and the results contained in the descriptive analysis of this chapter, however, point to the contrary. The poor in Ghana are predominantly rural, unskilled and employed relatively intensively in agriculture (mostly as landless peasant food crop farmers). It is for this reason that the results in Table 7 are especially important.

---

32   The only exceptions are households engaged in export farming (predominantly cocoa farmers). Aryeetey (2005) has argued, however, that one of the reasons why the export farming sector performed relatively better than food crop farmers is due to the fact that in the face of the severe agricultural import liberalization, the export farmers have been benefiting from governmental support in terms of technical training and other export promotion packages.

Table 7: Contribution of Trade Protection to Household Income (Welfare)

	1991/92 Skill Type of Household			1998/99 Skill Type of Household		
	Unskilled	Semi-	Skilled	Unskilled	Semi-	Skilled
Actual Welfare (log)	13.875	14.456	14.324	13.981	14.586	14.482
Predicted Welfare (log)	13.870	14.480	14.378	13.984	14.571	14.458
Residual	0.004	-0.024	-0.055	-0.003	0.016	0.025
Contribution of Tariffs to Welfare	0.200	0.184	0.182	0.176	0.168	0.168
Number of Observations	3016	190	144	3869	294	321

Note: Authors' calculations based on regression in column 1 of Table 6.
Figures are simple averages over all households in each skill type except tariff which is over households in traded sectors only.

In Table 7 we show the three skill types of all households in our regressions, along with their actual welfare as reported in the data and the predicted welfare from the regression in column 1 of Table 6. In addition, we estimate how much of the variation in within-household welfare is explained by trade policy. Overall, the model explains reasonably well the experience of all households irrespective of the skill type. The unexplained welfare (residual) is negligible, ranging between 0.3 percent and 5.5 percent in absolute terms. The first main message from this table is that for all households in traded sectors the contribution of protection to welfare is positive. Second, the results in this table corroborate the non-linear specification employed in column 2 of Table 6 (the model with the interactive term). We find that the contribution of tariffs to welfare is relatively higher (20 percent) for unskilled households. Without any special safety nets or complementary policies, one can expect that trade liberalisation, alone, would have disproportionate negative consequences for households in this skill type, *ceteris paribus*. Finally, the results reveal that over the period of seven years, the contribution of tariffs to welfare has fallen for all skill types while average welfare for each skill type has increased slightly. This seems to suggest, perhaps unsurprisingly, that in the medium to long run there appears to be a negative relationship between trade protection and welfare. If this were the case, it would be good news for free trade protagonists. The second and final messages from this table are the basis for the subsequent empirical analysis in this chapter. First, we investigate further the apparent, non-linear tariff-welfare relationship. Then, given the inherent dynamics in our model, we estimate the long-run welfare responses to trade protection.

5.1 Non-linearity

It appears reasonable to expect that trade protection and, for that matter, trade liberalization will impact differentially, either by direction or magnitude, on households with different levels of education. To examine how the effects of trade liberalization on households may vary by education, we have hypothesized a potential contingency in the relationship between protection (liberalization) and welfare. To attempt to capture this contingency, we introduced an interaction term between *Tariff* and *Skill* which is a categorical dummy variable constructed from the highest education completed dummies. The interaction term is meant to capture the non-linearity in the impact of trade policy on poverty, in order to ascertain whether the impact of greater openness is borne disproportionately by different skill groups[33]. Evidence of a contingent relationship is provided by a significant coefficient on the interaction term suggesting an un-modelled contingency bias in the results discussed previously.

The results reported in column 2 of Table 6 are quite revealing. This specification reveals a significant interaction effect under which the marginal impact of tariffs on welfare is decreasing in skill. We find that the positive tariff effect applies to all households but is more pronounced for less skilled households, suggesting that greater openness is likely to be associated with significantly lower returns to households with lower levels of education (the unskilled). This leads to the inference that households with higher education (skilled) in highly protected industries have lower welfare than households with only one of those attributes. A corollary is that unskilled households in highly protected industries enjoy relatively higher welfare than they otherwise would. Hence, trade liberalization would worsen their plight disproportionately. It is therefore reasonable to suppose that only skilled households (because they are more educated and more mobile) would have benefited from trade liberalization in the 1990s. This evidence on the differential impact of trade protection on poverty is consistent with our earlier descriptive results concerning the finding that the rural, food crop farmers and non-farm self-employed, all of whom are relatively unskilled, benefited the least from the trade reforms in the 1990s. Trade liberalization in Ghana seems to accord with an increase in income inequality in favour of skilled households.

---

33 Alternatively, we could simply conduct separate regressions for households in different skill categories. However, this approach would impose too much restriction on the data and would also not permit us to explore how the marginal effect of trade policy varies for more-skilled and less-skilled households.

Table 8: **Marginal and Long-run Effects of Trade Protection on Income (Welfare)**

	Unskilled	Semi-skilled	Skilled
Marginal Effects	0.01 (2.01)**	0.009 (1.92)*	0.006 (1.20)
Long-run Effects	0.016 (1.45)	0.01 (1.45)	0.01 (1.11)

Note: *Absolute t-ratios in parentheses, * denotes significant at 10%; ** denotes significant at 5%.*

In order to test the hypothesis that the simple slope (marginal effect of tariffs) differs from zero, we approximate the standard error of the simple slope by the following equation: $s_b = sqrt\left[s_{11} + 2Zs_{12} + Z^2 s_{22}\right]$, where s_{11} is the variance of the tariff coefficient (i.e., the squared standard error of δ_1), s_{22} is the variance of the interaction coefficient (i.e., the squared standard error of δ_2) and s_{12} is the covariance of the two. These values are obtained from the asymptotic covariance matrix based on our regression model in Table 6 column 2.

These results imply that the impact of trade protection on household welfare is a function both of the level of restriction and of the level of education (skill). To evaluate this conditional hypothesis, we use the three values for *Skill* (1 for unskilled; 2 for semi-skilled; 3 for skilled) to compute the marginal effects of trade policy and report the results in the first row of Table 8. From equation (19), the derivative of *welfare* with respect to *Tariff* is calculated as

$$\frac{\partial welfare}{\partial Tariff} = \delta_1 + \delta_2 \left(Skill\right)$$

(20)

Evaluated at *Unskilled* and *Semi-skilled*, we find a positive and statistically significant tariff effect. However, evaluated at *Skilled*, the marginal effect of *Tariff* becomes statistically insignificant. Thus, the regression indicates that the derivative of welfare with respect to tariffs is a decreasing and linear function of the level of skill. We know from the fact that the coefficient on the interaction term is negative that the positive effect of trade protection declines as the level of skill increases. Consequently, the potential adjustment costs resulting from any given trade policy reforms will not be universal across different skill groups. Thus, for two households with similar characteristics, affiliated to the same sector (and thus facing similar tariffs) but belonging to different skill groups (unskilled and skilled), a tariff reduction in that sector will have different effects on their respective welfare. Skilled households stand to benefit more than unskilled households. Alternatively, unskilled households will benefit the least relative to skilled households.

5.2 Long-run Effects of Trade Protection

The analysis so far has been restricted to the short-run impact of trade policy. While the short-run is definitely important and merits analysis, many economic policies have important long-run perspectives which equally deserve scrutiny. Most often, these long-run impacts are ignored by researchers and policy analysts. This is partly because of data constraints or because the electoratesonly cares about the short-run costs and benefits of public policy. However, to the extent that it is possible, we need to investigate the long-run impacts as well. In our empirical application, we are interested in knowing whether the long-run effects of trade policy are the same as the short-run consequences already documented. Specifically, we want to see whether the positive impact of tariffs on welfare weakens over time. Fortunately, the dynamic specifications employed in Table 6 allow us to explore this. The estimated significant coefficient on the lagged dependent variable is 0.386 with a standard error of 0.156. This suggests that past shocks to household welfare do affect current levels of welfare, above and beyond the influence of household-specific characteristics. The estimated tariff coefficient is 0.012 with a standard error of 0.005. This estimate divided by one minus the coefficient estimate on the lagged dependent variable yields the *long-run* effect of trade protection on welfare. The last row of Table 8 reports this long-run impact for all three skill groups. There is an interesting twist. None of the long run tariff effects is statistically distinguishable from zero. In other words, conditional on controls for the persistence of household welfare the positive and significant tariff effect disappears. Hence, it seems reasonable to speculate that the arguments for protection are valid (especially for poor unskilled labour households) so long as the short run is the period of interest. In the long run, however, it is highly unlikely for any household, irrespective of the skill type and industry affiliation, to benefit from protectionism. Trade liberalization has therefore, a potential role in enhancing welfare in the long run.

Results for the other control variables are also of interest. Household welfare correlates positively and significantly with land value. As expected, household size correlates negatively and significantly with welfare. The education variables show the expected pattern. All the estimated coefficients are positive and statistically significant, indicating that, other things being equal, all levels of education (relative to no education) of the household head improve welfare. It turns out that the returns to having progressively higher education are larger. The strong positive effect of education on welfare increases with the level of completed education of the household head. The incremental gain in welfare is smallest for households with heads with basic education and largest for graduate-headed households. Note that the effects of post-basic education (i.e., secondary, post-secondary and tertiary) are quantitatively the largest of all included explanatory variables. Hence, education emerges as the fundamental household characteristic determining the probability that a household experiences a reduction in welfare, *ceteris paribus*.

6. Further Robustness Checks

To verify our main findings, we now turn to a number of robustness checks. Our first check was to take seriously the measurement error problem raised in the pseudo-panel literature and reviewed in Section 4.1. We are interested in finding out whether the results are sensitive to the construction of the pseudo-panel. With an average cell size of 52 we may worry that the measurement error problem could be an issue in the results in Table 5. However, since the main conclusions in this chapter are based on Table 6 in which the regressions are based on the underlying micro data (not on cell means), we can safely ignore the measurement error problem. Nevertheless, we follow most researchers in this field (upon the advice of Verbeek and Nijman, 1993) and divide the sample into a smaller number of cohorts to ensure that observations per cell are reasonably large. To do this, we construct a new pseudo-panel by taking 10-year generation bands while maintaining the regional (10) and gender (2) categories[34]. Cohorts are defined by the interaction of four age intervals (GLSS 1991/92: 18-27, 28-37, 38-47 and 48-57; GLSS 1998/99: 25-34, 35-44, 45-54 and 55-64), two gender categories (male and female) of head and 10 geographic regions (see Table A5 in the Appendix for details). For example, the first cohort here is aged 18-27 in 1991/92 and 25-34 in 1998/99. By so doing, the average number of observations per cell increases to 104 at the expense of a relatively small total number of observations (a potential of 160 but 148 realized). Tables B3 to B5 in the Appendix replicate all the regressions in Tables 5 and 6 using this new data. In all cases, we find that cohort selection issues are not driving the results. Our results remain largely unaltered. Both the signs and statistical significance of the coefficients are preserved in most cases. Thus the model parameters are robust in that they show little sensitivity to changes in the data construction. We still find convincing evidence of a positive and statistically significant correlation between tariffs and welfare which is contingent on skill (human capital). In fact, the orders of magnitude of the estimated tariff coefficient have actually become larger.

Next, we used the estimator proposed by Verbeek and Vella (2005) as a robustness check on using Moffit's version of estimating dynamic models from RCS. Our aim is to check if failure to instrument *Tariff* and the lag of the dependent variable as the authors suggest affected the estimated parameters. In effect, we relax the assumption that the (predicted) lagged dependent variable is uncorrelated with the prediction error. Essentially, we estimated (19) using standard IV methods with cohort dummies interacted with time dummies, serving as instruments for both lagged welfare and tariffs. The results are presented in Table B6 in the Appendix. We found no big difference in the estimated coefficients. In other words, we did not have any major changes in significance or signs of the estimated coefficients in Table 6. In fact, the estimated coefficients on tariffs and the interaction term becomes stronger and both are significant at the 1 percent level. Hence, our results are not driven by model specification and the choice of estimator.

We also test for the joint significance of the industry fixed effects. The null hypothesis of the joint insignificance of the industry fixed effects (i.e., that each of the coefficients for the industry

---

34 The choice of 10-year intervals is essentially arbitrary, but meets the requirements for the cell sizes to be reasonably large (on average) so that the measurement error problem discussed previously is negligible.

dummies is not significantly different from zero) is safely rejected for all relevant specifications. The specifications controlling for unobserved industry heterogeneity are thus retained as our preferred models. The fit of the models is good, with R^2 ranging from 0.32 to 0.74. With only a few exceptions, the signs on the parameters are as expected, and the relative magnitudes of the parameters are reasonable.

7. Conclusions

In this chapter, we have presented one of the first direct microeconometric studies of the impact of trade protection on household income in Ghana. We matched tariff measures at the two-digit ISIC level to household survey data for 1991/92 and 1998/99 to represent the tariff for the industry in which the household head is employed. We examined the possibility that the effect of protection on income might not be uniform across households characterized by different education (skill) levels. We have presented both descriptive and econometric evidence to show that trade policy reforms in Ghana during the 1990s could have resulted in increases in poverty among certain sections of the population, especially the rural unskilled-labour households. Unskilled households, predominantly employed in agriculture, would experience the largest increases in poverty. This is consistent with the observations made by Aryeetey and McKay (2004) that the poorest of the poor participated much less in the growth and poverty reduction over this period.

In the econometric section of this chapter, we regressed the living standards indicator, consumption per equivalent adult, on household-specific demographic characteristics, tariffs and industry indicators. In particular, we allowed the relationship between welfare and trade policy to differ for households with different levels of education. The econometric results confirmed our previous descriptive findings and suggest that higher tariffs are associated with higher incomes for households employed in the sector, implying that some of the economic rents are shared with labour, so that liberalisation could reduce incomes and potentially increase poverty, at least in the short run, but with differing effects across skill groups. We find that the positive effect of protection is disproportionately greater for low-skilled labour households, suggesting an erosion of welfare of unskilled-labour households would result from trade liberalization. In the short run, all households regardless of skill type would have lost out from trade liberalization, but the poor unskilled households (because they are sector-specific and less mobile) would lose disproportionately. The results suggest that within the same sector, a trade reform may lead to differing impacts on households with similar attributes but different skills. Moreover, education emerge as the fundamental household characteristic determining the probability that a household experiences poverty, *ceteris paribus*. From a policy standpoint, we conclude that contemplating trade liberalization without recognizing the complementary role of human capital investment may be a sub-optimal policy for the poor, at least in the short run.

APPENDIX A: Data and Descriptive Statistics

Table A1: Inter-Industry Trade Protection (Liberalisation) during the 1990s

Industry Classification (26)	Tariff (%) 1992/93	1999/00	Tariff Change (%)
Traded Sectors (19)			
Agric, Forestry and Fishing (3) *of which*			
Agriculture Crop & Livestock	23.2	19.44	-16.18
Forestry & Logging	24.77	20	-19.27
Fishing	20.34	13.97	-31.36
Average (unweighted)	22.77	17.8	-22.27
Manufacturing (14) *of which*			
Food	18.94	24.94	31.63
Beverages	20.45	21.43	4.76
Furniture	19.73	27.84	41.1
Electrical	12.63	10.86	-14.08
Metals	7.89	11.03	39.83
Chemicals	10.61	12.08	13.84
Plastics	14.39	17.17	19.34
Footwear	19	20	5.26
Textiles	21.35	23.04	7.93
Wood	18	16.89	-6.16
Apparel	24.44	22.22	-9.09
Printing	20	23.33	16.67
Rubber	10	10	0
Other manufacturing	11.21	13.76	22.75
Average (unweighted)	16.33	18.19	12.41
Mining & Quarrying	9.77	11.64	19.14
Utilities	12.14	10.71	-11.76

Source: Authors' calculations using SITC 2-digit level tariff data from the (UNCTAD) TRAINS Database.

Note: The other seven Non-traded sectors including Trading, Construction, Restaurant & hotel, Transport & communication, Financial services, Other services and Community & social care were all assigned a tariff of zero.

Table A2: Industry Employment Shares by Skill Levels

Industry Name	1991/92 Share of different skill levels in industry			1998/99 Share of different skill levels in industry			1991/92 Share of industry in total employment	1998/99 Share of industry in total employment
	Un-skilled	Semi-	Skilled	Un-skilled	Semi-	Skilled		
Agriculture Crop & Livestock	0.982	0.014	0.004	0.969	0.022	0.010	0.481	0.486
Forestry & Logging	0.903	0.065	0.032	0.833	0.056	0.111	0.009	0.004
Fishing	0.960	0.000	0.040	0.988	0.000	0.012	0.015	0.018
Food	0.983	0.017	0.000	0.967	0.016	0.016	0.035	0.041
Beverages	0.957	0.000	0.043	0.903	0.065	0.032	0.007	0.007
Furniture	0.885	0.038	0.077	0.895	0.053	0.053	0.008	0.008
Electrical	0.667	0.000	0.333	0.000	1.000	0.000	0.001	0.000
Metals	0.889	0.111	0.000	0.810	0.143	0.048	0.005	0.005
Chemicals	1.000	0.000	0.000	0.500	0.500	0.000	0.001	0.000
Plastics	1.000	0.000	0.000	0.500	0.000	0.500	0.001	0.001
Footwear	1.000	0.000	0.000	0.818	0.182	0.000	0.001	0.002
Textiles	0.800	0.200	0.000	0.679	0.214	0.107	0.006	0.006
Wood	0.833	0.000	0.167	0.826	0.087	0.087	0.002	0.005
Apparel	0.944	0.037	0.019	0.882	0.082	0.035	0.016	0.019
Printing	0.571	0.429	0.000	0.545	0.273	0.182	0.002	0.002
Rubber	0.857	0.143	0.000	0.730	0.135	0.135	0.006	0.008
Other Manufacturing	0.968	0.000	0.032	0.769	0.154	0.077	0.009	0.012
Mining & Quarrying	0.636	0.273	0.091	0.733	0.133	0.133	0.003	0.003
Utilities	1.000	0.000	0.000	0.500	0.500	0.000	0.001	0.000
Trading	0.931	0.063	0.006	0.877	0.085	0.038	0.142	0.147
Construction	0.931	0.056	0.014	0.793	0.103	0.103	0.021	0.026
Restaurants & Hotels	0.955	0.000	0.045	0.889	0.056	0.056	0.007	0.004
Transport & Communication	0.879	0.093	0.029	0.800	0.103	0.097	0.042	0.039
Financial Services	0.357	0.429	0.214	0.286	0.457	0.257	0.004	0.008
Other Services	0.796	0.122	0.082	0.632	0.211	0.158	0.015	0.013
Community & Social	0.632	0.163	0.206	0.540	0.138	0.322	0.160	0.134
Total	0.900	0.057	0.043	0.863	0.066	0.072	1.000	1.000

Source: Authors' calculations from GLSS surveys. These are the 26/68 sectors for which we successfully matched households by the main employment of head.

Figure A1: The Pattern of Trade Protection in Ghana during the 1990s

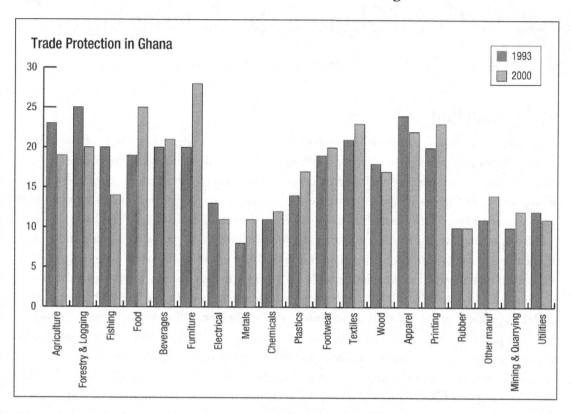

Note: These are all the 19 tradable sectors in our data. There are seven non-traded sectors with tariffs coded as zero.

Trade, Trade Policy and Total Factor Productivity: The Case of Ghanaian Manufacturing Firms

Charles Ackah, Ernest Aryeetey and Oliver Morrissey

1. Introduction

Since the 1980s most countries in sub-Saharan Africa (SSA), under the auspices of the Bretton Woods institutions and within the framework of the Structural Adjustment Programmes (SAPs), have departed from inward-looking protectionist development strategies, as a reaction to the disappointment of previous import-substitution industrialization policies. Trade policy reforms – tariff reduction and removal of non-tariff barriers - were an important element of SAPs. There is by now a rapidly growing literature on the impact of trade liberalization on productivity levels and growth in the manufacturing sectors of developing countries. The conventional theoretical argument is that trade liberalization would lead to significant gains in productivity. However, the theoretical literature has not yielded a definite prediction on the direction of causality (see Rodrik, 1988, 1992, and Tybout 1992). Supporters of trade liberalization claim that liberalization will raise productivity through at least two pathways. First, increased foreign competitive pressure faced by domestic producers from import competition can result in higher productivity supposing the producers eliminate slack, cut costs and use inputs more efficiently to remain competitive. This effect is referred to in the literature as the elimination of 'X-inefficiency' among firms in import-competing industries (Fenandes, 2003, 2007). A process of selection is expected to occur following trade liberalization during which the most productive firms survive and thrive while the inefficient ones exit. As a result, the average productivity across firms increases (Melitz, 2003). Secondly, trade liberalization may result in productivity gains through more access to foreign technology (Grossman and Helpman, 1991). This may occur through the importation of capital goods and intermediate inputs embodying technologies previously unavailable to the domestic firms. Also, trade liberalization may increase productivity through technology diffusion by allowing domestic producers to learn from imported finished goods as well as from exporting.

Given the apparent ambiguity in the theoretical literature summarized above, the relationship between trade liberalization and productivity appears an empirical matter. However, the available empirical evidence on the issue has been far from conclusive.[35] Unlike other regions, there exists a paucity of empirical research on how trade reforms have impacted firm performance in SSA.

---

35 In recent year in particular, considerable attempts have been made to investigate the channels through which trade liberalisation affects firm productivity in developing countries. Good examples are the studies of Pavcnik (2002), Topalova (2004), Amiti and Konings (2007) and Fernandes (2007) for Chile, India, Indonesia and Colombia, respectively.

This is in part due to the non-availability of reliable firm-level panel data. In this chapter, we match manufacturing firm-level panel data with commodity-level disaggregated data on import tariffs to examine the effects of trade liberalization on firm performance in one of Africa's most devout reformers: Ghana – Africa's sometime adjustment star pupil. We investigate the effects of import tariff reductions on total factor productivity (TFP) of Ghanaian manufacturing firms over the period 1993-2002.

The results from the chapter contribute to the ongoing theoretical and empirical debate on trade openness, productivity and growth. We find relatively large positive effects of tariff reductions on total factor productivity, a result that is robust to various alterations of the base model, including treating tariffs as endogenous and employing different estimation techniques. We note that these effects seem consistent with the hypothesis that trade liberalization has increased productivity in the domestic market. These results indicate that firms that are overprotected, as illustrated by high import tariffs pertaining to the industries in which they operate, have a lower level of TFP than firms that are exposed to competition. We find also a strong effect of export intensity on productivity, both on its own and in conjunction with lower tariffs. Exporters appear to take more advantage of foreign competition than non-exporters and appear more sensitive to tariffs.

The remainder of the chapter is organized as follows: Section 2 presents background information on trade policy reforms and manufacturing performance in Ghana. Section 3 presents our empirical approach to productivity measurement and the examination of how trade policy affects measured productivity. Section 4 discusses the data used in the econometric analysis. The results are summarized in Section 5. Section 6 concludes.

2. Background: Trade Policy Reforms and Manufacturing Performance

a. Trade policy reform in Ghana

Prior to gaining independence from British colonial rule in 1957, Ghana operated a liberal external payments regime. This was followed after independence by the pursuit of an import-substitution industrialisation strategy by Ghana's first president, Dr. Kwame Nkrumah. However, following years of economic stagnation during the 1960s and 70s, the then president, J.J. Rawlings, had no choice than to agree to the World Bank/IMF prescribed economic recovery programme (ERP) in April 1983. Indeed, Ghana was categorized as a relatively successful adjuster for implementing what came to be called the Structural Adjustment Programme. These reforms, which were aimed at removing distortions in the economy, included trade and exchange rate liberalization. Trade policy under the programme included tariff adjustments, import liberalization, liberalization of foreign exchange, deregulation of domestic market prices and controls and institutional reforms that particularly affected revenue-generating bodies such as the Customs, Excise and Preventive Service (CEPS).

In the last five decades, Ghana's trade policy has evolved from a fairly liberal one in the 1950s through a significantly controlled regime in the 1970s to the priod in which the economy underwent major trade and economic reforms in the 1980s and 1990s followed by the liberalised trade regime currently in place. Significant trade liberalization began with the adjustment of tariff rates in 1983, downwards from 35 percent, 60 percent and 100 percent to 10 percent, 20 percent, 25 percent and 30 percent. Tariffs were further simplified and lowered to 0 percent, 25 percent and 30 percent the following year to create a uniform pattern of protection although some import controls remained in place. Further reductions occurred in 1986 when the higher rates were lowered to 20-25 percent. Between 1987 and 1991 further changes were made to the tariff structure. The tariff on luxury goods was lowered in 1988 but this was replaced with a super sales tax in 1990 which ranged from 50 percent to 500 percent. Imports of fruits such as bananas, plantain, pineapples and guavas were subject to a tax of 500 percent while vegetables such as onions, potatoes and beans were subject to an import tax of 100 percent. However, this was reduced to the range of 10 to 100 percent in 1991.

Further liberalisation occurred with the lowering of the import tax rate on raw materials and capital goods by 5 percentage points in 1990. The sales tax on imported basic consumer goods was also reduced between 1989 and 1994. However protective duty rates were introduced for specified goods in 1990 and in 1994 to help some import-substituting industries such as those producing vegetable oil and soap, which were being subjected to intense competition. In 1994 import duties on all goods which were imported under exemption were raised to 10 percent and goods classified as standard saw an increase from 20 percent to 25 percent. With all the reforms in the 1990s, Ghana's simple average tariff fell to 13 percent in January 2000 from a high of 17 percent in 1992. However, in April 2000 a 'special import tax' of 20 percent was re-introduced covering some 7 percent of tariff lines. This raised the tariff on many consumer goods to 40 percent - well above the previous rate of 25 percent and consequently raised the average tariff to 14.7 percent. In 2002, the 'special import tax' was abolished in an effort to bring the tariff structure into harmony with ECOWAS and WTO provisions. Ghana's current tariff structure comprises four bands of 0, 5, 10 and 20 percent. Finished/consumer goods attract the highest rate of 20 percent while raw materials and intermediate goods are either zero-rated or attract a tariff of 10 percent. This applies to all goods except for some petroleum products which face specific tariffs. The average applied tariff is now 12.7 percent, down from 14.7 percent in 2000.

b.   Ghana's manufacturing sector

The Ghanaian manufacturing sector has undergone tremendous changes and has been subjected to various policy prescriptions since independence in an attempt to make it the engine of growth and economic prosperity. At independence, Ghana had a relatively underdeveloped and very narrow manufacturing sector accounting for only 0.8 percent of GDP. Under an import-substitution industrialisation (ISI) strategy, the manufacturing sector between the early 1960s and the early 1970s saw tremendous changes, with the state taking an important and growing role in the process. According to Steel (1972), by 1962 state-owned firms were producing about 12 percent of manufacturing output and this increased to about 20 percent in 1966. At the beginning of the 1970s the ISI strategy had begun to fail and by 1983, the sector was in a bad shape with negative growth rates.

The ERP, initiated in 1983 to get the Ghanaian economy out of its predicament, seems to have had a mixed impact on the manufacturing sector. The reform effort in Ghana which begun in 1983 sought to arrest and reverse the economic turmoil of the mid-1970s and early 1980s. Industrial strategy over this period shifted from an import-substitution and over-protected strategy to an outward-oriented, less protected or liberalized strategy. The liberalized strategy emphasized two main areas: first, the development of a more internationally competitive industrial sector with emphasis on local resource-based industries with the capacity for increased exports and efficient import substitution and secondly, the introduction of measures that would attract entrepreneurs and investors, into all major sub-sectors, with special emphasis on the development of appropriate technologies in small- and medium-scale manufacturing industries (Asante and Addo, 1997).

The manufacturing sector initially responded positively to the various policy measures adopted under the reforms after several years of continuous decline. The period following the introduction of the ERP also saw the emergence of a new crop of dynamic entrepreneurs. This culminated in increased growth in manufacturing output to an average of about 5 percent per annum between 1984 and 1987 (Figure 1). Indeed, one of the initial benefits of liberalization that accrued to Ghana's manufacturing sector was the improved utilization of installed capacity. This was a direct result of foreign exchange reforms that were pursued as part of the adjustment process. Exchange rate liberalization in Ghana initially eased foreign exchange pressures that had built up during the early 1960s to late 1970s. The reduced foreign exchange pressure made available and accessible the foreign exchange required to import the needed inputs (i.e. raw materials, equipment, spare parts etc.) for efficient and effective utilization of the installed capacity of many import-competing industries.

On the other hand, other manufacturing industries such as textiles, garments and electrical did not perform well because of stiff competition from imports. In 1988, the growth rate of the industrial sector and the manufacturing sub-sector started slowing down. In the late 1990s, the performance of the manufacturing sub-sector was mixed with an annual average growth rate of 4.5 percent from 1995 to 2000 (Figure 1). During the latter part of the 1990s, the decline in the manufacturing sub-sector's growth rate was attributed to the increase in crude oil prices, high domestic interest rates, significant depreciation in the value of the cedi and the domestic energy crisis that hit the economy in 1998. In addition, manufacturing industries in the textile and garments sub-sectors experienced substantial declines in output as a result of the intense competition that they were exposed to from cheaper imports. The decade 1995-2004 saw the manufacturing sector growing at 4.4 percent on average.

Figure 1: Growth in Industry and Manufacturing , 1983-2002 (%)

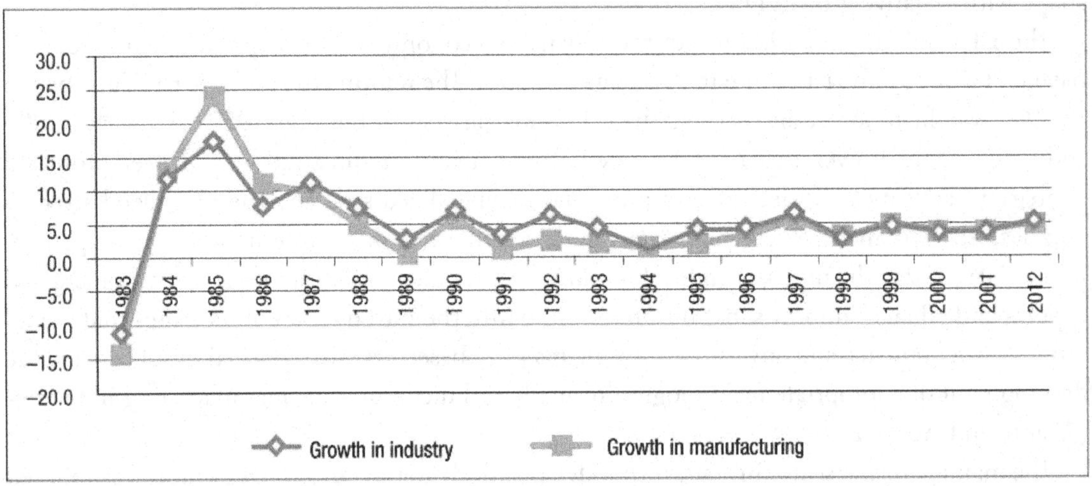

Source: Quarterly Digest of Statistics, GSS

3. Econometric Analysis

Our baseline specification is a standard Cobb-Douglas production function which links output with inputs and the firm's productivity as follows:

$$y_{ijt} = \beta_m m_{ijt} + \beta_l l_{ijt} + \beta_k k_{ijt} + w_{ijt} + \eta_{ijt} \tag{1}$$

where y_{ijt} denotes log real output, m_{ijt} is log intermediate materials, k_{ijt} is log physical capital, l_{ijt} is log employment, w_{ijt} is total factor productivity (TFP), η_{ijt} is a random disturbance, β_m, β_l, and β_k are input elasticities, and i, j, t denote firm, sector and time, respectively. If we assume that the share of intermediate input in output is constant, the output production function can be rewritten as a value-added specification. We report results for both specifications below.

Firm productivity is an unobservable firm characteristic, which can be recovered from estimating the production function (1) using actual input quantities. The basic problem in estimating (1) is that the input variables are in general correlated with the unobserved productivity shock, w_{ijt} but might not be observed by the econometrician, leading to the well-known simultaneity problem in production function estimation.[36] Several solutions have been proposed to address this econometric problem. In the most recent best-practices, firm-level TFP is calculated following the innovations espoused by Olley and Pakes (1996) that correct the simultaneity bias arising from the fact that firms choose their levels of input once they know their levels of productivity.[37] The method also corrects the selection bias induced by the fact that firms choose to stay or exit the market depending on their levels of productivity, which in turn depend on the levels of their fixed factor input, namely capital stock. The authors propose to overcome the simultaneity problem by using the firm's investment as a proxy for unobserved productivity shocks.

Other best-practice methods such as the within-group and GMM-type estimators (e.g., Arellano and Bond, 1991) have also been extensively employed to correct for simultaneity biases but it is believed that (if properly done) the Olley-Pakes estimator has several advantages as it does not assume that the firm-specific productivity component w_{ijt} "reduces to a 'fixed' (over time) firm effect...........and hence is a less costly solution to the omitted variable and/or simultaneity problem" (Frazer, 2005:592).[38] The problem with the Olley-Pakes estimator is that the procedure requires strictly positive investment, meaning that all observations with zero investment have to be dropped from the data. This condition may imply a considerable drop in the number of observations because often, firms do not have positive investment in every year.[39] More recently, Levinsohn and Petrin (2003) propose an estimation methodology that corrects the simultaneity bias using intermediate input expenditures, such as material inputs, as a proxy. This is especially useful as there are many firm-level datasets containing significantly less zeroobservations in intermediate inputs than in firm-level investment.

---

36 There are problems with estimating equation (2) with OLS; the method could be biased and would yield biased estimates of TFP if it turns out that the productivity shock in (2) is not orthogonal to the factor inputs as is implicit in OLS. See Marschak and Andrews (1944); Olley and Pakes (1996); Griliches and Mairesse (1998); and Levinsohn and Petrin (2003).

37 For example, if more productive firms are more likely to hire more workers and invest more capital due to higher current and anticipated future profitability, estimation methods such as OLS will not be consistent and thereby result in biased coefficient estimates; the estimated input coefficients would be higher than their true values.

38 Others have raised doubts about the appropriateness of the estimator's " internal" instruments (past levels for current differences and past differences for current levels) as they are likely to possess little resolving power (see Griliches and Mairesse, 1998).

39 For example, in the specific case of the data set under examination, about 32 percent of observations has zero investment while a further 44 percent has "missing" investment and therefore much information would be lost in dropping these observations, as required by the Olley-Pakes technique.

For a start, we follow Bigsten, Gebreeyesus and Söderbom (2009) and Dovis and Milgram-Baleix (2009) and use the "direct approach" to estimating production functions to estimate (1). To account for the simultaneity of input choices and unobserved productivity, we use the System-GMM estimator of Blundell and Bond (1998). We use twice lagged inputs and output as instruments in the differenced equation and lagged first-differences of inputs are instruments in the level equation. For comparison, we also estimated (1) with OLS and Fixed-effects estimators. The results of these regressions are reported in Tables 4 and 5. To assess the robustness of the findings, we apply a methodology that is similar to the one used by Dovis and Milgram-Baleix (2009), Fernandes (2007), Amiti and Konings (2007), Topalova (2004), and Pavcnik (2002) to study the correlation between total factor productivity and tariffs --- a two-step estimation procedure as proposed by Olley and Pakes. Since the Levinsohn-Petrin technique imposes less stringent data requirements than the Olley-Pakes approach, we follow several recent studies by choosing to adopt the former for the estimations in this chapter.[40]

In the first step, we estimate the production function (1) to obtain a measure of total factor productivity. We use the Levinsohn-Petrin method to estimate (1) to correct for the presence of selection and simultaneity biases in the input coefficients required to construct the measure of TFP.[41] In the second stage, we relate TFP to 3-digit industry tariffs and a set of firm characteristics believed to explain firm productivity. To explain TFP at the firm level, we use the following framework:

$$TFP_{ijt} = \alpha_0 + \alpha_1 TFP_{ijt-1} + \beta' X_{ijt} + \theta T_{jt} + \tau_t + \gamma_j + \delta_{ij} + \varepsilon_{ijt} \tag{2}$$

where TFP_{ijt} is total factor productivity at the firm level, X_{ijt} is a vector of firm characteristics, T_{jt} is the tariff variable, τ_t is a time-specific effect which takes into account macroeconomic shocks common to all firms, γ_j is a sector-level fixed effect, δ_{ij} is a firm-level fixed effect, ε_{ijt} is unobserved time varying productivity, and α, β and θ are parameters to be estimated. We use the System-GMM method proposed by Blundell and Bond (1998) to deal with the possible endogeneity of observable firm characteristics. Arellano and Bond (1991) recommend using the lagged values of the explanatory variables in levels as instruments under the assumptions that there is no serial correlation in the error term ε_{ijt} and the right-hand side variables. Thus, the GMM estimation procedure simultaneously addresses the problems of correlation and endogeneity. The consistency of the GMM estimator depends on the validity of the assumption that the error term does not exhibit serial correlation and on the validity of the instruments. By construction, the test for the null hypothesis of no first-order serial correlation should be rejected

---

40   See Levinsohn and Petrin (2003) for further details on the methodology. We implement this procedure using the "levpet" command in STATA, which was written by Levinsohn, Petrin and Brian Poi (2004).

41   The coefficients of the variable and fixed factor inputs are estimated at this stage. The dependent variable we use is value added (rather than gross revenue) and the GMM estimator is used.

under the identifying assumption that the error is not serially correlated; but the test for the null hypothesis of no second-order serial correlation, should not be rejected. We use two diagnostics tests proposed by Arellano and Bond (1991) and Blundell and Bond (1998), the Sargan test of over-identifying restrictions, and whether the differenced residuals are second-order serially correlated. Failure to reject the null hypotheses of both tests gives support to our model. We also control for unobservable characteristics that may explain current intra-firm productivity by taking into account the lagged value of TFP. The results from this estimation procedure are reported in Table 6.

4. Data Description

The data that is used in this chapter is from the World Bank Regional Project on Enterprise Development (RPED) dataset. The data is available from the Centre for the Study of African Economies at Oxford University. It is a panel survey of Ghanaian manufacturing firms covering the period from 1991 to 2002 and includes value of gross production, wage bill, number of employees, value of total raw materials, energy expenses, 4-digit industry dummies, value of fixed assets, and investment among other variables. We focus on the 1993-2002 period, since data on import tariffs are available only after 1992 for most of the firms. Box 1 provides more information about the data while Table A1 in the Appendix gives the definitions of all variables used in the analyses. The firm-level data is matched with commodity-level disaggregated data on import tariffs to examine the effects of trade liberalization on firm performance during the 1993-2002 period. This period is characterised by Ghana's increasing openness to trade; the significant phase of trade liberalisation in Ghana was undertaken during the 1980s, while the process to dismantle trade barriers in the framework of adhesion to WTO and ECOWAS protocols concluded in the early 2000s.

Table 1 shows total real output, real value added and real inputs from 1993 to 2002. A large degree of firm heterogeneity is found in inputs and outputs. Both real total output and real value added increased by more than twice over the period. Real output per worker and real value added per worker also increased by 17 percent and 55 percent respectively over this period, suggesting that Ghana experienced a high productivity gain. The productivity gains seem to have reflected in firms becoming relatively more capital intensive – real mean capital stock increased by more than 150 percent while employment increased by about 45 percent over the decade. Tariffs declined from an average of 20 percent in 1993 to 17 percent in 2002 while imports increased by just 5 percent during the period. Tariffs for 1993 and 2002 by industry are displayed in Table 2. For the period under study, Ghanaian MFN tariffs diminished slightly in all industries except for chemical products which remained at the same level.

Table 1: Summary Statistics

	1993	2002	% Change
Value Added	5,720	12,900	126
Output/Worker	182	212	17
Value added/Worker	60	93	55
Capital Stock	11,600	29,500	154
Employment	46	67	45
Intermediate Input	5,900	8,690	47
Tariff	20	17	13
Imports	1,460	1,528	5

Source: Authors' calculations from RPED data.

Note: Output, value added, intermediate input and capital stock in real Ghana cedis.

Table 2: Nominal MFN Tariffs and Imports

	Tariff (%)		Imports (000$)	
Manufacture of:	1993	2002	1993	2002
Textile & Apparel	22	19	998	619
Wood & Wood products	24	19	111	114
Basic metals	20	17	1,897	1,433
Machinery & Equipment	23	16	2,784	2,369
Chemicals	19	19	1,697	1,668
Food & Beverages	13	12	2,156	2,893
Average	20	17	1,460	1,528

Source: Tariff data are obtained from Ghana's Ministry of Trade; import data are from WITS

5. Empirical Results

In this section, we present the results of the estimation procedure described in Section 3, as well as results from OLS and firm fixed-effects. Table 4 reports results obtained from estimating a direct production function with real total output as the dependent variable. The productivity of a firm is determined by a set of regressors that may explain heterogeneity of firm performance. These include firm characteristics as well as the characteristics of the external environment in which the firm operates that can affect performance. Table 4 presents five different specifications of the determinants of firm productivity. The first and second columns present results from the estimation of the production function (1) by OLS and firm fixed-effects respectively. We introduced our trade policy measure, tariff, as an additional variable to test the correlation between trade protection and firm productivity. Specification 3 expands the base model with additional covariates and estimation is done by the SYS-GMM to deal with the potential endogeneity of the input variables and tariffs. If more employees are hired and more raw materials are consumed in periods of high productivity, OLS estimates of inputs' coefficients would be upwardly biased. In all specifications, we treat the input variables as endogenous using the lagged levels dated $t-2$ and before as instruments for the first-differenced equations and the lagged first-differences as instruments for the levels equations.

Next, we investigate if our results are robust to treating the tariff variable as endogenous. It is conceivable that the policy maker may increase trade protection in response to lobbying pressures from firms in industries with lower productivity.[42] In such a case, tariffs become endogenous and one needs to resort to instrumental variable regressions to get consistent estimates for the tariff coefficient. In specification 4, we replace the contemporaneous tariffs with lagged tariffs as a way of partly mitigating the potential bias. Then, in specification 5, we address the problem directly by estimating a specification where tariffs are instrumented by the Blundel and Bond procedure using the lagged levels dated $t-2$ and before as instruments for the first-differenced equations. For the levels equations we use the lagged first-differences as instruments. The validity of the instruments is checked by the Sargan test of over-identifying restrictions. The estimated models also satisfy the absence of second-order autocorrelation in the residuals. In all cases, the *m2* test does not indicate problems with the specification or validity of instruments.

The combined results from Table 4 confirm our *a priori* expectations. The inputs' coefficients are precisely estimated at the 1 percent confidence level. The export share and firm age variable are included in the estimations because exporters and older firms are generally expected to be relatively more productive than average. The export share has a positive and significant impact even at the 1 per cent level. This is in line with the vast literature, which has shown that exporters are typically more productive than non-exporters (see Greenaway and Kneller, 2007, for a survey). Firm age also has a positive sign, indicating that firms that have operated in Ghana for a longer have higher productivity, compared to those that have been around for just a while. Concerning the effect of trade policy, the results provide robust evidence that indicate a large, negative and statistically significant effect of tariffs on productivity, suggesting that trade liberalization may have increased productivity in the Ghanaian manufacturing sector.

---

42 Jones *et al* (2008) argue that such political economy mechanisms have played a limited role in explaining the pattern of protection and tariff reform in Africa during the 1990s. In that case, it would seem reasonable to argue that trade policy reforms were essentially exogenous.

Table 3: Tariffs and Firm-level Productivity – Output Regressions

VARIABLES	OLS 1	Fixed-Effects 2	SYS-GMM 3	SYS-GMM 4	SYS-GMM 5
Real Output $_{t-1}$			0.351***	0.349***	0.338***
			(0.00234)	(0.00232)	(0.00157)
Employment	0.231***	0.177***	0.107***	0.114***	0.117***
	(0.0154)	(0.0246)	(0.00376)	(0.00312)	(0.00382)
Capital Stock	0.0938***	0.00529	0.0982***	0.0977***	0.100***
	(0.00661)	(0.0222)	(0.00217)	(0.00272)	(0.00185)
Raw Materials	0.756***	0.699***	0.458***	0.454***	0.470***
	(0.00837)	-0.0112	(0.00204)	(0.00131)	(0.00176)
Tariff	-0.104***	0.00843	-0.152***		-0.0955***
	(0.0352)	(0.0608)	(0.00563)		(0.00394)
Tariff $_{t-1}$				-0.162***	
				(0.00475)	
Export Share			0.00156***	0.00164***	0.00129***
			(0.000112)	(0.00012)	(0.00009)
Firm Age			0.00445***	0.00443***	0.00399***
			(0.000215)	(0.00022)	(0.00025)
Accra			0.151***	0.141***	0.151***
			(0.00799)	(0.0114)	(0.0114)
Kumasi			0.157***	0.153***	0.162***
			(0.00866)	(0.00935)	(0.00911)
Takoradi			0.0679***	0.0494***	0.0621***
			(0.0105)	(0.0124)	(0.0113)
Constant	2.354***	5.138***	1.227***	1.344***	1.304***
	(0.117)	(0.399)	(0.0339)	(0.0309)	(0.0367)
Year Effects	yes	yes	yes	yes	yes
Observations	1,539	1,539	1,255	1,255	1,255
R-squared	0.97	0.79			
m2			0.793	0.819	0.759
Sargan			0.410	0.286	0.473

Source: Authors' calculations.

Notes:
1.   Dependent variable is log real output. All inputs and tariff are in logs.
2.   Standard errors are in parentheses. * Significant at 10%, ** at 5%, *** at 1%.
3.   The Sargan test is for the validity of the set of instruments.
4.   The test for 2nd (m2) - order serial correlation is asymptotically distributed as standard normal variables (see Arellano and Bond, 1991). The p-values report the probability of rejecting the null hypothesis of serial correlation, where the first differencing will induce (MA1) serial correlation if the time-varying component of the error term in levels is a serially uncorrelated disturbance.

Table 5 presents results for the value added (rather than output) specification of equation (1). The resulting tariff effects are qualitatively similar to those in Table 4. In both tables, most parameter estimates take on values within reasonable ranges, when compared to other productivity studies for African countries. In specification 6, we estimate an alternative specification allowing for a non-linear relation between productivity and export intensity. We hypothesize that the effect of trade policy on productivity may differ according to the degree of export intensity of the firm. Exporting firms may benefit more from trade liberalization as they are more subject to foreign competition (in foreign markets) and may be more exposed to advanced technologies. We test this hypothesis by introducing an interaction between tariffs and the export-to-output variables to allow productivity responses to vary between exporting and non-exporting firms. We are assuming that the productivity responses to trade liberalization may depend on the mode of globalization of the firm. The results of this estimation reported in column 6 confirm the previous finding of a negative and statistically significant coefficient on tariff, suggesting that in general, a cut in tariffs increases productivity. The results further indicate a strong effect of export intensity on productivity, both on its own and in conjunction with lower tariffs. The coefficient on the interactive term is negative and statistically significant, suggesting that greater openness is likely to be associated with significantly higher productivity for exporting firms. This means that high exporters found in low-tariff sectors enjoy relatively higher productivity than low exporters and non-exporting firms. Hence, further trade liberalization will increase their productivity disproportionately, *ceteris paribus*. These findings are generally consistent with studies that have documented a positive relationship between exporting and productivity in African manufacturing industries (Bigsten *et al*, 2004; Biesebroeck, 2005; Bigsten and Gebreeyesus, 2009).

Finally, in column 7, we introduce squared tariff in the model in order to test for nonlinearities. The estimated coefficients on both tariffs and its squared term are negative and statistically significant, suggesting that higher tariffs are particularly adverse for productivity.

Table 4: Tariffs and Firm-level Productivity – Value- added Regressions

VARIABLES	OLS 1	FE 2	SYS-GMM 3	SYS-GMM 4	SYS-GMM 5	SYS-GMM 6	SYS-GMM 7
Value added $t-1$			0.581***	0.579***	0.607***	0.609***	0.579***
			(0.00919)	(0.011)	(0.00388)	(0.00419)	(0.00908)
Employment	0.887***	0.558***	0.329***	0.331***	0.426***	0.392***	0.320***
	(0.0395)	(0.069)	(0.0234)	(0.0234)	(0.00663)	(0.00749)	(0.0246)
Capital Stock	0.238***	0.0474	0.135***	0.130***	0.0613***	0.0766***	0.149***
	(0.0184)	(0.0643)	(0.0158)	(0.0164)	(0.00669)	(0.0074)	(0.0152)
Tariff	-0.763***	-0.284	-0.148***		-0.194***	-0.135***	-0.878***
	(0.0992)	(0.174)	(0.0304)		(0.00697)	(0.00838)	(0.129)
Export Share			0.00194**	0.00231***	0.00153***	0.0189***	0.00512**
			(0.000798)	(0.000777)	(0.000195)	(0.000841)	(0.00204)
Tariff $t-1$				-0.150***			
				(0.0329)			
Tariff * Export Share						-0.0736***	-0.0169**
						(0.00261)	(0.00799)
Tariff Squared							-0.202***
							(0.0368)
Firm Age			0.00327***	0.00357***	0.00291***	0.00316***	0.00306***
			(0.00115)	(0.00112)	(0.000652)	(0.000628)	(0.00119)
Accra			0.306***	0.306***	0.353***	0.361***	0.277***
			(0.0522)	(0.0526)	(0.016)	(0.0273)	(0.0506)
Kumasi			0.375***	0.368***	0.391***	0.387***	0.360***
			(0.0545)	(0.0543)	(0.0158)	(0.0171)	(0.0534)
Takoradi			0.190***	0.195***	0.220***	0.223***	0.133**
			(0.0703)	(0.071)	(0.0269)	(0.0417)	(0.0646)
Constant	8.147***	13.28***	2.775***	2.905***	3.165***	3.055***	2.001***
	(0.254)	(1.081)	(0.263)	(0.242)	(0.0936)	(0.0955)	(0.281)
Year effects	yes	yes	yes	yes	yes	yes	yes
Industry effects	yes	yes	yes	yes	yes	yes	yes
Observations	1,462	1,462	1,162	1,162	1,162	1,162	1,162
R-squared	0.741	0.101					

VARIABLES	OLS 1	FE 2	SYS-GMM 3	SYS-GMM 4	SYS-GMM 5	SYS-GMM 6	SYS-GMM 7
m2			0.862	0.864	0.847	0.868	0.862
Sargan			0.198	0.177	0.561	0.628	0.217

Source: Authors' calculations.

Notes:
1. Dependent variable is log real value added. All inputs and tariff are in logs.
2. Standard errors are in parentheses. * Significant at 10%, ** at 5%, *** at 1%.
3. The Sargan test is for the validity of the set of instruments.
4. The test for 2nd (m2) - order serial correlation is asymptotically distributed as standard normal variables (see Arellano and Bond, 1991). The p-values report the probability of rejecting the null hypothesis of serial correlation, where the first differencing will induce (MA1) serial correlation if the time-varying component of the error term in levels is a serially uncorrelated disturbance.

We now turn to the results from the two-step estimation procedure described in Section 3. Table 6 reports the estimation results from several specifications where we relate TFP obtained through the Levinsohn and Petrin technique to 3-digit industry tariffs and a set of firm characteristics believed to explain firm productivity. The highly significant coefficients of the import tariffs display the expected signs, confirming our previous findings. Again from the relevant specification, we find that the effects of tariffs are higher for the firms that are more globalized (export a larger share of output). In all specifications, productivity increases with the age of the firm and the share of output that is exported. The effect of tariffs on firm productivity is always negative and precisely estimated at the 1 percent confidence level or better. Tariffs are measured in fractional terms so a percentage point reduction in nominal tariffs changes productivity by θ percent. Thus, the coefficient in column 5 implies that a reduction in tariffs by say 10 percentage points would result in an increase in firm productivity of about 1.2 percent. The results in column 7 again confirm the nonlinearities in the tariff-productivity relationship. The estimated coefficients on both tariffs and their squared term confirm that higher tariffs are particularly distortionary. The overall results provide robust support for the hypothesis that firms operating in industries less protected from foreign competition exhibit higher productivity, *ceteris paribus*.

Table 5: Tariffs and Total Factor Productivity

VARIABLES	OLS 1	FE 2	SYS-GMM 3	SYS-GMM 4	SYS-GMM 5	SYS-GMM 6	SYS-GMM 7
TFP $_{t-1}$			0.735***	0.738***	0.662***	0.661***	0.633***
			(0.0335)	(0.0343)	(0.0199)	(0.019)	(0.00584)
Tariff	-0.953***	-0.317*	-0.340***		-0.125**	-0.128**	-0.493***
	(0.108)	(0.175)	(0.0939)		(0.0543)	(0.0529)	(0.06)

VARIABLES	OLS 1	FE 2	SYS-GMM 3	SYS-GMM 4	SYS-GMM 5	SYS-GMM 6	SYS-GMM 7
Export Share			0.00185*	0.00190*	0.00231***	0.0142***	0.00492***
			(0.00107)	(0.00108)	(0.00076)	(0.00247)	(0.00073)
Tariff $_{t-1}$				-0.320***			
				(0.088)			
Tariff * Export Share						-0.0470***	-0.00844***
						(0.0104)	(0.00245)
Tariff Squared							-0.132***
							(0.0167)
Firm Age			0.00265	0.00224	0.00564***	0.00572***	0.00595***
			(0.00291)	(0.00294)	(0.00186)	(0.00183)	(0.00129)
Accra			0.271***	0.272***	0.248***	0.262***	0.256***
			(0.0648)	(0.0638)	(0.0508)	(0.0573)	(0.035)
Kumasi			0.230***	0.236***	0.278***	0.291***	0.265***
			(0.0655)	(0.0633)	(0.053)	(0.0577)	(0.0383)
Takoradi			0.109	0.114	0.112	0.141	0.156**
			(0.123)	(0.122)	(0.0872)	(0.0875)	(0.0627)
Constant	8.317***	9.641***	1.629***	1.726***	2.509***	2.500***	2.565***
	(0.212)	(0.306)	(0.319)	(0.311)	(0.227)	(0.224)	(0.106)
Year Effects	yes	yes	yes	yes	yes	yes	yes
Industry Effects	no	no	no	no	yes	yes	yes
Observations	1,462	1,462	1,149	1,149	1,149	1,149	1,149
R-squared	0.066	0.049					
m2			0.695	0.692	0.715	0.727	0.731
Sargan			0.490	0.606	0.599	0.713	0.384

Source: Authors' calculations.

Notes:
1. Dependent variable is $\ln(TFP_{it})$ from the Levinsohn and Petrin (2003) method. All inputs and tariff are in logs.
2. Standard errors are in parentheses. * Significant at 10%, ** at 5%, *** at 1%.
3. The Sargan test is for the validity of the set of instruments.
4. The test for 2nd (m2) - order serial correlation is asymptotically distributed as standard normal variables (see Arellano and Bond, 1991). The p-values report the probability of rejecting the null hypothesis of serial correlation, where the first differencing will induce (MA1) serial correlation if the time-varying component of the error term in levels is a serially uncorrelated disturbance.

6. Conclusion

The role of trade policy in forging economic growth and development has been an enduring area of research for economists since the industrial revolution of the 17th century. How does trade liberalization affect firm-level productivity? This is one of the most important questions in international economics, one that has generated a vast theoretical and empirical literature. Yet, the question remains controversial. This chapter empirically investigates the effects of trade liberalization on firm-level productivity in Ghana. We find, in the case of Ghanaian manufacturing, that it does affect firm-level productivity. We examine Ghanaian trade policy from 1993 to 2002, a period during which trade liberalization alternates with increased trade protection in varied ways across industries, to investigate the link between trade policy and firm productivity. Using a reasonably rich panel of manufacturing firms, we find a strong negative impact of nominal tariffs on firm productivity controlling for observed and unobserved firm characteristics and industry heterogeneity. The results from the chapter contribute to the ongoing theoretical and empirical debate on trade openness, productivity and growth. We find relatively large positive effects of tariff reductions on total factor productivity, a result that is robust to various alterations of the base model, including treating tariffs as endogenous and employing different estimation techniques. We note that these effects seem consistent with the hypothesis that trade liberalization has increased productivity in the domestic market. These results indicate that firms that are overprotected, as illustrated by high import tariffs pertaining to the industries in which they operate, have a lower level of TFP than firms that are exposed to competition.

We find also a strong effect of export intensity on productivity, both on its own and in conjunction with lower tariffs. Exporters appear to take more advantage of foreign competition than non-exporters and appear more sensitive to tariffs. The negative impact of trade protection on productivity is stronger for exporting firms (or firms that export larger shares of their output) relative to non-exporting firms. The use of lagged tariffs and instrumental variable estimation techniques and the evidence on the political economy of tariff determination in Ghana allow us to argue that the negative impact of tariffs is unlikely to reflect the endogeneity of protection.

References

Amiti, M. and J. Konings (2007), "Trade Liberalization, Intermediate Inputs and Productivity: Evidence from Indonesia", *American Economic Review*, 97(5), 1611–38.

Asante, Y. and S.E Addo, (1997): *"Industrial Development: Policies and Options"* in *Policies and Options for Ghanaian Economic Development* ed. Nyanteng, V.K. Institute of Statistical, Social and Economic Research, University of Ghana, Legon.

Asante, Y., F. Nixson and K. Tsikata (2000): "The Industrial Sector Policies & Economic Growth in Ghana" in *Economic Reforms in Ghana: The Miracle and the Mirage* ed. Aryeetey, E. Harrigan J. and Nissanke J. Woeli Publishing Services, Accra and Africa World Press, Trenton, NJ.

Bigsten, A. and M. Gebreeyesus (2009), "Firm Productivity and Exports: Evidence from Ethiopian Manufacturing", *Journal of Development Studies* 45(10), 1594-1614.

Bigsten, A., P. Collier, S. Dercon, M. Fafchamps, B. Gauthier, J. Gunning, A. Oduro, R. Oostendorp, C. Pattillo, M. Soderbom, F. Teal, and A. Zeufack (2004), "Do African Manufacturing Firms Learn from Exporting?", Journal of Development Studies, 40(3), 115-141.

Dovis, Marion and Juliette Milgram-Baleix, (2009), "Trade, Tariffs and Total Factor Productivity: The Case of Spanish Firms", *The World Economy*, pp. 575-605.

Greenaway, D., Gullstrand, J., & R. Kneller, (2003), "Exporting May Not Always Boost Firm Level Productivity", GEP Research Paper 2003/26.

Greenaway, David and Richard Kneller, (2004), Exporting and Productivity in the United Kingdom, Research Paper 2004/34.

Grossman, Gene and Elhana Helpman, (1991), *Innovation and Growth in the Global Economy, MIT Press*.

ISSER: *The State of the Ghanaian Economy*, 1997 to 2007 Issues: Chapters on the Industrial Sector. Institute of Statistical, Social and Economic Research, University of Ghana, Legon.

Levinsohn, J. and A. Petrin (2003), "Estimating Production Functions Using Inputs to Control for Unobservables", *Review of Economic Studies* 70(2), 317-341.

Melitz, Marc (2003) "The Impact of Trade on Intra-industry Reallocations and Aggregate Industry Productivity", *Econometrica*, Vol. 71, pp.1695-1725.

Olley, G. Steven and Ariel Pakes, (1996) "The Dynamics of Productivity in the Telecommunications Equipment Industry", *Econometrica*, Vol. 64, No. 6, pp. 1263-1297.

Pavcnik, N. (2002), "Trade Liberalisation, Exit and Productivity Improvements: Evidence from Chilean Plants", *Review of Economic Studies*, 69, 245–76.

Topalova, Petia (2004) "Trade Liberalization and Firm Productivity: The Case of India", IMF Working Paper 04/28.

Wangwu, S. and H. Semboja, (2002): "Impact of Structural Adjustment on Industrialization and Technology in Africa" in *African Voices on Structural Adjustment: Companion to our Continent our future* eds. by Mkandawire T. and Soludo C. IDRC/CODESRIA/Africa World Press.

Appendix

Table A1: List of Variables and Definitions - RPED Panel Data

Variable Name	Variable Description
Total Factor Productivity (TFP)	Calculated using the Levinsohn and Petrin (2003) methodology
Output	Real value of firm's total production during previous year
Physical Capital Stock	Real value of firm's total physical capital stock
Intermediate Input	Real value of firm's raw material cost
Employment	Firm's total employment level
Firm Age	Age of firm
Export Share	Share of exports in firm's total output
Tariff	Nominal MFN tariff at the 3-digit level
Location	A dummy for each of the following regions: Accra, Kumasi, Takoradi. The omitted region is Cape Coast.

Box 1: RPED Manufacturing Panel Survey

The World Bank Regional Project on Enterprise Development (RPED) survey is a comprehensive panel dataset from surveys of the Ghanaian manufacturing sector conducted in seven rounds between 1991 and 2002. The data was collected by a team from the Centre for the Study of African Economies (CSAE), University of Oxford, the University of Ghana, Legon, and the Ghana Statistical Service. The first sample of firms was drawn randomly from the Census of Manufacturing Activities conducted in 1987. The firms were categorized based on sector and location. In total, there are nine sectors including textiles and garments and metal works. They were also categorized by location: Accra, Cape Coast, Kumasi and Takoradi, all of which constitute major industrial centres in Ghana. The coverage of this dataset is quite extensive as most of the major manufacturing sectors at the time under investigation are represented. When firms exited from the sample, they were replaced with firms of the same size category, sector, and location, so that approximately (but not exactly) 200 firms were sampled in each year. The dataset has the advantage of containing a reasonably large number of firms, by African standards, over a long period of time and information on many firm characteristics. The data collected span all major investment climate topics, ranging from infrastructure and access to finance to corruption and crime. Detailed productivity information includes firm finances, costs such as labour and materials, sales, and investment. For more information, including details on the sampling procedure, visit http://www.csae.ox.ac.uk/

The Impact of the Elimination of Trade Taxes on Poverty and Income Distribution in Ghana

Vijay Bhasin

1. Introduction

Developing countries have witnessed major macroeconomic shocks that have had significant impact on the level of poverty and the distribution of incomes. In order to understand the linkages between macroeconomic shocks and their impact at the micro level, Computable General Equilibrium (CGE) models are required. CGE models are preferred to the partial equilibrium models because they can explain the inter linkages among the various sectors of the economy and the agents present in the model. The effects of trade liberalization on poverty and income distribution can be examined by using Social Accounting Matrices (SAM) and CGE models. The SAM is a comprehensive, disaggregated, consistent and complete data system that captures the interdependence that exists within a socio-economic system. CGE models have been widely used to simulate the impact of macroeconomic policies on income distribution and poverty. One can identify three types of CGE models that try to address this question. The first type considers only the representative agent and provides information on inequalities between groups without giving any results in terms of poverty. This strand of literature includes Adelman and Robinson (1979) for Korea; Dervis, de Melo and Robinson (1982) and Gunning (1983) for Kenya; Thorbecke (1991) for Indonesia; Morrisson (1991) for Morocco; Chia, Wahba and Whalley (1994) for Cote d'Ivoire, and Obi (2003) for Nigeria. The second type of modelling is grounded on the previous one but includes information on intra group income distributions and endogenises poverty. This strand of literature includes de Janvry, Sadoulet and Fargeix (1991), Decaluwe, Patry, Savard and Thorbecke (1999); Azis and Thorbecke (2001); Aka (2006), and Bhasin and Annim (2005). The third type of modelling is based on the second type but endogenises both the intra-group income distribution and poverty. This strand of literature includes Cogneau and Robillard (1999), Decaluwe, Dumont and Savard (1999), and Chitiga, *et al* (2005). The present study uses the second type of modelling approach. However, it should be mentioned that this approach by itself will not be able to capture all channels by which trade liberalization will impact on poverty and income distribution because the model being used is a static model.

It is generally believed that expanded trade holds the key to prosperity for developing countries. According to this view, if the industrialised countries would eliminate their trade barriers, especially in apparel and agriculture, this would provide a basis for growth in developing countries, pulling hundreds of millions of people out of poverty. According to the World Bank (2002), a reduction in world barriers to trade could accelerate growth, provide stimulus to new forms of productivity-enhancing specialization, and lead to a more rapid pace of job creation and poverty reduction around the world. Weisbrot and Baker (2002) have argued that most of the projected gains from trade liberalization do not come from the removal of trade barriers in the industrialized countries . The biggest source of gains to developing countries is the removal of their own barriers to trade. In principle, these gains would be available whether or not the industrialized countries also followed a path of trade liberalization. They also look at the reasons why developing countries may choose not to liberalize, in spite of the potential gains. The two most important considerations are the loss of revenue due to tariff reductions, and the economic and social disruptions caused by rapid displacement of workers from agriculture. This raises the question of what type of fiscal reforms should be adopted by developing countries to liberalize their trade and reap the benefits of trade. According to Baker and Weisbrot (2001), this type of fiscal reform could be where the lost tariff revenue is replaced by an increase in non-distortionary lump sum taxes. The other alternative is to finance trade liberalization through foreign capital inflows.

Foreign capital inflows comprise remittances from abroad, foreign aid, foreign direct investment (FDI), portfolio investment and commercial bank lending. Since the CGE model is a real model, we consider only the real components of foreign capital inflows, e.g. foreign remittances, foreign aid and foreign direct investment. The financial inflows e.g. portfolio investment and commercial bank lending are not considered in the CGE model. Remittances from the rest of the world to households directly affect their incomes and can reduce poverty (Gustafsson and Makonnen, 1993; Siddiqui and Kemal, 2002a; Taylor, Mora and Adams, 2005; Adams, 2005; and Bhasin and Obeng, 2006). Foreign aid can reduce poverty through its impact on household income via public current spending and capital expenditures (Anderson and Evia, 2003). It is argued that a direct link between FDI and poverty reduction does not exist, while three indirect links are possible. First, FDI-induced increases in national income offer a potential benefit to the poor. Secondly, well-developed linkages between foreign firms and local suppliers may generate employment opportunities for the poor. Thirdly, FDI may lead to higher wages. FDI can affect household income and reduce poverty through additional private and public investment (Siddiqui and Kemal, 2002b; and Arbenser, 2004).

Trade liberalization in Ghana was characterized by the removal of quantitative restrictions on the current (import licences and banned items) and capital accounts (restrictions on the repatriation of profits), simplification of the tariff structure, and lowering the level and range of tariffs. However, in the present study we define trade liberalization as the removal of import and export tariffs on agricultural and industrial goods as well as the removal of restrictions on the capital account of the balance of payments. Moreover, the trade liberalization is unilateral and partial sector-wise because only one form of trade-related tariff on agricultural and industrial goods is eliminated at a point of time.

Despite the adoption of trade-related reforms and fiscal reforms in Ghana, growth has not accelerated and poverty remains widespread and pervasive, particularly in the rural areas. Trade and fiscal reforms are recognised as a potent tool for enhancing growth, redistributing income and reducing poverty. It is generally believed that trade liberalization is poverty alleviating in the long run and may be poverty enhancing in the short run. Moreover, the impact of trade liberalization on the poor also depends on the sectors in which trade reforms take place. Multilateral agencies such as the World Bank and the International Monetary Fund (IMF) have been making their funding operations in developing countries conditional on the progress achieved nationally with respect to poverty reduction policies and trade liberalization measures. This requires an assessment and the quantification of the impact of economic policies on the poor.

Trade liberalization envisages a fall in tax revenue that can be compensated by foreign savings or domestic savings. Foreign capital inflows generally come to the developing countries with conditionality. If the developing country does not want to accept the conditional funding then it may have to finance trade liberalization through domestic resources. One of the ways is to raise the value-added tax (VAT) to finance trade liberalization. This chapter tries to provide answers to the following questions. What is the relationship between trade liberalization and poverty and income distribution in Ghana? Is it poverty alleviating or poverty enhancing? What is the contribution of trade liberalization to poverty? What is the contribution of foreign capital inflows to poverty? What is the contribution of value-added tax to poverty? What is their combined effect on poverty and income distribution?

The basic objective of the chapter is to assess the impact of partial sector-wise trade liberalization on poverty and income distribution of households in Ghana. Specifically, this is achieved by considering three scenarios. Elimination of import and export tariffs on agricultural and industrial goods (final goods as well as inputs) is considered in the first scenario. In the second scenario, partial sector-wise trade liberalization is combined with foreign capital inflows. In the third scenario, partial sector-wise trade liberalization is combined with value-added tax.

2. Trade Liberalization and Poverty Reduction in Ghana

Import controls were introduced in Ghana through import licences and the policy of import controls was continued from 1961-1983. During the period 1961-69, a mixed policy was adopted with respect to foreign capital inflows and as a result, Ghana was successful in attracting foreign direct investment and foreign aid. However, during the period 1969-83, restrictive policy was adopted with respect to foreign capital inflows and as a result Ghana was not successful in attracting FDI and Foreign Aid. Ghana pursued a more liberalized policy on the current as well as capital accounts of the balance of payments after 1983 and was successful in attracting foreign resources. After 1986, most of the quantitative restrictions, including import licensing, were eliminated along with the simplification of the tariff structure and reduction in the level and range of tariffs in Ghana.

Poverty in Ghana has many dimensions. Poor communities are characterised by low-income, malnutrition, ill health, illiteracy, and insecurity. There is also a sense of powerless and isolation. These different aspects interact and keep households and communities in persistent poverty. Using the Ghana Living Standards Surveys data, the Ghana Statistical Service (2000) classified the incidence, the depth, and severity of poverty into two broad groups, rural and urban. Each of these groups was in turn subdivided into forest, coastal and savannah regions, with the capital, Accra, standing alone. It also gave the contribution of ecological zones to total poverty in the country. Both the food energy intake and the cost of basic needs methods were used in determining the poverty lines in the construction of the poverty profile. Upper and lower poverty lines were set, with the lower line as the extreme or critical poverty line. A comparison was also made between poverty in 1991/92 and 1998/99. The overall trend in poverty during the 1990s broadly favourable in Ghana. Taking the upper poverty line of GHc 90, the percentage of the Ghanaian population defined as poor fell from almost 52 percent in 1991-92 to just fewer than 40percent in 1998-99. At the national level, the incidence of consumption poverty fell by 12.2 percent over this seven-year period. It was found that poverty is substantially higher in rural areas than urban areas and is disproportionately concentrated in the rural savannah. The decline, however, is not evenly distributed according to ecological zones and regions.

The incidence of poverty in Ghana is still very high and there is a need to reduce poverty. In the present study, the monetary poverty line of GHc 66.53 per annum was obtained from the consumption basket of the bottom 20percent of the distribution of individuals by their standard of living, which provided 2,900 kilocalories per equivalent adult per day. The commodities that were included in this consumption basket numbered about 120 and come from the agricultural, industrial and services sectors.

3. Literature Review

According to Bourguignon (2002 and 2004) absolute poverty reduction could be achieved through two effects: (i) the growth effect, i.e. the effect of the growth rate of the mean income of the population; and (ii) the distribution effect, i.e., the change in income distribution. In order to analyze and understand the impact of openness on poverty and income distribution, both these links have to be scrutinized. The first link is from openness to growth. The main manifestation of openness is through trade and capital movement liberalization which in turn is presumed to affect growth directly through three sub-channels: exports, imports and capital inflows. Trade liberalization policies encourage exports which benefit export industries and contribute to GDP growth. A second sub-channel links increased imports to growth. A country that switches from a regime of import substitution to one of trade liberalization will, in the short run, hurt previously protected domestic industries, and suffers from a fall in fiscal revenues as a result of lower tariffs. However, the initial negative consequences on output are likely to be more than compensated through a more efficient allocation of resources and benefits of competition, leading to a higher growth path. The third sub-channel operates through the impact of foreign direct investment (FDI) and portfolio and other capital flows on domestic output and growth. If FDI takes the form of 'Greenfield' investment as opposed to investment through merger and acquisition, much of the capital inflow from transnational corporations (TNCs) tends to be converted directly into factories producing new products.

According to Winters *et al.* (2004), trade liberalization could impact poverty through economic growth, households and markets, wages and employment, and government revenue and spending. Trade liberalization and openness stimulate long-run growth and incomes, sustained growth requires increases in productivity, and macroeconomic volatility may have adverse effects on growth. Trade liberalization could affect poverty through changes in the sources of incomes of households, consumption and investment decisions, transmission of price changes, response of markets, spillover benefits, and the vulnerability of households. The other channel through which trade liberalization can impact poverty is through wages, employment, and transitional unemployment. Lastly, trade liberalization affects poverty through changes in government revenue and spending.

The second link is between income distribution and poverty. The income distribution effects induced by a shift in relative product prices in the process of the opening up of trade are well-known, as postulated in the Stolper-Samuelson theorem of international trade. The losers (especially the poor residing in either urban or rural areas) may be vulnerable to these induced effects in addition to changes in absolute and relative prices of wage goods (Williamson, 2002). Thus, trade liberalization can affect poverty directly through relative price changes in factor markets and goods markets. According to the Stolper-Samuelson theorem as applied to within-country inequality, developing countries well endowed with unskilled labour should experience a decline in income inequality through an increased demand for unskilled labour, while unskilled labour in developed countries would lose out, with an adverse effect on equity.

CGE models have been used extensively to investigate the effects of policy change within an economy since they take into account interactions and interdependencies within the economy. Bussolo and Round (2003) have used a CGE model and the 1993 SAM for Ghana to investigate the possible effects of a range of budget-neutral redistributive income transfers on poverty. The classification of households was based on agriculture-non-agriculture, savannah, forest and Coast. Four financing schemes for the short-run and long-run factor market adjustment rules were simulated. The results indicated that poverty outcomes were different according to which of the four rules, i.e. income taxation, corporate taxation, indirect taxes, and tariffs, were chosen in the period under consideration. In this respect, the authors found tariffs as the financing scheme with the largest reduction in poverty, followed by indirect taxes, corporate taxes and household direct taxes in that order under the long-run factor market closure rule. The short-run outcomes were not very clear, except that there appeared to be an increase in overall poverty under the corporate tax financing rule. The reduction in the incidence of poverty ranged from 0.4 percentage points to 4.8 percentage points and the increase in the incidence of poverty ranged from 1.3 percentage points to 7.6 percentage points due to an increase in tariffs. On the other hand, the reduction in the incidence of poverty ranged from 0.7 percentage points to 11.3 percentage points and the increase in the incidence of poverty ranged from 6.1 percentage points to 16.4 percentage points due to an increase in indirect taxes.

Arbenser (2004) examined the impact of FDI on incomes of households in Ghana using the 1993 SAM. In the model, the author disaggregated households into four groups, namely, household urban skilled, household urban non-skilled, household rural agriculture and household rural non-agriculture. Three counterfactual simulations were carried out: simulation 1 consisted of 50 percent increase in FDI inflows with an endogenous foreign exchange rate and fixed current account balance. The second simulation involved 50 percent cut in tariffs with flexible government savings and mobile factors. The third simulation was a mixture of simulations 1 and 2. Arbenser (2004) shows that increase in FDI inflows raise the household income by more than 1.3 percent; urban skilled households register the highest percentage increase in income followed closely by rural agricultural households , and the lowest income gain accrues to urban non-skilled households . It also establishes that increase in FDI inflows and a reduction of tariff levels are complementary policies that enhance household welfare.

Bhasin and Annim (2005) used the 1999 SAM for Ghana and static CGE model to analyze the impact of the elimination of trade taxes accompanied by an increase in VAT on the incidence, depth, and severity of poverty and income distribution of five categories of households: agriculture farmers, private sector employees, public sector employees, non-farm self employed and non-working. They analyzed the impact of two shocks on poverty and income distribution. The first shock takes the form of elimination of trade-related import taxes on goods and services accompanied by an increase in VAT by 100 percent. The second shock involves the elimination of export taxes on goods and services accompanied by an increase in VAT by 100 percent. The chapter shows that the first shock reduces the incidence, depth, and severity of poverty, and improves the income distribution of households. In the first simulation, reduction in the incidence of poverty ranges from 0.71 percentage points to 1.50 percentage points, the depth of poverty ranges from 0.25 percentage points to 0.67 percentage points, and the severity of poverty ranges from 0.25 percentage points to 0.38 percentage points. The mean income improvement ranges from 1.31 percent to 3.86 percent. Although this result may appear to be unconventional, it is obtained because of the closure rule that allows a transfer of VAT revenue to households in Ghana through poverty alleviation programmes. Bhasin and Annim (2005) also show that the second type of shock increases the incidence, depth, and severity of poverty, and worsens income distribution of households. In the second simulation, theincrease in the incidence of poverty ranges from 0.18 percentage points to 0.22 percentage points, the depth of poverty ranges from 0.04 percentage points to 0.11 percentage points, and the severity of poverty ranges from 0.03 percentage points to 0.09 percentage points. The mean income reduction ranges from 3.81 percent to 4.08 percent.

Chitiga, et al (2005) used a CGE model and a SAM for 1995 to study the impact of trade liberalization on poverty in Zimbabwe. The model contained 16 production sectors, four factors of production, namely skilled labour, unskilled labour, capital and land and 14,006 households categorized by location and skill. The authors employed a micro-simulation approach where household data was incorporated into the CGE model and simulated with individual households. The simulation that was conducted involved total removal of import tariffs. The complete removal of tariffs reduced overall poverty in the economy, falling more in the urban than in the rural areas, while inequality hardly changed. The decrease in the incidence of poverty ranges from 0.01 percent to 0.02 percent, the depth of poverty ranges from 0.003 percent to 0.01 percent, and the severity of poverty ranges from 0.002 percent to 0.01 percent. The Gini index shows that the decrease in inequality ranges between 0.002 percent and 0.003%.

Aka (2006) used a CGE model to analyze the effects of removing trade taxes and instituting some fiscal reform on inequality and poverty in Cote d'Ivoire. The author used an aggregated SAM with three tradable sectors and a non-tradable sector, nine groups of households based on the ENV 1998 survey data and SCN 1993 Cote d'Ivoire national accounts. Four simulations were carried out; the first simulation considered the elimination of taxes on agricultural exported goods; the second simulation involved the elimination of taxes on agricultural exported goods combined with an increase of 20 percent in indirect taxes; the third simulation considered the elimination of taxes on agricultural exported goods combined with the elimination of taxes on imported goods, and the fourth simulation involved the third simulation with an increase of 20 percent in indirect taxes. Poverty increases for all categories of households in simulations one and two. The increase in the incidence of poverty ranges from 0.31 percentage points to 4.05 percentage points, the depth of poverty ranges from 0.63 percentage points to 1.69 percentage points, and the severity of poverty ranges from 0.48 percentage points to 0.92 percentage points in simulations one and two. In simulations 3 and 4, poverty decreases for all the groups, except for other food crop farmers and agricultural workers. The decrease in the incidence of poverty ranges from 0.01 percentage points to 1.48 percentage points, the depth of poverty ranges from 0.19 percentage points to 0.53 percentage points, and the severity of poverty ranges from 0.14

percentage points to 0.27 percentage points in simulations 3 and 4. The Gini index shows that inequality increases for all the socioeconomic groups in these simulations.

4. Features of the Model and Methodology

The general equilibrium model presented here is based on the works of Decaluwe, Patry, Savard, and Thorbecke (1999); Siddiqui and Kemal (2002b); Aka (2006) and Bhasin and Annim (2005). This model represents a small open economy that has no influence on international markets. The model is developed in such a way that it is consistent with the Social Accounting Matrix of Ghana (SAM) for the year 1999 and Ghana Living Standards Survey 4 for the year 1999. The integrated SAM for 1999 is adopted from Bhasin and Annim (2005). The CGE model for Ghana is presented in Appendix A. In the CGE model, there are 51 basic equations, comprising 10 equations for production and trade block; 16 equations for income, taxes, savings, and investment block; 8 equations for demand for commodities block; 12 equations for prices; and 5 equations for equilibrium conditions and macroeconomic closures. Since there are three production activities and five categories of households, the total numbers of equations to be solved are 147. There are 147 endogenous variables and 33 exogenous variables. The model is just identified as containing as many endogenous variables as equations.

The model is calibrated to a 1999 dataset. The GAMS software is used to check for the consistency of the data with the equilibrium conditions and to perform the simulations. The benchmark equilibrium must be replicated with the use of calibrated parameters and base-year data. The pre-shock values for the variables are obtained from the solution of the specified model. The post-shock effects of these simulations are used to find the effects on the poverty line and the incomes of households. The DAD software is used to evaluate the poverty measures and PCGIVE software is used to plot the income distribution of households before and after the exogenous shocks. The pre-shock and post-shock poverty levels are obtained using Foster, Greer and Thorbecke (FGT) poverty measures

$$POV_{k,h} = \int_0^z [(z - y_h)/z]^k f(y_h) \, dy_h, \, k = 0,1,2$$

where y_h is the income of household h , k is a poverty-aversion parameter, z is the endogenously determined poverty line. The incidence of poverty is indicated by $k = 0$. The depth of poverty is indicated by $k = 1$, and the severity of poverty is indicated by $k = 2$.

Since CGE models are fully calibrated on the basis of an initial year SAM that provides a set of consistent initial conditions and the SAM does not contain information on intra socio-economic household group income distribution, it is advisable to generate the intra group income distribution in the same base year as that of the SAM to calibrate the general equilibrium model. Several approaches have been used in the literature to describe and define intra-group distribution of income in a CGE framework. For example, de Janvry *et al.* (1991) used both a lognormal and a Pareto distribution function to depict income distribution. Decaluwe, Patry, Savard, and Thorbecke (1999) and Aka (2006) used the Beta distribution to represent the intra -group income distribution. Unlike the lognormal, the Beta function is much more flexible when it comes to the asymmetric forms it can adopt. However, since we know very little about the probability density functions of the incomes of households, density functions may be interpolated to give a clearer picture of the implied distributional shape. To estimate the density functions without imposing too many assumptions about its properties, a non-parametric approach is used in PCGIVE based on a kernel estimator of density function $f(Y_h)$.

The kernel estimator of the density f is defined by:

$$f(Y_h) = (1/Tu) \sum_{t=1}^{T} K\{(1/u)(Y_h - y_{ht})\}$$

where $K\{\}$ is the kernel function and u is a 'window width' or smoothing parameter and corresponds to the width of histogram bars. The kernel K used is the Normal or Gaussian kernel.

5. Analysis of Simulation Results

In the first simulation, we eliminate the trade-related import tariff on agricultural goods (final goods as well as inputs). In the second simulation, we eliminate the trade-related import tariff on agricultural goods that is compensated for by an increase in foreign capital inflows by 0.63 percent, which are redistributed to households in the form of transfer payments in proportion to their share in the transfer payments. The reduction in government income is compensated by an equivalent amount of foreign capital inflows and that gives us 0.63 percent. In the third simulation, we eliminate the trade-related import tariff on agricultural goods and increase the value-added tax by 50 percent and this tax revenue is redistributed to households in the form of transfer payments in proportion to their share in total transfer payments. The reduction in government income is compensated for by an increase in VAT by 50 percent. Table 1 indicates the effects of these simulations on macroeconomic variables.

Table1: **Simulation Results for the Elimination of Import Tariffs on Agricultural Goods**

Variables	Base level	Simulation 1: Elimination of import tariffs on agricultural goods	Percentage Increase or Decrease	Simulation 2: Elimination of import tariffs on agricultural goods and 0.63% increase in foreign capital inflows	Percentage Increase or Decrease	Simulation: 3. Elimination of import tariffs on agricultural goods and 50% increase in value added tax	Percentage Increase or Decrease
Government Income	631.43	612.19	-3.05	613.11	-2.90	675.84	7.03
Income of Agricultural Households	314.40	316.17	0.56	322.52	2.58	326.32	3.79
Income of Public Sector Employees	283.82	285.53	0.60	289.12	1.87	291.27	2.62
Income of Private Sector Employees	246.14	247.64	0.61	250.28	1.68	251.87	2.33
Income of Non-farm Self Employed	264.28	265.86	0.60	269.13	1.84	271.09	2.58
Income of Non-working	271.50	273.08	0.58	277.57	2.24	280.26	3.23
Composite Price of Agricultural Goods	0.576	0.550	-4.51	0.551	-4.34	0.552	-4.17
Composite Price of Industrial Goods	0.707	0.707	0.00	0.708	0.14	0.709	0.28
Composite Price of Services	0.817	0.819	0.24	0.819	0.24	0.819	0.24

In these simulations, elimination of import tariffs on agricultural goods leads to a reduction in the prices of imported agricultural goods. As a result, imports of agricultural goods become cheaper and consumers substitute imported agricultural goods for the domestically produced agricultural goods, thereby causing the demand for agricultural imports to increase. Since the industrial goods and services are used in the production of agricultural goods (input-output linkages), it is likely that the imports of industrial goods and services (wholesale and retail trade services) will increase along with the increase in imports of agricultural goods even though there are no cuts in the import tariffs on industrial goods and services. The reduction in domestic costs caused by cuts in agricultural import tariffs increases the profitability of the agricultural sector. This leads to increased production of agricultural goods, thereby causing the exports of agricultural goods to increase in the first two simulations. Due to the production linkages between the agriculture and services sectors, the production of services also increases in the second and third simulation. However, due to the increased domestic supply of services and the non-tradable nature of some services, exports of services decline. Since the agricultural and services sectors are expanding in the second and third simulations, this increases the demand for labour and capital in these two sectors. As labour and capital move away from the industrial sector, production in the industrial sector declines, thereby causing the exports of industrial goods to decline. Due to this sectoral reallocation of labour and capital, returns to labour and capital increase. The incomes of all types of households increase because of an increase in factor prices, reallocation of existing resources and inflows of foreign direct investment, and remittances received from abroad and transfer payments received from the government that arise due to foreign aid or additional tax revenue. The cut in import tariffs on agricultural goods reduces the prices of composite goods in the agricultural sector and increases the prices of composite goods in the industrial and services sectors. However, the net effect of these changes in the prices of composite goods is to reduce the poverty line by 2.83 percent, 2.66 percent, and 2.54 percent in the first, second and third simulations, respectively. Changes in households' incomes and poverty line determine the net effect on the incidence, depth, and severity of households' poverty.

Table 2 presents information on the incidence, depth, and severity of poverty for the base year and variations in these measures for the simulations relating to import tariffs on agricultural goods. In the base year, the incidence, depth, and severity of poverty is highest among the private sector employees. The incidence, depth, and severity of poverty is lowest among agricultural households. In these simulations, changes in the prices of composite goods reduce the poverty line and incomes of all households increase. This causes the incidence, depth, and severity of poverty for all categories of households to be reduced. The maximum reduction in the incidence of poverty is noticed for the non-farm self-employed, whereas the maximum reduction in the depth and severity of poverty is observed for the private sector employees. The lowest reduction in the incidence of poverty is for the public sector employees, whereas the lowest reduction in the depth of poverty is observed for the agricultural households in the first simulation, and public sector employees in the second and third simulations. The lowest reduction in the severity of poverty is noticed for agricultural households in the first simulation, and public sector employees in the second and third simulations. The difference between the base and the first simulation captures the effect of elimination of import tariffs of agricultural goods on poverty. The difference between the first simulation and the second simulation captures the effect of foreign capital inflows on poverty. The difference between the first simulation and the third simulation captures the effect of value-added tax on poverty. These effects vary across households.

Table 2: Poverty Measures for the Base Year and Simulations for Import Tariffs on Agricultural Goods

		Agricultural Households Employees	Public Sector Employees	Private Sector Employed	Non-farm Self-	Non-Working
Incidence of Poverty						
(alpha=0)	base	17.29%	19.28%	25.36%	21.04%	20.00%
	Simulation 1	16.52%	18.75%	24.31%	19.67%	19.36%
		(-0.77%)	(-0.53%)	(-1.05%)	(-1.37%)	(-0.64%)
	Simulation 2	16.35%	18.57%	24.10%	19.48%	18.94%
		(-0.94%)	(-0.71%)	(-1.26%)	(-1.56%)	(-1.06%)
	Simulation 3	16.11%	18.57%	24.10%	19.41%	18.94%
		(-1.18%)	(-0.71%)	(-1.26%)	(-1.63%)	(-1.06%)
Depth of Poverty						
(alpha=1)	base	7.15%	9.02%	9.85%	8.56%	7.99%
	Simulation 1	6.82%	8.66%	9.33%	8.15%	7.59%
		(-0.33%)	(-0.36%)	(-0.52%)	(-0.41%)	(-0.40%)
	Simulation 2	6.64%	8.55%	9.20%	8.03%	7.42%
		(-0.51%)	(-0.47%)	(-0.65%)	(-0.53%)	(-0.57%)
	Simulation 3	6.54%	8.49%	9.12%	7.96%	7.32%
		(-0.61%)	(-0.53%)	(-0.73%)	(-0.60%)	(-0.67%)
Severity of Poverty						
(alpha=2)	base	4.16%	5.30%	5.41%	4.96%	4.30%
	Simulation 1	3.97%	5.09%	5.11%	4.73%	4.06%
		(-0.19%)	(-0.21%)	(-0.30%)	(-0.23%)	(-0.24%)
	Simulation 2	3.87%	5.02%	5.04%	4.66%	3.96%
		(-0.29%)	(-0.28%)	(-0.37%)	(-0.30%)	(-0.34%)

		Agricultural Households Employees	Public Sector Employees	Private Sector Employed	Non-farm Self-	Non-Working
	Simulation 3	3.81%	4.98%	4.99%	4.62%	3.90%
		(-0.35%)	(-0.32%)	(-0.42%)	(-0.34%)	(-0.40%)
Mean Income	base (GH Cedis)	276.57	253.41	220.65	236.01	239.84
	Simulation 1	278.12	254.93	222.00	237.42	241.23
		(0.56%)	(0.60%)	(0.61%)	(0.60%)	(0.58%)
	Simulation 2	283.72	258.15	224.36	240.35	245.21
		(2.58%)	(1.87%)	(1.68%)	(1.84%)	(2.24%)
	Simulation 3	287.05	260.05	225.79	242.10	247.59
		(3.79%)	(2.62%)	(2.33%)	(2.58%)	(3.23%)
Poverty Line	base (GH Cedis)	66.53	66.53	66.53	66.53	66.53
	Simulation 1	64.64	64.64	64.64	64.64	64.64
		(-2.83)	(-2.83)	(-2.83)	(-2.83)	(-2.83)
	Simulation 2	64.76	64.76	64.76	64.76	64.76
		(-2.66%)	(-2.66%)	(-2.66%)	(-2.66%)	(-2.66%)
	Simulation 3	64.84	64.84	64.84	64.84	64.84
		(-2.54%)	(-2.54%)	(-2.54%)	(-2.54%)	(-2.54%)

The partial unilateral trade liberalization of imported agricultural goods alone is a poverty alleviating policy. The decline in the incidence of poverty ranges from 0.53 percentage points to 1.37 percentage points; the depth of poverty ranges from 0.33 percentage points to 0.52 percentage points; and the severity of poverty ranges from 0.19 percentage points to 0.30 percentage points. This finding is similar to Chitiga et al. (2005). The partial unilateral trade liberalization of imported agricultural goods with an increase in foreign capital inflows is also a poverty-alleviating policy. The contribution of foreign capital inflows to the reduction in the incidence of poverty ranges from 0.17 percentage points to 0.42 percentage points; the depth of poverty ranges from 0.11 percentage points to 0.18 percentage points; and the severity of poverty ranges from 0.07 percentage points to 0.10 percentage points. This finding is in conformity with the studies by Gustafsson and Makonnen, 1993; Siddiqui and Kemal, 2002a; Taylor, Mora and Adams, 2005; Adams, 2005; and Bhasin and Obeng, 2006; Anderson and Evia, 2003; Siddiqui and Kemal, 2002b; and Arbenser, 2004, which examine different components of foreign capital inflows. The partial unilateral trade liberalization of imported agricultural goods with an increase in value-added tax is also a poverty-alleviating policy. The contribution of VAT to the reduction in the incidence of poverty ranges from 0.18 percentage points to 0.42 percentage points; the depth of poverty ranges from 0.17 percentage points to 0.28 percentage points; and the severity of poverty ranges from 0.11 percentage points to 0.16 percentage points. This finding is in line with the finding of Bhasin and Annim (2005) and Aka (2006). The new finding of this chapter is that financing of partial (reduction in import tariffs on agricultural goods) unilateral trade liberalization through domestic resources could have a greater impact on poverty alleviation than through foreign resources.

In the fourth simulation, we eliminate the trade-related export tariff on agricultural goods (final goods as well as inputs). In the fifth simulation, we eliminate the trade-related export tariff on agricultural goods that is compensated for by an increase in the foreign capital inflows by 0.87 percent, which are redistributed to the households in the form of transfer payments in proportion to their share in the transfer payments. In the sixth simulation, we eliminate the trade-related export tariff on agricultural goods and increase the value-added tax by 50 percent and this tax revenue is redistributed to households in the form of transfer payments in proportion to their share in total transfer payments. Table 3 indicates the effects of these simulations on macroeconomic variables.

Table 3: Simulation Results for the Elimination of Export Tariffs on Agricultural Goods

Variables	Base level	Simulation 4: Elimination of export tariffs on agricultural goods	Percentage Increase or Decrease	Simulation 5: Elimination of export tariffs on agricultural goods and 0.87% increase in foreign capital inflows	Percentage Increase or Decrease	Simulation: 6.: Elimination of export tariffs on agricultural goods and 50% increase in value added tax	Percentage Increase or Decrease
Government Income	631.43	604.95	-4.19	606.64	-3.93	667.61	5.73
Income of Agricultural Households	314.40	321.32	2.20	330.05	4.98	332.68	5.81
Income of Public Sector Employees	283.82	290.46	2.34	295.39	4.08	296.88	4.60
Income of Private Sector Employees	246.14	252.00	2.38	255.63	3.86	256.73	4.30

Variables	Base level	Simulation 4: Elimination of export tariffs on agricultural goods	Percentage Increase or Decrease	Simulation 5: Elimination of export tariffs on agricultural goods and 0.87% increase in foreign capital inflows	Percentage Increase or Decrease	Simulation: 6.: Elimination of export tariffs on agricultural goods and 50% increase in value added tax	Percentage Increase or Decrease
Income of Non-farm Self Employed	264.28	270.46	2.34	274.94	4.03	276.31	4.55
Income of Non-working	271.50	277.58	2.24	283.74	4.51	285.62	5.20
Composite Price of Agricultural Goods	0.576	0.579	0.52	0.581	0.87	0.582	1.04
Composite Price of Industrial Goods	0.707	0.715	1.13	0.716	1.27	0.717	1.41
Composite Price of Services	0.817	0.822	0.61	0.823	0.73	0.823	0.73

The effect of the imposition of an export tax is to reduce the domestic price of exports in relation to the world price of exports. In these simulations, export tariffs on agricultural goods are eliminated and this raises the domestic price of agricultural exports to equal the world price of agricultural exports. A higher domestic price for agricultural exports increases the profitability of agricultural goods. This leads to increased production of agricultural goods, thereby causing the exports of agricultural goods to increase. Increased production of agricultural goods creates more demand for imported agricultural goods (consumer goods such as rice, sugar, etc). Since industrial goods and services are used in the production of agricultural goods (input-output linkages), imports of industrial goods (pesticides and other agro-chemical products) and services (wholesale and retail trade services) increase along with the increase in imports of agricultural goods in the fifth and sixth simulations. However, in the fourth simulation, imports of industrial goods decrease and imports of services increase. Due to the production linkages between the agriculture and services sectors, the production of services also increases in the fifth and sixth simulations but not in the fourth simulation. However, due to the increased domestic supply of services and the non-tradable nature of some services, exports of services decline. Since the agricultural and services sectors are expanding, this increases the demand for labour in the agricultural sector and demand for capital in the agriculture and service sectors. As labour and capital move away from the industrial sector, production in the industrial sector declines, thereby causing the exports of industrial goods to decline. Due to this sectoral reallocation of labor and capital, returns to labour increase and returns to capital decrease. The incomes of all types of households increase because of changes in factor prices, reallocation of existing resources and inflow of foreign direct investment, and remittances received from abroad and transfer payments received from the government that arise due to foreign aid and additional tax revenue . The cut in export tariffs on agricultural goods increases the prices of composite goods in all the three sectors that increase the poverty line by 0.61 percent, 0.87 percent, and 0.95percent in the fourth, fifth and sixth simulations, respectively. Again, changes in household'incomes and poverty line determine the net effect on the incidence, depth, and severity of household poverty.

Table 4: Poverty Measures for the Base Year and Simulations for Export Tariffs on Agricultural Goods

		Agricultural Households	Public Sector Employees	Private Sector Employees	Non-farm Self-Employed	Non-Working
Incidence of Poverty						
(alpha=0)	base	17.29%	19.28%	25.36%	21.04%	20.00%
	Simulation 4	16.96%	19.11%	24.74%	20.39%	19.79%
		(-0.33%)	(-0.17%)	(-0.62%)	(-0.65%)	(-0.21%)
	Simulation 5	16.42%	18.75%	24.31%	19.87%	19.15%
		(-0.87%)	(-0.53%)	(-1.05%)	(-1.17%)	(-1.85%)
	Simulation 6	16.38%	18.75%	24.31%	19.67%	19.15%
		(-0.91%)	(-0.53%)	(-1.05%)	(-1.37%)	(-1.85%)
Depth of Poverty						
(alpha=1)	base	7.15%	9.02%	9.85%	8.56%	7.99%
	Simulation 4	7.00%	8.84%	9.59%	8.35%	7.80%
		(-0.15%)	(-0.18%)	(-0.26%)	(-0.21%)	(-0.19%)
	Simulation 5	6.76%	8.70%	9.41%	8.19%	7.58%
		(-0.39%)	(-0.32%)	(-0.44%)	(-0.37%)	(-0.41%)
	Simulation 6	6.70%	8.65%	9.36%	8.14%	7.51%

		Agricultural Households	Public Sector Employees	Private Sector Employees	Non-farm Self-Employed	Non-Working
		(-0.45%)	(-0.37%)	(-0.49%)	(-0.42%)	(-0.48%)
Severity of Poverty						
(alpha=2)	base	4.16%	5.30%	5.41%	4.96%	4.30%
	Simulation 4	4.08%	5.22%	5.26%	4.85%	4.19%
		(-0.08%)	(-0.08%)	(-0.15%)	(-0.11%)	(-0.11%)
	Simulation 5	3.94%	5.12%	5.16%	4.75%	4.05%
		(-0.22%)	(-0.18%)	(-0.25%)	(-0.21%)	(-0.25%)
	Simulation 6	3.90%	5.09%	5.13%	4.72%	4.01%
		(-0.26%)	(-0.21%)	(-0.28%)	(-0.24%)	(-0.29%)
Mean	base (GH Cedis)	276.57	253.41	220.65	236.01	239.84
Income	Simulation 4	334.68	259.34	265.84	241.53	245.21
		(2.20%)	(2.34%)	(2.38%)	(2.34%)	(2.24%)
	Simulation 5	343.79	263.75	269.69	245.52	250.66
		(4.98%)	(4.08%)	(3.86%)	(4.03%)	(4.51%)
	Simulation 6	346.51	265.07	270.83	246.74	252.31
		(5.81%)	(4.60%)	(4.30%)	(4.55%)	(5.20%)
Poverty	base (GHc)	66.53	66.53	66.53	66.53	66.53
Line	Simulation 4	66.93	66.93	66.93	66.93	66.93
		(0.61%)	(0.61%)	(0.61%)	(0.61%)	(0.61%)
	Simulation 5	67.10	67.10	67.10	67.10	67.10
		(0.87%)	(0.87%)	(0.87%)	(0.87%)	(0.87%)
	Simulation 6	67.16	67.16	67.16	67.16	67.16
		(0.95%)	(0.95%)	(0.95%)	(0.95%)	(0.95%)

Table 4 presents information on the incidence, depth, and severity of poverty for the base year and variations in these measures for the simulations relating to export tariffs on agricultural goods. In these simulations, changes in the prices of composite goods increase the poverty lines and incomes of all households increase. These changes cause the incidence, depth, and severity of poverty for all categories of households to decrease. The maximum reduction in the incidence of poverty is noticed for the non-farm self employed, whereas the maximum reduction in the depth and severity of poverty is observed for private sector employees. The smallest reduction in the incidence and severity of poverty is observed for public sector employees, whereas the smallest reduction in the depth of poverty is for agricultural households in the fourth simulation and public sector employees in the fifth and sixth simulations. The difference between the base and the fourth simulation captures the effect of the elimination of export tariffs on agricultural goods on poverty. The difference between the fourth simulation and the fifth simulation captures the effect of foreign capital inflows on poverty. The difference between the fourth simulation and the sixth simulation captures the effect of value-added tax on poverty. These effects vary across households.

The partial unilateral trade liberalization of exported agricultural goods alone is a poverty alleviating policy. The decline in the incidence of poverty ranges from 0.17 percentage points to 0.65 percentage points; the depth of poverty ranges from 0.15 percentage points to 0.26 percentage points; and the severity of poverty ranges from 0.08 percentage points to 0.15 percentage points. The partial unilateral trade liberalization of exported agricultural goods with an increase in foreign capital inflows is also a poverty-alleviating policy. The contribution of foreign capital inflows to the reduction in the incidence of poverty ranges from 0.36 percentage points to 1.64 percentage points; the depth of poverty ranges from 0.14 percentage points to 0.24 percentage points; and the severity of poverty ranges from 0.10 percentage points to 0.14 percentage points. This finding is in conformity with the study by Bhasin and Obeng (2006). The partial unilateral trade liberalization of exported agricultural goods with an increase in value-added tax is also a poverty-alleviating policy. The contribution of VAT to the reduction in the incidence of poverty ranges from 0.36 percentage points to 1.64 percentage points; the depth of poverty ranges from 0.19 percentage points to 0.30 percentage points; and the severity of poverty ranges from 0.13 percentage points to 0.18 percentage points. This finding is different from the findings of Bhasin and Annim (2005) and Aka (2006). However, this finding is in conformity with Bussolo and Round (2003).

In the seventh simulation, we eliminate the trade-related import tariff on industrial goods (final goods as well as inputs). In the eighth simulation, we eliminate the trade-related import tariff on industrial goods that is compensated for by an increase in foreign capital inflows by 0.64 percent, which are redistributed to the households in the form of transfer payments in proportion to their share in the transfer payments. In the ninth simulation, we eliminate the trade related import tariff on industrial goods and increase the value-added tax by 50 percent and this tax revenue is redistributed to the households in the form of transfer payments in proportion to their share in total transfer payments. Table 5 indicates the effects of these simulations on macroeconomic variables.

Table 5: Simulation Results for the Elimination of Import Tariffs on Industrial Goods

Variables	Base level	Simulation 7: Elimination of import tariffs on industrial goods	Percentage Increase or Decrease	Simulation 8: Elimination of import tariffs on industrial goods and 0.64% increase in foreign capital inflows	Percentage Increase or Decrease	Simulation: 9. Elimination of import tariffs on industrial goods and 50% increase in value added tax	Percentage Increase or Decrease
Government Income	631.43	611.88	-3.10	612.81	-2.95	676.73	7.17
Income of Agricultural Households	314.40	316.44	0.65	322.90	2.70	327.61	4.20
Income of Public Sector Employees	283.82	285.79	0.69	289.45	1.98	292.11	2.92
Income of Private Sector Employees	246.14	247.86	0.70	250.55	1.79	252.55	2.60
Income of Non-farm Self Employed	264.28	266.11	0.69	269.43	1.95	271.87	2.87
Income of Non-working	271.50	273.37	0.69	277.93	2.37	281.27	3.60
Composite Price of Agricultural Goods	0.576	0.580	0.69	0.581	0.87	0.582	1.04
Composite Price of Industrial Goods	0.707	0.678	-4.10	0.679	-3.96	0.680	-3.82

Variables	Base level	Simulation 7: Elimination of import tariffs on industrial goods	Percentage Increase or Decrease	Simulation 8: Elimination of import tariffs on industrial goods and 0.64% increase in foreign capital inflows	Percentage Increase or Decrease	Simulation: 9. Elimination of import tariffs on industrial goods and 50% increase in value added tax	Percentage Increase or Decrease
Composite Price of Services	0.817	0.817	0.00	0.817	0.00	0.817	0.00

These simulations lead to a reduction in the prices of imported industrial goods. As a result, imports of industrial goods become cheaper and consumers substitute imported industrial goods for domestically produced industrial goods, thereby causing the demand for industrial imports to increase. Since agricultural goods and services are used in the production of industrial goods (input-output linkages), it is likely that imports of agricultural goods and services (wholesale and retail trade services) will increase along with the increase in imports of industrial goods even though there are no cuts in the import tariffs on agricultural goods and services. The reduction in domestic costs caused by cuts in industrial import tariffs increases the profitability of the industrial sector (provided that the revenue effect offsets the cost effect). This leads to increased production of industrial goods, thereby causing exports of industrial goods to increase. Due to the production linkages between the industrial and services sectors, the production and export of services also increases. Since the industrial and services sectors are expanding, this increases the demand for labour and capital in the industrial sector, whereas the demand for labour increases and the demand for capital decreases in the services sector. As labour and capital move away from the agricultural sector, agricultural production declines, thereby causing exports of agricultural goods to decline. Due to this sectoral reallocation of labour and capital, returns to labour and capital increase. The incomes of all types of households increase because of an increase in factor prices, reallocation of existing resources and inflows of foreign direct investment, remittances received from abroad and transfer payments received from the government that arise due to foreign aid and additional tax revenue. The cut in import tariffs on industrial goods reduces the prices of composite goods in the industrial sector and increases the price of composite goods in the agricultural sector. However, the net effect of these changes in the prices of composite goods is to reduce the poverty lines by 0.26 percent and 0.07 percent in the seventh and eighth simulation, respectively, and increase the poverty line by 0.07 percent in the ninth simulation. Changes in household incomes and poverty lines determine the net effect on the incidence, depth, and severity of household poverty.

Table 6: Poverty Measures for the Base Year and Simulations for Import Tariffs on Industrial Goods

		Agricultural Households Employees	Public Sector Employees	Private Sector Employed	Non-farm Self-Employed	Non-Working
Incidence of Poverty						
(alpha=0)	base	17.29%	19.28%	25.36%	21.04%	20.00%
	Simulation 7	17.20%	19.28%	25.16%	20.65%	20.00%
		(-0.09%)	(-0.00%)	(-0.20%)	(-0.39%)	(-0.00%)
	Simulation 8	16.62%	18.93%	24.74%	20.13%	19.36%
		(-0.67%)	(-0.35%)	(-0.62%)	(-0.91%)	(-0.64%)
	Simulation 9	16.42%	18.93%	24.31%	19.93%	19.36%
		(-0.87%)	(-0.35%)	(-1.05%)	(-1.11%)	(-0.64%)
Depth of Poverty						
(alpha=1)	base	7.15%	9.02%	9.85%	8.56%	7.99%
	Simulation 7	7.07%	8.92%	9.71%	8.45%	7.88%
		(-0.08%)	(-0.10%)	(-0.14%)	(-0.11%)	(-0.11%)
	Simulation 8	6.89%	8.81%	9.58%	8.32%	7.71%
		(-0.26%)	(-0.21%)	(-0.27%)	(-0.24%)	(-0.28%)
	Simulation 9	6.76%	8.73%	9.48%	8.23%	7.58%
		(-0.39%)	(-0.29%)	(-0.37%)	(-0.33%)	(-0.41%)
Severity of Poverty						
(alpha=2)	base	4.16%	5.30%	5.41%	4.96%	4.30%
	Simulation 7	4.11%	5.28%	5.33%	4.90%	4.24%
		(-0.05%)	(-0.02%)	(-0.08%)	(-0.06)	(-0.06%)
	Simulation 8	4.01%	5.20%	5.25%	4.83%	4.13%
		(-0.15%)	(-0.10%)	(-0.16%)	(-0.13%)	(-0.17%)
	Simulation 9	3.93%	5.14%	5.19%	4.78%	4.06%
		(-0.23%)	(-0.16%)	(-0.22%)	(-0.18%)	(-0.24%)
Mean	base (GH Cedis)	276.57	253.41	220.65	236.01	239.84
Income	Simulation 7	278.37	255.16	222.20	237.63	241.49
		(0.65%)	(0.69%)	(0.70%)	(0.69%)	(0.69%)
	Simulation 8	284.04	258.43	224.60	240.61	245.52

		Agricultural Households Employees	Public Sector Employees	Private Sector Employed	Non-farm Self-Employed	Non-Working
		(2.70%)	(1.98%)	(1.79%)	(1.95%)	(2.37%)
	Simulation 9	288.18	260.81	226.39	242.78	248.47
		(4.20%)	(2.92%)	(2.60%)	(2.87%)	(3.60%)
Poverty	base (GH Cedis)	66.53	66.53	66.53	66.53	66.53
Line	Simulation 7	66.35	66.35	66.35	66.35	66.35
		(-0.26)	(-0.26)	(-0.26)	(-0.26)	(-0.26)
	Simulation 8	66.48	66.48	66.48	66.48	66.48
		(-0.07%)	(-0.07%)	(-0.07%)	(-0.07%)	(-0.07%)
	Simulation 9	66.57	66.57	66.57	66.57	66.57
		(0.07%)	(0.07%)	(0.07%)	(0.07%)	(0.07%)

Table 6 presents information on the incidence, depth, and severity of poverty for the base year and variations in these measures for the simulations relating to import tariffs on industrial goods. In these simulations, the incidence, depth, and severity of poverty for all categories of households are reduced. The maximum reduction in the incidence of poverty is noticed for the non-farm self-employed, whereas the maximum reduction in the depth and severity of poverty is observed for private sector employees in the seventh simulation and non-working in the eighth and ninth simulations. The lowest reduction in the incidence and severity of poverty is noticed for public sector employees, whereas the lowest reduction in the depth of poverty is noticed for agricultural households in the seventh simulation and public sector employees in the eighth and ninth simulations. The difference between the base and the seventh simulation captures the effect of the elimination of import tariffs on industrial goods on poverty. The difference between the seventh simulation and the eighth simulation captures the effect of foreign capital inflows on poverty. The difference between the seventh simulation and the ninth simulation captures the effect of value-added tax on poverty. These effects vary across households. Moreover, it is observed that financing of partial (reduction in import tariffs on industrial goods) trade liberalization through domestic resources could have a greater impact on poverty alleviation than through foreign resources because of greater linkages via domestic transmission than through foreign capital inflows.

The partial unilateral trade liberalization of imported industrial goods alone is a poverty alleviating policy. The decline in the incidence of poverty ranges from 0.00 percentage points to 0.39 percentage points; the depth of poverty ranges from 0.08 percentage points to 0.14 percentage points; and the severity of poverty ranges from 0.02 percentage points to 0.08 percentage points. This finding is similar to Chitiga et al. (2005). The partial unilateral trade liberalization of imported industrial goods with increase in foreign capital inflows is also a poverty alleviating policy. The contribution of foreign capital inflows to the reduction in the incidence of poverty ranges from 0.35 percentage points to 0.64 percentage points; the depth of poverty ranges from 0.11 percentage points to 0.18 percentage points; and the severity of poverty ranges from 0.07 percentage points to 0.11 percentage points. The partial unilateral trade liberalization of imported industrial goods with increase in value-added tax is also a poverty-alleviating policy. The contribution of VAT to the reduction in the incidence of poverty ranges from 0.35 percentage points to 0.85 percentage points; the depth of poverty ranges from 0.19 percentage points to 0.31 percentage points; and the severity of poverty ranges from 0.12 percentage points to 0.18 percentage points. This finding is in line with the finding of Bhasin and Annim (2005) which showed that the reduction in import tariffs on goods and services along with an increase in VAT by 100 percent reduces the incidence of poverty between 0.71 percentage points and 1.50 percentage points, the depth of poverty between 0.25 percentage points and 0.67 percentage points, and the severity of poverty between 0.25 percentage points and 0.38 percentage points. Moreover, this finding is also in conformity with the finding of Aka (2006). The study shows that financing of partial (reduction in import tariffs on industrial goods) unilateral trade liberalization through domestic resources could have a greater impact on poverty alleviation than foreign resources.

In the tenth simulation, we eliminate the trade-related export tariff on industrial goods (final goods as well as inputs). In the eleventh simulation, we eliminate the trade-related export tariff on industrial goods that is compensated for by an increase in foreign capital inflows by 0.33 percent, which are redistributed to households in the form of transfer payments in proportion to their share in the transfer payments. In the twelfth simulation, we eliminate the trade related export tariff on industrial goods and increase the value-added tax by 50 percent and this tax revenue is redistributed to the households in the form of transfer payments in proportion to their share in total transfer payments. Table 7 indicates the effects of these simulations on macroeconomic variables.

Table 7: Simulation Results for the Elimination of Export Tariffs on Industrial Goods

Variables	Base level	Simulation 10: Elimination of export tariffs on industrial goods	Percentage Increase or Decrease	Simulation 11: Elimination of export tariffs on industrial goods and 0.33% increase in foreign capital inflows	Percentage Increase or Decrease	Simulation: 12. Elimination of export tariffs on industrial goods and 50% increase in value added tax	Percentage Increase or Decrease
Government Income	631.43	621.51	-1.57	622.06	-1.48	698.20	10.57
Income of Agricultural Households	314.40	319.16	1.51	322.45	2.56	333.35	6.03
Income of Public Sector Employees	283.82	288.43	1.62	290.29	2.28	296.49	4.46
Income of Private Sector Employees	246.14	250.13	1.62	251.51	2.18	256.08	4.04
Income of Non-farm Self Employed	264.28	268.58	1.63	270.28	2.27	275.93	4.41
Income of Non-working	271.50	276.10	1.69	278.43	2.55	286.15	5.40
Composite Price of Agricultural Goods	0.576	0.599	3.99	0.600	4.17	0.602	4.51
Composite Price of Industrial Goods	0.707	0.703	-0.57	0.704	-0.42	0.706	-0.14
Composite Price of Services	0.817	0.829	1.47	0.829	1.47	0.829	1.47

In these simulations, export tariffs on industrial goods are eliminated and this raises the domestic price of industrial exports to equal the world price of industrial exports. A higher domestic price for industrial exports increases the profitability of industrial goods. This leads to increased production of industrial goods, thereby causing exports of industrial goods to increase. Increased production of industrial goods creates more demand for imported intermediate industrial goods resulting in increased imports of industrial goods. Since agricultural goods and services are used in the production of industrial goods (input-output linkages), it is likely that imports of agricultural goods and services (wholesale and retail trade services) will increase along with the increase in imports of industrial goods. The expansion of the industrial sector results into the contraction of the services sector. As a result, the production and export of services decline. Expansion of the industrial sector causes the demand for labour and capital to increase. On the other hand, the contraction of the services sector causes the demand for labour to increase and the demand for capital to decrease. At the same time, labour and capital move away from the agricultural sector, agricultural production declines, thereby causing exports of agricultural goods to decline. Due to this sectoral reallocation of labour and capital, returns to labour and capital increase. The incomes of all types of households increase because of changes in factor prices, reallocation of existing resources and inflow of foreign direct investment, remittances received from abroad and transfer payments received from the government that arise due to foreign aid and additional tax revenue . The cut in export tariffs on industrial goods reduces the prices of composite goods in the industrial sector and increases the prices of composite goods in the agricultural and services sectors that increase the poverty lines by 2.71 percent, 2.80 percent, and 3.11 percent in the tenth, eleventh, and twelfth simulations, respectively. Again, changes in household incomes and poverty lines determine the net effect on the incidence, depth, and severity of households' poverty.

Table 8: Poverty Measures for the Base Year and Simulations for Export Tariffs on Industrial Goods

		Agricultural Households	Public Sector Employees	Private Sector Employees	Non-farm Self-Employed	Non-Working
Incidence of Poverty						
(alpha=0)	base	17.29%	19.28%	25.36%	21.04%	20.00%
	Simulation 10	17.67%	19.46%	26.00%	21.37%	20.21%
		(0.38%)	(0.18%)	(0.64%)	(0.33%)	(0.21%)
	Simulation 11	17.47%	19.46%	25.58%	21.24%	20.00%
		(0.18%)	(0.18%)	(0.22%)	(0.20%)	(0.00%)
	Simulation 12	16.59%	19.11%	25.16%	20.59%	19.36%
		(-0.70%)	(-0.17%)	(-0.20%)	(-0.45%)	(-0.64%)
Depth of Poverty						

		Agricultural Households	Public Sector Employees	Private Sector Employees	Non-farm Self-Employed	Non-Working
(alpha=1)	base	7.15%	9.02%	9.85%	8.56%	7.99%
	Simulation 10	7.28%	9.13%	10.03%	8.70%	8.12%
		(0.13%)	(0.11%)	(0.18%)	(0.14%)	(0.13%)
	Simulation 11	7.18%	9.07%	9.95%	8.63%	8.03%
		(0.03%)	(0.05%)	(0.10%)	(0.07%)	(0.04%)
	Simulation 12	6.88%	8.88%	9.72%	8.41%	7.73%
		(-0.27%)	(-0.14%)	(-0.13%)	(-0.15%)	(-0.26%)
Severity of Poverty						
(alpha=2)	base	4.16%	5.30%	5.41%	4.96%	4.30%
	Simulation 10	4.24%	5.42%	5.51%	5.05%	4.38%
		(0.08%)	(0.12%)	(0.10%)	(0.09%)	(0.08%)
	Simulation 11	4.18%	5.38%	5.47%	5.01%	4.33%
		(0.02%)	(0.08%)	(0.06%)	(0.05%)	(0.03%)
	Simulation 12	4.00%	5.25%	5.33%	4.88%	4.15%
		(-0.16%)	(-0.05%)	(-0.08%)	(-0.08%)	(-0.15%)
Mean	base (GH Cedis)	276.57	253.41	220.65	236.01	239.84
Income	Simulation 10	280.74	257.52	224.23	239.85	243.89
		1.51%	(1.62%)	i.62%	1.63%	1.69%
	Simulation 11	283.65	259.19	225.46	241.36	245.96
		(2.56%)	(2.28%)	(2.18%)	(2.27%)	(2.55%)
	Simulation 12	293.25	264.71	229.57	246.41	252.79
		(6.03%)	(4.46%)	(4.04%)	(4.41%)	(5.40%)
Poverty	base (GH Cedis)	66.53	66.53	66.53	66.53	66.53
Line	Simulation 10	68.33	68.33	68.33	68.33	68.33
		(2.71%)	(2.71%)	(2.71%)	(2.71%)	(2.71%)
	Simulation 11	68.39	68.39	68.39	68.39	68.39
		(2.80%)	(2.80%)	(2.80%)	(2.80%)	(2.80%)
	Simulation 12	68.59	68.59	68.59	68.59	68.59
		(3.11%)	(3.11%)	(3.11%)	(3.11%)	(3.11%)

Source: Authors compution

Table 8 presents information on the incidence, depth, and severity of poverty for the base year and variations in these measures for the simulations relating to export tariffs on industrial goods. In these simulations, changes in the prices of composite goods increase the poverty lines ,and incomes of all households increase. These changes cause the incidence, depth, and severity of poverty for all categories of households to increase, with the exception of the incidence of poverty of non-working, in the tenth and eleventh simulations. In contrast, these changes cause the incidence, depth and severity of poverty of all categories of households to decrease in the twelfth simulation. The maximum increase in the incidence and depth of poverty is noticed for private sector employees, whereas the maximum increase in the severity of poverty is observed for public sector employees. The lowest increase in the depth of poverty is observed for public sector employees in the tenth simulation and agricultural households in the eleventh simulation. The lowest increase in the severity of poverty is noticed for agricultural households. The maximum reduction in the incidence, depth, and severity of poverty is noticed for agricultural households. The lowest reduction in the incidence and severity of poverty is observed for public sector employees and depth of poverty for private sector employees. The difference between the base and the tenth simulation captures the effect of elimination of export tariffs on industrial goods on poverty. The difference between the tenth simulation and the eleventh simulation captures the effect of foreign capital inflows on poverty. The difference between the tenth simulation and the twelfth simulation captures the effect of value-added tax on poverty. These effects vary across households.

The partial unilateral trade liberalization of exported industrial goods alone is a poverty enhancing policy. The increase in the incidence of poverty ranges from 0.18 percentage points to 0.64 percentage points; the depth of poverty ranges from 0.11 percentage points to 0.18 percentage points; and the severity of poverty ranges from 0.08 percentage points to 0.12 percentage points. The partial unilateral trade liberalization of exported industrial goods with increase in foreign capital inflows is also a poverty-enhancing policy. The contribution of foreign capital inflows to the increase in the incidence of poverty ranges from 0.00 percentage points to 0.42 percentage points; the depth of poverty ranges from 0.06 percentage points to 0.10 percentage points; and the severity of poverty ranges from 0.04 percentage points to 0.06 percentage points. This finding is not in conformity with the study by Bhasin and Obeng (2006). However, the partial unilateral trade liberalization of exported industrial goods with an increase in value-added tax is a poverty-alleviating policy. The contribution of VAT to the reduction in the incidence of poverty ranges from 0.35 percentage points to 1.08 percentage points; the depth of poverty ranges from 0.25 percentage points to 0.40 percentage points; and the severity of poverty ranges from 0.17 percentage points to 0.24 percentage points. This finding is different from the findings of Bhasin and Annim (2005). However, this finding is in conformity with Bussolo and Round (2003). The study contributes to the literature by showing that financing of partial (reduction in export tariffs on industrial goods) unilateral trade liberalization through domestic resources could have a greater impact on poverty alleviation than through foreign resources.

In all the simulations, the density functions for all categories of households shift to the right with higher mean incomes. However, the effect on the poverty line differs across these simulations. The poverty lines are reduced in simulations 1, 2, 3, 7 and 8, whereas the poverty lines increase in simulations 4, 5, 6, 9, 10, 11, and 12. This causes a reduction of the population below the poverty line in each household group in simulations 1, 2, 3, 4, 5, 6, 7, 8, 9, and 12, with the exception of public sector employees and non-working in simulation 7. In contrast there is an increase in the population below the poverty line in simulations 10 and 11. The mean incomes of the private sector employees improve to a larger extent in simulations 1, 4, and 7, whereas the mean incomes of the non-working improve to a large extent in simulation 10 when trade liberalization in isolation is considered. On the other hand, the income distribution of agricultural households improves to a larger extent in simulations 2, 5, 8 and 11 when trade liberalization is combined with foreign capital inflows as well as in simulations 3, 6, 9 and 12 when trade liberalization is combined with value-added tax. This finding is in conformity with Arbenser (2004) and Bhasin and Obeng (2006).

6. Conclusions and Policy Implications

To analyze the impact of partial trade liberalization alone, combined with foreign capital inflows, and value-added tax on the incidence, depth, and severity of poverty and income distributions of households, the chapter used a CGE framework. The chapter analyzed the impact of 12 simulations on poverty and income distribution. The first shock takes the form of elimination of trade-related import tariffs on agricultural goods. The second shock takes the form of elimination of trade-related import tariffs on agricultural goods accompanied by an increase in real foreign capital inflows by 0.63 percent. The third shock takes the form of elimination of trade-related import tariffs on agricultural goods accompanied by an increase in value-added tax by 50 percent. The fourth shock involves the elimination of export tariffs on agricultural goods. The fifth shock involves the elimination of export tariffs on agricultural goods accompanied by an increase in real foreign capital inflows by 0.87 percent. The sixth shock involves the elimination of export tariffs on agricultural goods accompanied by an increase in value-added tax by 50 percent. The seventh shock takes the form of elimination of trade-related import tariffs on industrial goods. The eighth shock takes the form of elimination of trade related import tariffs on industrial goods accompanied by an increase in real foreign capital inflows by 0.64 percent. The ninth shock takes the form of elimination of trade related import tariffs on industrial goods accompanied by an increase in value-added tax by 50 percent. The tenth shock involves the elimination of export tariffs on industrial goods. The eleventh shock involves the elimination of export tariffs on industrial goods accompanied by an increase in real foreign capital inflows by 0.33 percent. The twelfth shock involves the elimination of export tariffs on industrial goods accompanied by an increase in value-added tax by 50 percent%.

The chapter shows that elimination of trade-related import and export tariffs on agricultural goods and import tariffs on industrial goods in isolation combined with foreign capital inflows and value-added tax reduces the incidence, depth, and severity of poverty of all categories of households, with the exception of the incidence of poverty of public sector employees and non-working when import tariffs on industrial goods are eliminated in isolation. In particular, a regressive tax (VAT) as a revenue replacement makes poor people better off because of the neoclassical assumptions and transfers of VAT revenue to households. On the other hand, elimination of trade-related export tariffs on industrial goods in isolation and combined with foreign capital inflows increases the incidence, depth and severity of poverty of all categories of households, with the exception of the incidence of poverty of non-working. Moreover, the elimination of trade-related export tariffs on industrial goods combined with value-added tax reduces the incidence, depth and severity of poverty of all categories of households. The impact of trade related fiscal reforms on poverty differs across households. The most significant beneficiaries of the simulations related to the elimination of trade-related import tariffs on agricultural goods are the non-farm self-employed and the private sector employees. The most significant beneficiaries of the simulations related to the elimination of trade related export tariffs on agricultural goods and import tariffs on industrial goods are private sector employees, non-farm self employed and non-working. The most significant beneficiaries of the simulation related to the elimination of trade-related export tariffs on industrial goods are agricultural households.

The chapter shows that financing of partial sector-wise unilateral trade liberalization through domestic resources could have a greater impact on poverty alleviation and improvement in the mean incomes of households than foreign resources. This is due to the fact that a fall in government revenue due to trade liberalization is compensated for by a budget-neutral increase in foreign capital inflows that are redistributed to households in the form of transfer payments in proportion to their share in total transfer payments from the government to households. On the other hand, when trade liberalization is combined with an increase in VAT, a fall in government revenue due to trade liberalization is not compensated for by a budget-neutral increase in VAT but rather a 50 percent increase in VAT. The increase in the transfer payments to households in the case of VAT is higher than in the case of foreign capital inflows. Thus the increase in the incomes of households is larger in the VAT case in comparison to the foreign capital inflows case and that is why poverty falls more in case of VAT increase rather than an increase in foreign capital inflows.

The impact of trade-related fiscal reforms on income distribution differs across households. The mean incomes of private sector employees and non-working improve to a larger extent when trade liberalization in isolation is considered. On the other hand, the mean incomes of agricultural households improve to a larger extent when trade liberalization is combined with foreign capital inflows and value-added tax. The government of Ghana should not eliminate export tariffs on industrial goods in isolation even when combined with foreign capital inflows because these are not poverty-reducing policies. The government should try to finance its unilateral trade liberalization through domestic resources instead of through foreign resources in order to have greater impact on poverty reduction and improvement in the incomes of households.

References

Adams, R. (2005) "Remittances, Selection Bias and Poverty in Guatemala", Washington, D.C.:World Bank,

Adelman, I. and S. Robinson (1979). "Income Distribution Policy: A Computable General Equilibrium Model of South Korea" in Adelman, I., *The Selected Essays of Irma Adelman, Vol. 1. Dynamics and Income Distribution*. Aldershot: Economists of the Twentieth Century Series, Aldershot, 256-89.

Aka, B. F. (2006). "Poverty, Inequality and Welfare Effects of Trade Liberalization in Cote d'Ivoire: A CGE Model Analysis", AERC Research Paper No. 160, Nairobi,

Anderson, L. E., and J. Evia. (2003). "The Effectiveness of Foreign Aid in Bolivia", Research Paper No. 10, Insttituto de Investigaciones Socio Economicas, Documento de Trabajo, Bolivia.

Arbenser, L.(2004). "A General Equilibrium Analysis of the Impact of Inward FDI on Ghana: The Role of Complementary Policies", Eco Mod Net, September 2-4, Brussels.

Azis, I. and E. Thorbecke. (2001). "Modelling the Socio-Economic Impact of the Financial Crisis: The Case of Indonesia", Mimeo, Cornell University.

Bhasin, V. and S. Annim. (2005). "Impact of Elimination of Trade Taxes on Poverty and Income Distribution in Ghana", GDN Report, 1-42.

Bhasin, V. and C. Obeng. (2006). "Trade Liberalization, Remittances, Poverty and Income Distributions of Households in Ghana." In Judith Shaw (ed.): *Remittances, Microfinance and Development: Building the Links. Volume 1: A Global View*, The Foundation for Development Co-operation, Brisbane, Australia, 2005, 33-45. (ISBN 0-9586728-7-3).

Bourguignon, F. (2002). "The Growth Elasticity of Poverty Reduction: Explaining Heterogeneity Across Countries and Time-Periods", Paris.: DELTA Working Paper.

Bourguignon, F. (2004). "The Poverty-Growth-Inequality Triangle", Paper presented at the Indian Council for Research on International Economic Relations, New Delhi.

Bussolo, M. and Round, J. (2003). "Poverty Reduction Strategies in a Budget-Constrained Economy: The Case of Ghana". OECD Development Centre Working Paper No 220.

Chia, N., Wahba, S., and J. Whalley. (1994). "Poverty Reduction Targeting Programs: A General Equilibrium Approach", *Journal of African Economies*, Vol. 3, No. 2, 309-38.

Chitiga, M., Kandiero, T., and R. Mabugu. (2005) "Computable General Equilibrium Microsimulation Analysis of the Impact of Trade Policies on Poverty in Zimbabwe". PEP Working Paper, No.1.

Cogneau, D. and A. S. Robillard. (1999). "Income Distribution, Poverty and Growth in Madagascar: *Micro simulations in a General Equilibrium Framework*", Mimeograph.

Decaluwe, B., Dumont, J., and L. Savard. (1999). "Measuring Poverty and Inequality in a Computable General Equilibrium Model", CREFA, Working Paper 99-20,Quebec: Department of Economics, University of Laval.

Decaluwe, B., Party, A., Savard, L. and E. Thorebecke. (1999). "Poverty Analysis Within a General Equilibrium Framework", CREFA, Working Paper 99-09, Quebec: Department of Economics, University of Laval.

de Janvry, A., E. Sadoulet, and A. Fargeix. (1991). "Adjustment and Equity in Ecuador", Paris: OECD Development Center..

De Maio, L., Stewart, F., and R. Van Der Hoeven. (1999). "Computable General Equilibrium Models, Adjustment and the Poor in Africa", *World Development*, Vol. 27, No. 3, 453-70.

Dervis, K., DeMelo, J., and S. Robinson. (1982). *General Equilibrium Models for Development Policy*, Cambridge, London:Cambridge University Press

,Ghana Statistical Service (2000). *Poverty Trends in Ghana in the 1990s*. Accra: GSS.

Gunning, W. J. (1983). "Income Distribution and Growth: A Simulation Model for Kenya" in D.G. Greene. *Growth and Structural Change*, Vols 1 and 2, World Bank, Washington, DC, 487-621.

Gustafsson, B. and N. Makonnen. (1993) "Poverty and Remittances in Lesotho", *Journal of African Economies*, Vol. 2, 49-73.

Morrisson, C. (1991). "Adjustment and Equity in Morocco", Paris: OECD Development Center..

Obi, B. P. (2003). "Fiscal Policy and Income Distribution: Some Policy Options for Nigeria". Final Report, Nairobi: AERC.

Siddiqui,R., and A. Kemal. (2002a) 'Remittances, Trade Liberalization, and Poverty in Pakistan: The Role of Excluded Variables in Poverty Change Analysis', Study No. 1, London: Department for International Development

Siddiqui, R., and A. Kemal. (2002b). " Poverty Reducing or Poverty Inducing? A CGE Based Analysis of Foreign Capital Inflows in Pakistan", Globalization and Poverty in South Asia, DFID Project,U.K.

Taylor, E., Mora, J. and R. Adams. (2005) "Remittances, Inequality and Poverty: Evidence from Rural Mexico", University of California.

Thorbecke, E. (1991). "Adjustment, Growth and Income Distribution in Indonesia", *World Development*, Vol. 19, No. 11, 1595-1614.

Weisbrot, M. and D. Baker. (2002). "The Relative Impact of Trade Liberalization On Developing Countries", Washington, D.C.: Centre for Economic and Policy Research,

Williamson, J. (2002). "Winners and Losers over Two Centuries of Globalization", WIDER Annual Lecture No. 6, Helsinki:UNU-WIDER.

Winters, A., McCulloch, N. and McKay, A. (2004) "Trade Liberalization and Poverty: The Evidence So Far", *Journal of Economic Literature*, Vol. XLII, 72-115.

World Bank. (2002). *Global Economic Prospects and the Developing Countries*, Washington, D.C.

Appendix : Computable General Equilibrium Model for Ghana

I Sets definition

$i \in I =$ {AGR, IND, SER}, Goods (AGR: Agriculture, IND: Industry, SER: Services).

$j \in J =$ {AGR, IND, SER}, Production Sectors

$h \in H =$ {AGRF, PUBE, PRIE, NFSE, NW}, Households (AGRF: Agricultural Household, PUBE: Public Sector Employee, PRIE: Private Sector Employee, NFSE: Non-farm Self Employed, NW: Non-Working).

II Parameters

Λ_j	Share of Value Added in Total Output
c_j	Scale Coefficient of Cobb–Douglas Function
aij	Quantity of Good i used in the Production of Good j
α_j	Elasticity Parameter of Cobb–Douglas Function
$\ddot{O}_i$	Scale Coefficient of CET Function
γ_i	Distributive Parameter of CET Function
R_i	Transformation Parameter of CET Function
η_i	Elasticity of Transformation
λ_i	Scale Coefficient of CES Function
δ_i	Distributive Parameter of CES Function
ρ_i	Substitution Parameter
σ_i	Elasticity of Substitution
Ω_1	Firms Share in Total Capital Income
Ω_2	Govt. Share in Total Capital Income
s_h	Share of Household h in Labor Income
k_h	Share of Household h in Total Capital Income
ty_h	Tax Rate on Household h Income
dvr_h	Dividend Rate for Household h
Ψ_h	Marginal Propensity to Save of h Household
Ψ_f	Marginal Propensity to Save of Firms
Ψ_g	Marginal Propensity to Save of Government
ty_f	Tax Rate on Firm Income
tm_i	Tax Rate on Import of Good i
te_i	Tax Rate on Export of Good i
tx_i	Value Added Tax Rate on Good i
β^c_{ih}	Share of Good i in Household h Consumption
β^f_i	Share of Good i in Firm consumption

β^g_i Share of Good i in Government Consumption

$C^{MIN}_{i,h}$ Household Minimum Consumption of Good i

ϕ_j Share of Sector j in Total Investment

μ_i Share of Good i in Value Added

III Endogenous Variables

XS_j	Production of Sector j	3
VA_j	Value Added of Sector j	3
PV_j	Value Added Price of Sector j	3
LD_j	Labor Demand of Sector j	3
w_j	Wage Rate of Sector j	3
w	Average Wage Rate	1
KD_j	Capital Demand of Sector j	3
r_j	Rate of Return to Capital in Sector j	3
r	Average Rental Rate	1
$DI_{i,j}$	Intermediate Demand for Good i in Sector j	9
DI_i	Intermediate Demand for Good i	3
E_i	Export Supply of Good i	3
DS_i	Domestic Supply of Good i	3
PE_i	Domestic Export Price of Good i	3
PL_i	Producer Price of Domestic Good i	3
Q_i	Demand for Composite Good i	3
PC_i	Price of Composite Good i	3
M_i	Import Demand of Good i	3
DD_i	Domestic Demand of Good i	3
PD_i	Domestic Price of Good i	3
PM_i	Domestic Import Price of Good i	3
YH_h	Income of Household h	5
YDH_h	Disposable Income of Household h	5
DTH_h	Direct Taxes on Household h Income	5
SH_h	Savings of Household h	5
$CTFH_h$	Current Transfers from Firms to Household h	5
SH	Savings of Households	1
YF	Income of Firms	1
DTF	Direct Taxes on Firms Income	1
YDF	Disposable Income of Firms	1

SF	Savings of Firms	1
TIM_i	Indirect Taxes on Imports of Good i	3
TIE_i	Indirect Taxes on Exports of Good i	3
$TIVA_i$	Value added Taxes on Good i 3	
P_i	Price of Aggregate Output of Good i 3	
YG	Government Income 1	
SG	Savings of Government 1	
CTH_h	Total Consumption of Household h 5	
$C_{i,h}$	Consumption of Good i of Household h 15	
CT_i	Total Consumption of Good i 3	
CF_i	Firm Consumption of Good i 3	
GC_i	Government Consumption of Good i 3	
I	Total Investment 1	
S	Total Savings 1	
I_j	Investment of Sector j 3	
P_{INV}	Investment Price Index 1	
$PINDEX$	Price Index	1
B	Balance of Payments 1	
z	Poverty Line 1	

Number of Endogenous Variables	147

IV Exogenous Variables Number

LS	Labor supply	1
KS	Capital Supply	1
e	Nominal Exchange Rate	1
PWE_i	World Price of Exports of Good i	3
PWM_i	World Price of Imports of Good i	3
$CTGH_h$	Current Transfers from Govt. to Household h	5
$CTWH_h$	Current Transfers from ROW to Household h	5
$CTHF_h$	Current Transfers from Household h to Firms	5
$CTHW_h$	Current Transfers from Household h to ROW	5
$CTGF$	Current Transfers from Govt. to Firms	1
$CTWF$	Current Transfers from ROW to Firms	1
FB	Foreign Borrowing	1
FKI	Foreign Capital Inflows	1

Number of Exogenous Variables	33

V Equations

Production and Trade	Number

1. $XS_j = VA_j / \Lambda_\varphi$ ... 3

2. $VA_j = c_j \, LD_j^{\alpha j} \, KD_j^{1-\alpha j}$ ... 3

3. $DI_{i,j} = a_{ij} XS_j$ ... 9

4. $DI_i = \sum_j DI_{i,j}$ ... 3

5. $LD_j = \alpha_j \, PV_j \, VA_j / w_j$ ... 3

6. $KD_j = (1-\alpha_j) \, PV_j \, VA_j / r_j$ ... 3

7. $XS_i = \ddot{O}_i \, [\gamma_i E_i^{R_i} + (1-\gamma_i) \, DS_i^{R}i \,]^{1/R_i}$ ... 3

8. $E_i = DS_i \, [\, PE_i / PL_i) \, \{(1-\gamma_i)/(\gamma_i)\} \,]^{\eta_i}$ ... 3

9. $Q_i = \lambda_i \, [\, \delta_i \, M_i^{\rho_i} + (1-\delta_i) \, DD_i^{\rho_i} \,]^{-1/\rho_i}$ ... 3

10. $M_i = DD_i \, [(\, PD_i / PM_i) \, \{\delta_i / (1-\delta_i)\} \,]^{\sigma_i}$ ... 3

Income, Taxes, Savings and Investment

11. $YH_h = s_h \sum_j w_j LD_{\cdot j} + k_h \sum_j r_j KD_{\cdot j} + CTGH_h + CTFH_h + CTWH_h$ ... 5

12. $CTFH_h = dvr_h \, YF$ ... 5

13. $DTH_h = ty_{\cdot h} \, YH_h$ ... 5

14. $YDH_h = YH_h (1 - ty_{\cdot h})$ ... 5

15. $SH_h = YDH_h - \sum_i PC_i C_{ih} - CTHF_h - CTHW_h$ ... 5

16. $SH = \sum_h SH_h$ ... 1

17. $YF = \Omega_{\cdot 1} \sum_j r_j KD_j + \sum_h CTHF_h + CTGF + CTWF$ ... 1

18. $DTF = ty_f \, YF$ ... 1

19. $YDF = YF (1 - ty_f)$ ... 1

20. $SF = YDF - \sum_h CTFH_h - \sum_i PC_i CF_i$ ... 1

21. $TIM_i = tm_i \, e \, PWM_i M_i$ ... 3

22. $TIE_i = te_i \, PE_{\cdot i} E_{\cdot i}$ ... 3

23. $TIVA_i = tx_i \, PC_i Q_i$ ... 3

24. $YG = \Omega_{\cdot 2} \sum_j r_j KD_j + \sum_i TIM_i + \sum_i TIE_i + \sum_i TIVA_i + \sum_h DTH_h + DTF + FB$ ... 1

25. $SG = YG - \sum_h CTGH_h - CTGF - \sum_i PC_i GC_i$ ... 1

26. $S = SH + SF + SG + FKI$ ... 1

Demand for Commodities

27. $CTH_{\cdot h} = YDH_h - SH_h$ ... 5

28. $PC_i C_{i,h} = PC_i C_{i,h}^{MIN} + \beta^c_{j,h} (CTH_{\cdot h} - \sum_i PC_i C_{i,h}^{MIN})$ ... 15

29. $z = \sum_i PC_i C_{ih}^{MIN}$ ... 1

30 $CF_i = \beta^f_i (1 - \Psi_f) YDF / PC_i$ 3
31 $GC_i = \beta^g_i (1 - \Psi_g) YG / PC_i$ 3
32 $CT_i = \sum_h C_{i,h} + CF_i + GC_i$ 3

33 $I_i = [\phi_i I] / P_{INV}$ 3
34 $I = \sum_i I_i$ 1

Prices

35 $PV_i = [P_i X\tilde{S}_i - \sum_j PC_i DI_{i,j}] / VA_i$ 3

36 $PM_i = PWM_i (1 + tm_{.i})(1 + tx_i) e$ 3
37 $PE_i = (PWE_i e) / (1 + te_i)$ 3
38 $PC_i = (PD_i DD_{.i} + PM_i M_i) / Q_i$ 3
39 $PD_i = (1 + tx_i) PL_i$ 3
40 $P_i = (PL_i DS_i + PE_i \tilde{E_i}) / XS_i$ 3
41 $w_j = (PV_j VA_j - r_j KD_j) / LD_j$ 3
42 $w = \sum_j w_j / 3$ 1

43 $r_j = (PV_j VA_j - w_j LD_j) / KD_j$ 3
44 $r = \sum_j r_j / 3$ 1

45 $P_{INV} = \Pi_i [PC_i / \phi_i]^{\phi i}$ 1

46 $PINDEX = \sum_i \mu_i PV_i$ 1

Equilibrium Conditions and Macroeconomic Closure

47 $Q_i = DI_i + CT_i + I_i$ 3
48 $LS = \sum_j LD_j$ 1

49 $KS = \sum_j KD_j$ 1

50 $I = S$ 1
51 $B = e \sum_i PWM_i M_{.i} - e \sum_i PWE_i E_i + \sum CTHW_h - \sum CTWH_h - CTWF$

     $- FB - FKI = 0$ 1

Number of Independent Equations   *147*

Food Prices, Tax Reforms and Consumer Welfare in Ghana during the 1990s

Charles Ackah and Simon Appleton

1. Introduction

The pattern of food consumption is an important indicator of household welfare. However, in spite of the general concerns expressed in many quarters, relatively little is known about the consumption patterns of households in Ghana and how households have adjusted to price changes in the 1990s, which to some extent, resulted from policy reforms. This chapter aims to fill some of the gaps in the literature by analyzing the food consumption behaviour of Ghanaian households using the Almost Ideal Demand System (AIDS) model developed by Deaton and Muellbauer (1980b) to obtain price and income elasticity estimates for six major food categories, which together comprise the basic subsistence staples for most poor households. The estimated price elasticities are then utilized to evaluate the welfare implications of the relative food price changes in terms of compensating variation. We then assess the extent to which welfare changes can be explained by agricultural trade policy reforms using counterfactual simulation analysis.

Typically, there are a number of factors that determine the extent to which households are impacted by food price shocks, including the magnitude of the relative price changes, the relative importance of different food commodities in the consumption basket of different households as well as the degree to which households are compensated for the price shocks by changes in income. This chapter concentrates on the partial equilibrium welfare effects of food price changes, given the food consumption choices of households in Ghana. In essence, we focus on changes in consumer welfare resulting from the variations in food price changes, assuming an absence of income effects. While it would be appropriate to estimate the overall welfare changes (i.e. including producer welfare or allowing for income responses), we do not pursue this line of enquiry in this chapter due to data limitations including adequate producer price data. Our analysis does not account for supply responses through production and labour adjustments. The results must therefore be interpreted with these caveats in mind. However, the data constraints notwithstanding, our simple partial equilibrium analysis provides useful insights into household food consumption behaviour and the distributional implications of the variation in food price changes for household welfare in Ghana during the 1990s – a decade of remarkable food price inflation reminiscent of the economic crisis that precipitated the Structural Adjustment Programmes (SAPs) in the early 1980s.

The remainder of this chapter is organized as follows. Section 2 provides a review of the literature on demand system analysis and household welfare. Section 3 presents the econometric model and describes the methodology used to measure welfare changes facing Ghanaian households during the 1990s. Section 4 discusses the dataset and sources and Section 5 reports the elasticity estimates and the welfare analysis due to the price changes in the 1990s. This section also assesses the impact of simulated trade policy reform. Section 6 concludes with some policy implications of the findings.

2. Literature Review

In a number of studies, Deaton (1988, 1990 and 1997) propose a unique methodology to estimate demand elasticities using only a single cross-section of household budget survey data. His approach is based on the notion that prices for comparable goods can vary greatly across space in developing countries due to the fact that survey data are often collected in clusters of households in the same village. Deaton's two-stage estimation procedure first purges the unit value data of quality effects and then uses the cross-spatial variation in the 'corrected' unit values to identify own-price or cross-price elasticities. The main advantage of using unit values in demand analysis derives from the substantial cross-sectional variability, but it may give biased results (Deaton, 1990, 1997). Many commentators have argued that unit values, unlike market prices, are error-ridden and subject to sample selection problems as they are unavailable for non-purchasing households. The problem with unit value is that it is a function of expenditure and quantity, both of which are potentially measured with error in most household surveys (see Gibson and Rozelle 2002; Kedir 2001, 2005; and Niimi 2005.[1]

The most standard application of Deaton's approach follows the estimation of budget share and unit value equations such that for each household h in the cluster c, the M-good system of equations are given as:

$$w_{hc} = \alpha_1 + \beta_1 \ln x_{hc} + \delta_1 z_{hc} + \sum_{j=1}^{M} \gamma_j \ln p_{jc} + f_c + u_{1hc} \qquad (1)$$

$$\ln v_{hc} = \alpha_2 + \beta_2 \ln x_{hc} + \delta_2 z_{hc} + \sum_{j=1}^{M} \theta_j \ln p_{jc} + u_{2hc} \qquad (2)$$

where, w_{hc} is the budget share devoted to the good in question (good i), x_{hc} is total household expenditure, v_{hc} is unit value, z_{hc} is a vector of household characteristics, p_{jc} is the (unobserved cluster) price, f_c is the cluster fixed-effect, and the error terms of the two equations are u_{1hc} and u_{2hc} respectively. The estimation procedure follows two stages. Based on the assumption of no price variation in the same cluster, the main task in the first stage is to estimate total expenditure (or income) elasticities and the elasticity of unit values with respect to total expenditure (i.e., the quality effects) using the within-cluster variation in purchases and unit values. The second stage then involves estimating the price responses using the between-cluster information in the data. While the first-stage estimation is typically based on an OLS regression applied to the demeaned (at the cluster level) equations, an errors-in-variables regression is by necessity applied to the (corrected) budget shares and unit values.

Deaton (1997) provides an excellent empirical application of his estimation technique to examine the implications of tax reform in India and Pakistan. In Pakistan a reduction in the effective domestic subsidies to rice and wheat (due, in the case of rice, to export taxes) would be efficiency enhancing, but in both countries the burden falls relatively heavily on the poor, who have a high and relatively inflexible expenditure shares on these items.

Another example of this approach is Ravallion and van de Walle's (1991) study of Indonesian rice reform. They use detailed household survey data from the Indonesian National Socio-Economic Survey (SUSENAS) to estimate household demand equations that conform to the nonlinear version of the AIDS model (see Deaton and Muellbauer, 1980b) from which they derive the equivalent income function (as proposed by King, 1983). Assuming a hypothetical policy reform, Ravallion and van de Walle evaluate the partial equilibrium effects on poverty of changes in the price of Indonesia's main food staple (rice) by means of dominance tests. They show, *inter alia*, that the results depend partly on how the government passes the budget shock implied by rice price changes onto consumers and on what poverty line is used. The very poor are net consumers of rice and so suffer from the price rises, whereas farmers just below the standard poverty line are net producers and hence benefit and show positive chances of escaping from poverty.

In their study of the effect of the Indonesian economic crisis on poor households, Levinsohn, Berry, and Friedman (1999) employed the 1996 National Socio-Economic Survey (SUSENAS) data for 61,965 households, along with price changes caused by the 1997-1998 Asian currency crisis to estimate the distributional impact on households. Using only single pre-crisis cross-sectional consumption data, the authors estimate price elasticities for 22 composite goods - 21 aggregate food goods and a residual non-food consumption category. Matching the pre-crisis budget shares with post-crisis price changes, the authors then calculate the welfare impact of the price increases based on compensating variation (CV) and then explore the results further with non-parametric methods.[2] The main findings were that middle-income households were the most severely affected by the crisis. For the sample as a whole, they find that the CV has an inverted u-shape, with the poorest households (i.e. lowest expenditure decile) having an average CV of 73 percent of initial household expenditures, rising to 85 percent for those in the sixth, seventh, and eighth deciles, and falling to 77 percent for households in the top decile. Additionally, the consumer price impacts of the crisis were greater for urban than for rural areas, and greatest overall for the urban poor. From this perspective, it was the Indonesian households in the middle of the distribution that were most adversely impacted by the price changes. A further investigation revealed that it was the urban poor who tended to be hurt the most-needing, on average, 109 percent of their pre-crisis income in order to reach pre-crisis utility levels. The rural poor, on the other hand, require the lowest amount, only 70 percent of their pre-crisis income.

3. Empirical Methodology

3.1 The Demand Model

In this section, we discuss the estimation strategy used and some of the econometric issues encountered. We adopt the estimation of a linear *approximate* Almost Ideal Demand System (AIDS) for food demand using cross-sectional data. The AIDS model has been widely applied in many empirical studies of consumer behaviour using both cross-sectional and time series data. The model is adopted in this study because of its many attractive properties relative to other models for analyzing demand for food in developing countries (Deaton and Muellbauer, 1980b). An advantage of the AIDS model is that it is able to treat zero and non-zero consumption in the same way. Another desirable property of the AIDS model is that it is simple to estimate and free from the restrictive assumption of homotheticity, therefore allowing the model to capture any differences in the consumption bundles among different income groups. Other advantages include its tractability and flexibility in allowing us to overcome the problem of aggregation (see Deaton and Muellbauer 1980b).

The AIDS model with the addition of household demographic factors can be specified for the M-good system as

$$w_{ihc} = \alpha_i + \beta_i \ln\left(\frac{x_{hc}}{a(p)}\right) + \sum_{j=1}^{M} \gamma_{ij} \ln p_{jc} + \delta_1 Z_{hc} + u_{ihc} \tag{3}$$

where w_{ihc} is the share of the budget devoted to the ith commodity of household h in cluster c, x is the household's food expenditure, p_{jc} is the jth commodity price in cluster c and Z is a vector of household characteristics. α_i, β_i, γ_{ij} and δ_1 are parameters to be estimated, and u_{ihc} is the random error term with the standard properties. The aggregate price index, $a(p)$, used to normalize food expenditure x is defined as

$$\ln a(p) = \alpha_0 + \sum_{i=1}^{M}\alpha_i \ln p_i + \frac{1}{2}\sum_{i=1}^{M}\sum_{i=1}^{M}\gamma_{ij}\ln p_i \ln p_j \tag{4}$$

The Stone (1954) price index, which permits us to linearise the AIDS model as presented in equation (5) is used to approximate the price aggregator in equation (6) (Deaton and Muellbauer, 1980b). Thus, $\ln a(p)$ is substituted by the Stone price index defined as

$$\ln P_c^* = \sum_{i=1}^{M} \bar{w}_{ic} \ln p_{ic}$$

(5)

The Stone price index is computed using the cluster mean expenditure shares, $\bar{w}_{ic}$, and thus like all other price variables, is invariant within the same cluster.

The demand system is estimated for each of the seven food categories as listed in Table 2. While it would clearly be preferable to estimate the entire demand system, we do not have suitable price data for the important non-food items, e.g. housing, education and durable ownership. In the absence of such data (and in some cases, for simplicity) the usual practice, which is followed in this chapter, is to adopt weak separability as a working (and perhaps reasonable) assumption. By excluding non-food goods from the model, we are implicitly assuming that the utility of food is weakly separable from the quantities consumed of non-food. In other words, we assume that the demand for food does not depend on prices of non-food items given total food spending (or real income). We believe such a structure is plausible. However, we need to recognise that total food spending is necessarily endogenous. Hence, we allow for the endogeneity of all the food expenditures. Instruments include the logarithm of income (which should be correlated with food spending).

For the demand system to be theory-consistent, we impose the restrictions for implied by consumer demand theory, namely adding-up, homogeneity and symmetry. Adding-up is satisfied if $\sum_i w_i = 1$ for all x and p which requires $\sum_i \alpha_i = 1$, $\sum_i \beta_i = 0$ and $\sum_i \gamma_{ij} = 0$. We fulfil the condition of adding-up by dropping one of the M demand equations from the system and recovering the parameters of the omitted food equation from the estimates of the $M-1$ equations. The homogeneity property is satisfied by treating the price of the 'other foods' as a numeraire and setting its price to unity. In our empirical estimation, we omit the price term for the other food category and express the other price variables relative to the omitted price. Note that the demand functions are homogenous of degree zero in prices and income. This means that an equal proportional change in prices and income will leave commodity demands unchanged. (Slutsky) symmetry requires that $\gamma_{ij} = \gamma_{ji}$ which could be met by employing the Seemingly Unrelated Regressions (SUR) procedure to estimate the demand equations simultaneously.[43]

Beginning with a Stone approximation to $a(p)$, we estimate the remaining parameters by linear regression, imposing symmetry. We then update the linearly homogeneous price index $a(p)$ and repeat estimation until convergence. The income or expenditure, Marshallian (uncompensated) own-price and cross-price and the Hicksian (compensated) elasticities for equation (5) are computed at the sample means respectively as follows:

---

43 Consistent estimation of all parameters requires an iterative (maximum likelihood) method. Hence we employ Zellner's Iterative Seemingly Unrelated Regression (ITSUR) procedure. Formal tests based on the likelihood ratio test for the system as a whole fail to reject homogeneity and symmetry, implying that it is not unreasonable to impose these restrictions on the food demand system.

$$e_i = \frac{\partial \ln q_i}{\partial \ln x} = 1 + \frac{1}{w_i} \frac{\partial w_i}{\partial \ln x} = 1 + \frac{\beta_i}{w_i} \qquad (6)$$

$$\varepsilon_{ii} = \frac{\partial \ln q_i}{\partial \ln p_i} = -1 + \frac{1}{w_i} \frac{\partial w_i}{\partial \ln p_i} = -(1 + \beta_i) + \frac{\gamma_{ii}}{w_i} \qquad (7)$$

$$\varepsilon_{ij} = \frac{\partial \ln q_i}{\partial \ln p_j} = \frac{1}{w_i} \frac{\partial w_i}{\partial \ln p_j} = \frac{\gamma_{ij}}{w_i} - \beta_i \left(\frac{w_j}{w_i} \right) \qquad (8)$$

$$\varepsilon^*_{ij} = \varepsilon_{ij} w_j e_i \qquad (9)$$

where, q_i denotes quantity demanded of the ith commodity and all other variables are as previously defined.

3.2 Consumer Welfare Evaluation

This section describes the methodology used to determine welfare changes facing Ghanaian households during the 1990s. Since structural reforms are, in principle, designed to change prices, our interest is in linking observed food price changes to changes in household welfare, especially the partial equilibrium effects on welfare of changes in the prices of the main staple foods. Abstracting away from transmission mechanisms, we treat the policy-induced effect as captured by proportional changes in food prices. The welfare impact of food price changes on households can be measured in monetary terms by using the money metric indirect utility function. Using a set of reference prices, we can compute how well - or worse off households were, moving from their initial utility level to the new or post-reform utility level in response to the changes in food prices. Following the usual practice in this literature (Deaton, 1989 and 1997; Friedman and Levinsohn, 2002; and Niimi, 2005), we characterize the welfare effects of food price changes as the compensating variation (CV).

Suppose $c(u, p)$ denotes the expenditure function which defines the minimum expenditure required to achieve a specific utility level, u, at a given price vector p facing the household (see Deaton and Muellbauer, 1980a). Assume that prices change from p_0 to p_1 as a result of the removal of export tariffs or input subsidies. The money measure of the resultant welfare effect is the difference between the minimum expenditure required to achieve the original utility level, at the new prices, and the initial total expenditure. In other words, CV is the amount of money the household would need to be given at the new set of (higher) prices in order to attain the pre-reform initial level of utility. Subscripts refer to before (0) and after (1) prices, in this study 1991/92 and 1998/99 respectively. Hence, in terms of the expenditure (cost) function:

$$CV = c(p_1, u_0) - c(p_0, u_0) \qquad (10)$$

The CV can be approximated using a second order Taylor expansion of the minimum expenditure function as:

$$\Delta \ln c \approx \sum_{i=1} w_i \Delta \ln p_i + \frac{1}{2} \sum_{i=1} \sum_{j=1} w_i \varepsilon^*_{ij} \Delta \ln p_i \Delta \ln p_j \qquad (11)$$

where, w_i is the budget share of commodity i in the initial period (1991/92), $\Delta \ln p_i$ approximates the proportionate change in the price of commodity i, and ε^*_{ij} is the compensated price elasticity of commodity i with respect to the price change of good j. Clearly, equation (11) indicates that the impact of a price change upon a household is a function of both the magnitude of the price change as well as the relative importance of different food items in the consumption basket. The first-order effect is proportional to quantity consumed. The second-order effect depends on the compensated price elasticity. To account for consumption responses, we estimate first-and second-order impacts using the budget shares and the compensated demand elasticities.

4. Data Description and Sources

The GLSS datasets for 1991/92 and 1998/99 are used to match household-level data on food consumption with cluster-level information on food prices. A total of 4,523 households were surveyed in 1991/92 while 5,998 households were surveyed in 1998/99. The 1991/92 survey was conducted in about 400 clusters with 15 households per urban cluster and 10 households per rural cluster. In the case of the 1998/99 survey, 300 clusters were covered, each cluster containing about 20 households. These surveys contain detailed consumption data on about 100 food items. For estimation purposes, expenditures (including both cash purchases and imputed own-consumption) on various food commodities were aggregated into five composite categories: cereals, roots and tubers, fish, meat and alcohol. All remaining food items were aggregated into a miscellaneous category referred to as 'other food' giving a total of six food categories. The five main aggregates which are the focus of this study represent about 61 percent and 68 percent of the food consumption basket of households in 1991/92 and 1998/99 respectively. Unlike most household surveys in developing countries, the GLSS also include a community price questionnaire which collects data on prevailing prices of a variety of mainly food commodities and some non-food items in the local markets. In principle, these prices should reflect prices faced by households. In practice, there are some concerns about the reliability of such data as the prices may not refer to exactly the same type or quality of goods or that the prices quoted do not involve actual purchases (Deaton and Grosh, 2000). Nonetheless, this is a preferred source of price data when information regarding quantities is not collected from households as is the case of the GLSS (see Deaton and Zaidi, 2002).

4.1 Descriptive Statistics

Dependent and Explanatory Variables

The dependent variables in the demand analysis are the budget shares of the six food aggregates which are the shares of consumption expenditure of each food commodity in total food consumption expenditure. In addition to the price variables, the explanatory variables include total food expenditure and a set of demographic and household characteristics: (log) household size, age and squared age of the household head, regional and urban dummies.

Table 1 presents the mean budget shares for the overall sample while Tables 2 and 3 present the same information for households categorized into per capita household expenditure deciles.[44] The major components of food consumption in 1991/92 were: tubers (23.8 percent), fish (17.7 percent) and cereals (13.6%). A similar pattern was registered for 1998/99: tubers (23.5 percent), fish (19.9 percent) and cereals (17.1 percent). In general, consumption baskets in Ghana were remarkably uniform across income groups. However, there were considerable differences in the composition of the consumption basket between the richest 10 percent and the poorest 10 percent. As we would expect from Engel's law, poorer households spend a greater share of their budget on food than rich households in both survey years (71 percent for those in the bottom decile compared with 56 percent in the top decile in 1991/92, for example). As Tables A3 and A4 in the Appendix show, food consumption patterns vary considerably for the various regions and geographical locations in Ghana. Tubers and fish are consistently consumed largely by rural households. Cereals, meat and alcohol are consumed more intensively in the north (i.e., Northern, Upper East and Upper West). Tubers and fish on the other hand are not favourites in the north.

Table 1: Summary Statistics - Dependent Variables (Expenditure Shares)

Commodity Group	1991/92		1998/99	
	Mean	Std. Dev.	Mean	Std. Dev.
Cereals	0.136	0.126	0.171	0.115
Rice	0.036	0.047	0.056	0.057
Maize	0.044	0.077	0.053	0.080
Sorghum	0.011	0.050	0.007	0.036
Other cereal products				
Tubers & Starchy Roots	0.238	0.171	0.235	0.164

---

44 Summary statistics for all explanatory variables (except prices) are reported in the Appendix.

Commodity Group	1991/92		1998/99	
Cassava	0.084	0.099	0.090	0.104
Yam	0.048	0.091	0.047	0.076
Plantain	0.050	0.074	0.046	0.070
Other Starchy Roots				
Fish	0.177	0.118	0.199	0.118
Meat (Poultry)	0.020	0.045	0.027	0.047
Alcohol	0.041	0.078	0.044	0.071
Other Food	0.389	0.160	0.324	0.159
Oils & fats	0.032	0.032	0.001	0.007
Pulses	0.025	0.047	0.029	0.044
Prepared Meals	0.098	0.133	n/a	n/a
Other miscellaneous foods				

Source: Authors' calculations from GLSS 3 & 4.
Notes: n/a means data were not available.

Table 2: Expenditure Shares in Ghana, by Decile of Per Capita Consumption in 1991/92

	Poorest	2	3	4	5	6	7	8	9	Richest
Commodity										
Cereals	0.187	0.142	0.139	0.138	0.121	0.130	0.131	0.134	0.129	0.131
Rice	0.025	0.029	0.029	0.030	0.031	0.038	0.036	0.039	0.039	0.043
Maize	0.076	0.053	0.058	0.048	0.043	0.042	0.043	0.040	0.037	0.028
Sorghum	0.037	0.023	0.016	0.018	0.008	0.011	0.010	0.007	0.005	0.003
Tubers	0.230	0.280	0.277	0.289	0.264	0.252	0.248	0.230	0.225	0.175
Cassava	0.075	0.108	0.099	0.106	0.091	0.090	0.090	0.078	0.080	0.056
Yam	0.048	0.057	0.052	0.054	0.051	0.051	0.042	0.046	0.045	0.041
Plan	0.038	0.049	0.052	0.057	0.057	0.055	0.054	0.053	0.049	0.041
Fish	0.156	0.203	0.193	0.190	0.187	0.185	0.185	0.183	0.165	0.152
Meat	0.016	0.014	0.014	0.013	0.017	0.017	0.019	0.020	0.023	0.030
Alcohol	0.053	0.036	0.043	0.035	0.038	0.042	0.036	0.033	0.040	0.048
All Food	0.71	0.69	0.69	0.70	0.66	0.66	0.65	0.65	0.65	0.56

Source: Authors' calculations from GLSS 3.
Note: Deciles are by per-adult equivalent household expenditure.

Table 3: Expenditure Shares in Ghana, by Decile of Per Capita Consumption in 1998/99

	Poorest	2	3	4	5	6	7	8	9	Richest
Commodity										
Cereals	0.273	0.207	0.176	0.168	0.169	0.159	0.156	0.154	0.154	0.153
Rice	0.050	0.047	0.048	0.054	0.057	0.056	0.056	0.060	0.060	0.060
Maize	0.113	0.082	0.075	0.059	0.059	0.055	0.045	0.039	0.035	0.026
Sorghum	0.041	0.020	0.006	0.007	0.004	0.003	0.003	0.002	0.001	0.001
Tubers	0.138	0.216	0.266	0.268	0.261	0.275	0.262	0.249	0.235	0.195
Cassava	0.048	0.090	0.114	0.118	0.112	0.113	0.105	0.088	0.081	0.058
Yam	0.029	0.044	0.048	0.047	0.051	0.049	0.048	0.053	0.052	0.046
Plan	0.008	0.023	0.037	0.046	0.044	0.058	0.052	0.054	0.057	0.051
Fish	0.177	0.196	0.215	0.213	0.219	0.223	0.212	0.207	0.193	0.168
Meat	0.018	0.018	0.018	0.018	0.019	0.020	0.024	0.029	0.037	0.046
Alcohol	0.057	0.046	0.035	0.041	0.033	0.029	0.036	0.039	0.045	0.061
All Food	0.63	0.64	0.63	0.63	0.61	0.61	0.61	0.59	0.58	0.57

Source: Authors" calculations from GLSS 4.
Note: Deciles are by per-adult equivalent household expenditure.

Table 4 provides evidence on food price movements between 1991/92 and 1998/99. There is evidence that food prices fell relative to non-food prices during the 1990s. There are perceptible variations (across goods and location) in the degree of price changes observed. It is clear that there has been a significant increase in food price inflation, in both rural and urban areas, and across the country, with alcohol (178.4 percent), meat (173.4 percent) and fish (123.5 percent) registering the largest average increases. The prices of cereal and tubers, the two major staples in Ghana, increased by the lowest proportion of 3.1 percent and 7.9 percent respectively. This may be due partly to increased production and also imports, at least for rice. The real prices of all food commodities, except meat, increased the most in rural Ghana relative to urban locations. In fact, the real price of cereal fell by 18 percent in urban areas compared with an increase of about 14 percent in rural areas. It is the variation in these price changes that we seek to exploit in examining the distributional impact on household welfare of the food price changes.

Table 4: **Median Real Market Food Price Changes , 1991/92-1998/99(%)**

	Cereals	Tubers	Fish	Meat	Alcohol
Region					
Western	-17.5	22.9	129.2	177.7	161.4
Central	17.1	-1.7	134.0	208.4	197.7
Greater Accra	27.6	-2.7	124.1	196.3	113.9
Eastern	4.3	-6.7	132.5	166.5	165.1
Volta	10.7	4.7	101.8	180.4	167.6
Ashanti	-46.8	8.3	137.5	172.7	171.1
Brong Ahafo	50.5	29.5	115.2	115.5	207.8
Northern	0.5	26.8	69.2	135.1	201.4
Upper West	28.6	-9.8	119.2	160.1	211.1
Upper East	-5.1	-11.3	91.8	133.7	211.3
Locality					
Rural	13.9	6.9	126.9	168.8	192.1
Urban	-18.0	5.8	122.2	170.8	134.2
All Ghana	3.1	7.9	123.5	173.4	178.4

Source: Authors" calculations from GLSS 3 & 4

5. Empirical Results

Tables A2 and A3 in the Appendix report the structural parameters together with their p-values from the demand system estimated using the SURE procedure based on the 1991/92 and 1998/99 GLSS data respectively. The estimated coefficients obtained by imposing the conventional homogeneity and symmetry demand restrictions are mostly significant at the 5 percent level or better, indicating that the expenditure shares for each commodity are responsive to prices and income and to most of the household and demographic variables included in the model. With the budget shares as dependent variables (not the quantities consumed), a positive and statistically significant expenditure coefficient implies that the budget share increases with total food spending, suggesting that the expenditure elasticity would be greater than one and the commodity is a luxury good (see Table A8 in the Appendix). This is the case for meat and alcohol in 1991/92 and for meat, alcohol and tubers in 1998/99. Household size is a strong determinant of all expenditure shares. Household size is strongly negatively correlated with budget shares for meat and alcohol in both 1991/92 and 1998/99, implying that budget shares for these goods are falling with household size. Regional dummies and urban locality are also good determinants of household spending patterns. The estimates suggest that households located in the three northern regions have the largest budget shares for cereals, and the lowest shares for tubers and fish.[45]

5.1 Demand Elasticities

We now turn to the discussion of the estimated demand elasticities, which are needed to properly evaluate the welfare consequences of the reforms discussed earlier. The Marshallian (ordinary) elasticity matrices for 1991/92 and 1998/99 evaluated at the sample means are reported in Tables 5 and 6 respectively, which include the cross-price elasticity estimates. Tables A6 and A7 in the Appendix contain the Hicksian (income-compensated) demand elasticity matrices for 1991/92 and 1998/99 respectively. The expenditure (income) elasticities computed at the sample means using equation (8) are also presented in Table A8 in the Appendix.

As shown in Table 5, all the estimated Marshallian (uncompensated) own-price elasticities are negative. Consistent with consumer demand theory, there exists an inverse relationship between changes in own-price indexes and quantities demanded. In most cases the absolute value of the own-price elasticity is greater than unity, meaning that they are price elastic. The Hicksian (compensated) own-price elasticities reported in Tables A6 and A7 in the Appendix corroborate the information in Tables 5 and 8. As expected, in all cases, the compensated elasticities are lower than the uncompensated ones. Even after the income-compensation, tubers and meat (in 1991/92) remain the only commodities with own-price elasticity exceeding unity. For the remainder of the foods, the absolute values of the own-price elasticities are smaller than unity, meaning that they are not price elastic.

Several of the cross-price elasticities are particularly interesting in respect of the nature of the substitutability and complementarity between the various commodity groups (see Tables A6 and A7 in the Appendix). The compensated cross-price elasticities adjusted for real expenditure (income) changes appear to suggest, quite surprisingly, that cereal and fish, which constitute the core diet for the poorest households, were net substitutes in both years. Similarly, tubers and meat, consumed more intensively by the richest households, were net substitutes in 1998/99 but complements in 1991/92. The negative sign of the cross-price elasticities between cereals and tubers and between meat and fish suggests that these commodity groups are net complements.[46] Meat was a net complement to cereal in 1991/92 and fish was similarly a net complement to tubers in 1998/99. Alcohol was a net complement to all goods except meat in 1991/92. The

---

45   Although there are no accessible estimates for Ghana to be used as points of reference, we believe that the estimates are plausible and are generally consistent with a priori expectations.

46   A possible explanation of this phenomenon may be due to the fact that cassava and maize, which constitute about 9 percent and 5 percent respectively of the budget share for the average Ghanaian, are jointly used for the preparation of the some important local dishes (e.g. *banku* in the south and *tuozafi* in the north). It is also very common to find a combination of some meat (e.g. beef, chicken wings) and fish in most Ghanaian household meals.

nature of these commodities suggests that diets for poor and rich households are interrelated after all. This has implications for public policy in Ghana. The results seem to suggest that pro-poor policies targeted at individual commodities without recognising these interdependencies can be flawed. Elimination of protection in one market (say cereals) aimed to benefit the poor will have limited welfare impact if significant distortions persist in other markets (say meat).

For both 1991/92 and 1998/99 all goods had positive consumption expenditure elasticities, implying that no commodity was classified as "inferior"; all were "normal goods" (see Table A8 in the Appendix). The expenditure elasticities for all goods appear to change over the period, even if marginally. As expected, commodities that constitute the diet of poorer households have lower income elasticities. In 1991/92, cereals, tubers, fish and 'other food' were necessities ($e_i < 1$) while meat and alcohol were found to be luxury ($e_i > 1$). In 1998/99, cereals and fish remained necessities whereas the expenditure elasticity for tubers increased above unity. Recall that by the end of the 1990s cereals (27.3 percent) and fish (17.7 percent) alone constituted 45 percent of the food expenditures for the average poorest household.

Table 5: Marshallian (Ordinary) Demand Elasticity Matrix, 1991-92.

Commodity	With Respect to the Price of					
	Cereal	Tubers	Fish	Meat	Alcohol	Other Food
Cereals	-1.027	-0.304	-0.170	-0.034	-0.092	-0.349
Tubers	-0.066	-1.409	0.002	-0.031	-0.091	-0.198
Fish	-0.151	-0.257	-0.874	-0.062	-0.070	-0.437
Meat	-0.421	-0.156	-1.618	-2.014	0.452	0.691
Alcohol	-0.227	-0.085	-0.288	0.055	-0.969	-0.702
Other Food	-0.113	-0.204	-0.324	0.040	-0.083	-1.308

Source: Authors' calculations from GLSS 3.

Table 6: Marshallian (Ordinary) Demand Elasticity Matrix, 1998/1999

Commodity	With Respect to the Price of					
	Cereals	Tubers	Fish	Meat	Alcohol	Other Food
Cereal	-1.102	-0.328	-0.127	0.010	-0.088	-0.295
Tubers	-0.372	-1.037	-0.520	0.034	0.016	-0.370
Fish	-0.067	-0.433	-0.988	-0.114	-0.026	-0.203
Meat	-0.107	0.088	-0.935	-0.758	0.015	-0.718
Alcohol	-0.422	0.136	-0.217	0.040	-1.004	-0.615
Other Food	-0.175	-0.166	-0.190	-0.041	-0.071	-1.356

Source: Authors' calculations from GLSS 4.

5.2 Price Changes and Consumer Welfare

The estimated elasticities can be used to assess the welfare consequences of the food price changes that occurred during the 1990s. The measurement of the 'dynamic' household welfare effect, one that jointly considers (static) first-order effects in consumption as well as consumption responses, is the object of this sub-section. While the first term in equation (13) – the first-order approximation – may capture a large part of the impact of price changes on welfare, ignoring household behavioural responses in welfare analysis – the second order approximation - may lead to significant biases and inappropriate inferences (see Banks *et al.*, 1996; McCulloch, 2003; Niimi, 2005; Nicita, 2004b; Friedman and Levinsohn, 2002). The first-order approximation of impact of price changes implicitly assumes that households are unable to change their consumption patterns when prices change (equivalent to assuming that all elasticities are zero). Given the substantial observed price changes, substitution effects can be non-trivial, and therefore, first-order approximations can be seriously biased (Banks *et al.*, 1996). However, for purposes of comparison, we report results from both first-order and second-order approximations.

We utilize the estimated Hicksian (compensated) elasticities for 1991/92 to measure the welfare impact of the food price changes observed between 1991/92 and 1998/99. Following some recent literature (see Niimi, 2005; Nicita, 2004b; Friedman and Levinsohn, 2002; Minot and Goletti, 2000), we estimate the change in consumer welfare, measured as compensating variation (CV). The CV measures the total transfer required to compensate all households for the price changes they experienced between 1991/92 and 1998/99, as a percentage of their initial total expenditure. In doing this, we also recognise the importance of determining how different population groups are affected in different ways by these reforms. Thus, to illustrate which groups of households were relatively disadvantaged by the price changes, we disaggregate the CV measure by income group, locality and region. Table 7 presents the welfare measure as a share of total household expenditure in 1991/92. For comparison purposes, we also present estimates from a first-order approximation to the price changes, which disregards substitution effects in consumption. The first column presents the first-order effects computed using equation (11) for the various categories of households while the second column displays the full effects.

Table 7: Compensating Variation Implied by the Price Changes

Household Category	First-order Effects (%)	Full Effects (CV) (%)
Locality		
Rural	37.9	21.5
Urban	29.0	17.7

Household Category	First-order Effects (%)	Full Effects (CV) (%)
Income Group		
1st quartile	35.4	22.1
2nd quartile	35.2	20.4
3rd quartile	34.3	19.6
4th quartile	34.3	18.7
Poverty status		
Non-poor	34.6	19.4
Poor	35.2	21.5
Poverty status	Rural	Rural
Non-poor	39.3	21.7
Poor	36.6	21.4
Poverty status	Urban	Urban
Non-poor	29.2	16.7
Poor	28.1	22.1
Ghana	34.8	20.2

Source: Authors' calculations from GLSS 3 & 4.

Note: Compensating variation is measured as a proportion of 1991/92 total household expenditures.

The results suggest that all household groups suffered welfare losses arising from the food price increases during the 1990s. Consistent with our *a priori* expectations, it is clear that the first order effect overstates, albeit marginally, the welfare losses for all groups of households. On average, Ghanaian households need to be reimbursed to the tune of about 20.2 percent of their 1991/92 total household expenditures for the food price changes they faced during the 1990s. The results, however, reveal some heterogeneity in the impact of price variations on households. The results indicate that the burden of higher consumer prices fell largely on the poor and on rural households.[47] The distributional impacts of the price changes were quite similar for the rural poor and non-poor. However, within urban localities it is the poor who suffered disproportionately, requiring a compensation of about 22 percent of their 1991/92 household expenditures. It is probable that a combination of the relatively lower compensated own-price elasticities (see Table A9 in the Appendix), which means that households are unable to substitute away from high-priced goods, and the higher budget shares (see Table 2), contributed to relatively higher welfare losses for poor households. For rural households, it appears that the relatively higher price increases (see Table 4), coupled with lower compensating price elasticities and higher budget shares (see Table A9 in the Appendix) accentuated the welfare losses.

---

47 Poor households are defined as those whose per adult equivalent expenditure is below the lower poverty line of 700,000 cedis per year (in the constant prices of Accra in January 1999).

What can we infer from the results? As has already been noted, the linkage between policy reform and price changes is complex, especially when it involves the removal of quantitative restrictions. There could be a number of reasons that may account for welfare losses following the sharp food price changes such as exchange rate devaluation (depreciation), the abolition of fertilizer (and other input) subsidies or adverse weather conditions, which results in domestic production shortfalls. For example, while tariff liberalisation is expected to reduce the domestic price of imports, exchange rate devaluation (depreciation) would generally achieve the opposite. In essence, while it is difficult to attribute the price change and ,by implication, the welfare losses), to any particular policy *per se*, the results provide new insights into household consumption patterns and how household welfare was impacted by exogenous food price changes in the 1990s.[48] However, since our interest is in the effect of trade policy, the next sub-section adopts counterfactual experiments in an attempt to isolate the potential trade policy effects from those arising from other factors.

5.3 Trade Liberalisation and Consumer Welfare

In this sub-section, we use simulation techniques to analyse how trade liberalisation, defined here as tariff reductions, could have altered the effect of the actual food price changes that took place in the 1990s. Our motivation derives from the hypothesis that tariff reductions were possibly not dramatic enough to offset the price increases which, to some extent, resulted from other policy reforms. Alternatively, one could argue that tariff reductions notwithstanding, other factors could have prevented price transmission from the border to local prices. Lacking suitable data to estimate a tariff pass-through model, our approach is to follow the largest strand of the literature by using simulation analysis to explore the effect on welfare of a hypothetical trade policy reform (see for example, Porto, 2003; Minot and Goletti, 2000; Ravallion and van de Walle 1991). Having already estimated price elasticities of demand and using a partial equilibrium framework, we explore the potential distributional effects of further import tariff liberalisation on household welfare. For analytical convenience and due to data constraints, we assume that tariff reductions are fully transmitted to domestic prices. Further, for the model to be tractable, we abstract away from any potential general equilibrium effects on incomes, customs revenue and balance of payments, to mention just a few.

For the purpose of the simulations, a policy change is described as the change in the price of a good resulting from the tariff reform. We focus on a scenario in which all tariffs are cut by 50

---

48 We know from Table A12 that for all foods except poultry, the import tariff fell or was unchanged during the 1990s, which directly implies that consumer prices for such foods would have fallen, *ceteris paribus,* ruling out tariff reform as the culprit for the price increases and the subsequent welfare losses.

percent. For a small open economy the domestic price p_i^D for traded good i is related to the international price p_i^W through the following equation

$$p_i^D = p_i^W (1+t_i)$$ (12)

where t_i represents the *ad valorem* tariff rate applied to the import of good i. Following Porto (2003), we write the change in the (logarithmic) price of the ith good as

$$d \ln p_i^D = d \ln (1+t_i)$$ (13)

Using data on pre-reform tariffs and prices, we use (15) to compute the price changes that would result from the tariff reform. The tariffs that apply to each of the six composite goods (and their components) are listed in Table A12 in the Appendix. Equation (15) is estimated using the MFN tariff rates that prevailed in 1993 as the benchmark. The average tariff on food imports in 1993 ranges between 20 percent (for cereal, fish and meat) and 25 percent (for tubers and alcohol). Applying (15) to the hypothetical reform of 50 percent tariff reductions results in the prices of cereal, fish and meat declining by 8.7 percent and the prices of tubers and alcohol falling by 10.5 percent. These price changes are employed in re-estimating equation (13). Table 10 presents the simulation results of the effects of the 50 percent across-the-board tariff reductions.

The negative CV estimates indicate that all households would gain from further tariff reductions, suggesting that the tariff liberalisation in the 1990s was probably not large enough. Implementing the 50 percent across-the-board tariff cuts and thus reducing domestic prices by 8.7 percent to 10.5 percent could have offset the adverse effects of the price movements experienced in the 1990s. On average, the government would need to take away from each household about 6 percent of their 1991/92 total household expenditures to reduce its welfare to pre-reform levels. The experiment further suggests that poor consumers, especially in the rural areas, would be the major beneficiaries of further tariff liberalization. This means that tariff liberalisation would tend to benefit the poor (6.4 percent) over the rich (5.7 percent) and thereby potentially reduce inequality. Rural households also stand to gain substantially (6.5 percent), compared to their urban counterparts (5 percent). These findings indicate that trade policy may not have been responsible for the welfare losses observed in the previous analysis. The role of other factors and policies, such as the removal of fertilizer subsidies, exchange rate depreciation and domestic supply constraints could be decisive.

Tables 8 and 9 provide information on what happened to real incomes of households across the income distribution categories and in different sectors during the 1990s. We are interested in knowing whether real incomes increased enough to compensate households for the food price shocks and the implied welfare losses documented in Table 9. Table 9 shows a marginal increase in average real income by 2.5 percent between 1991/92 and 1998/99. However, across the income distribution categories and locality, the evidence indicates that it is not uniformly the case that all households experienced real income increase. Consistent with our *a priori* expectations, urban households in Ghana, especially the poorest (32.8 percent), had their real incomes falling substantially (10.7 percent) compared with an increase in real incomes for rural households (12.5 percent). In fact, it is non-poor rural households who saw the greatest improvement in income at 21 percent. These results show that even after allowing for real income increases, poor households, particularly in urban localities, were clearly disadvantaged by the rising consumer food prices.

Table 8: Compensating Variation due to Tariff Reform

Household Category	First-order Effects (%)	Full Effects (CV) (%)
Locality		
Rural	-6.3	-6.5
Urban	-4.8	-5.0
Income group		
1st quartile	-6.3	-6.5
2nd quartile	-6.1	-6.2
3rd quartile	-5.7	-5.9
4th quartile	-5.2	-5.4
Poverty status		
Non-poor	-5.5	-5.7
Poor	-6.2	-6.4
Poverty status	Rural	Rural
Non-poor	-6.2	-6.4
Poor	-6.5	-6.6
Poverty status	Urban	Urban
Non-poor	-4.8	-4.9
Poor	-5.2	-5.3
Ghana	-5.8	-6.0

Source: Authors' calculations from GLSS 3 & 4

Note: Compensating variation is measured as a proportion of 1991/92 total household expenditures.

Table 9: Household Income and Changes in the 1990s

Household Category	1991/92	1998/99	Changes (%)
Locality			
Rural	2,024,815	2,277,439	12.5

Household Category	1991/92	1998/99	Changes (%)
Urban	3,029,128	2,704,301	-10.7
Income group			
1st quartile	1,680,675	1,458,722	-13.2
2nd quartile	2,300,523	2,211,556	-3.9
3rd quartile	2,472,098	2,877,610	16.4
4th quartile	3,046,975	3,188,210	4.6
Poverty status			
Non-poor	2,712,510	2,831,827	4.4
Poor	1,865,052	1,573,762	-15.6
Poverty status	Rural	Rural	
Non-poor	2,276,180	2,753,458	21
Poor	1,784,633	1,583,733	-11.3
Poverty status	Urban	Urban	
Non-poor	3,202,658	2,927,371	-8.6
Poor	2,275,599	1,529,843	-32.8
Ghana	2,374,914	2,433,936	2.5

Source: *Author's calculations from GLSS 3 & 4.*
Note: *Amounts are stated in Cedis per annum in the constant prices of Accra in January 1999.*

6. Conclusion

In this study we had three main objectives: (1) to estimate for the first time a complete food demand system using recent household survey data for Ghana; (2) to measure the (consumer) welfare impact on households of food price changes in the 1990s; and (3) to assess the extent to which changes can be explained by trade and agricultural policy reforms. Using the linear approximate version of the AIDS model, we have calculated expenditure, own-price and cross-price demand elasticities for six food aggregates important for providing the calorific needs of most Ghanaian households. The results indicate that demand for most food commodities in Ghana is price sensitive. The estimated price and expenditure elasticities are plausible and consistent with economic theory: all own-price elasticities were negative and statistically significant. Similarly, estimated expenditure elasticities were positive and statistically significant for all food groups as is expected. The demand estimates presented in this chapter provide the first detailed information about the characteristics of food demand in Ghana.

With regard to our second and third objectives, we employed the estimated price elasticities to evaluate the welfare consequences of the relative food price changes in terms of compensating variation. Results suggest that Ghanaian household consumption did respond to relative price and real income changes, which to some extent resulted from policy reforms. We find that the remarkable increases in food prices resulted in severe erosion of real income and purchasing power for the urban poor in particular. Although the food price changes have had differential effects on the population, the general experience has been that, for the vast majority of households, the price changes have brought severe hardship through higher food prices. The results indicate that the burden of higher consumer food prices fell largely on urban poor households.

While it is difficult to attribute the food price changes, and by implication the welfare losses, to any particular policy *per se*, our counterfactual experiment indicates that trade liberalisation may not (for consumers) have been responsible for the welfare losses. The role of other factors and policies, such as the removal of fertilizer subsidies and exchange rate depreciation, could be decisive. The simulation exercise suggests that further tariff liberalisation would tend to offset the welfare losses of higher food prices for all household groups, although it is the poor and rural consumers that stand to gain the most. In sum, the results suggest, perhaps unsurprisingly, that although trade liberalisation may have a positive impact on welfare, at least from a consumption perspective, other factors may offset this, at least in the case of Ghana.

References

Ackah, Charles and Oliver Morrissey (2005), "Trade Policy and Performance in Sub-Saharan Africa since the 1980s", "*Economic Research Working Paper 78.*" African Development Bank (September).

Alderman, H. (1994), "Ghana: Adjustment's Star Pupil?" in Sahn (ed.), *Adjusting to Economic Failure in African Economies*, Ithaca and London: Cornell University Press.

Aryeetey, Ernest (2005), "Globalization, Employment and Poverty in Ghana", mimeo, Legon: Institute of Statistical, Social and Economic Research, University of Ghana.

Aryeetey, Ernest and Andrew McKay (2004), "Operationalising Pro-Poor Growth: Ghana Case Study", mimeo. AFD, BMZ, UK Department for International Development and World Bank.

Aryeetey, Ernest, Jane Harrigan and Machiko Nissanke (eds.) (2000), *Economic Reforms in Ghana: The Miracle and the Mirage*, Oxford and Accra: James Currey and Woeli Publishers.

Banks, J., Blundell, R. and A. Lewbel (1996), "Tax Reform and Welfare Measurement: Do We Need Demand System Estimation?", *The Economic Journal*, 106(438):1227-41.

Brooks, J., Croppenstedt, A., and Aggrey-Fynn, E. (2006), "Distortions to Agricultural Incentives in Ghana" unpublished manuscript. Rome: FAO,.

Coulombe, H. and A. McKay (2003), "Selective Poverty Reduction in a Slow Growth Environment: Ghana in the 1990s", Paper prepared for the World Bank, Human Development Network.

Cox, T. and M. Wohlgenant (1986), "Prices and Quality Effects in Cross-sectional Demand Analysis", *American Journal of Agricultural Economics* 68(4): 908-919.

Deaton, Angus (1985), "Panel Data from Time-series of Cross-sections", *Journal of Econometrics*, 30:109-126.

Deaton, Angus (1987), "Estimation of Own- and Cross-Price Elasticities from Household Survey Data", *Journal of Econometrics*, 36:7-30.

Deaton, Angus (1988), "Quality, Quantity and Spatial Variation of Price", *American Economic Review*, 78:418-430.

Deaton, Angus (1989), "Rice Prices and Income Distribution in Thailand: A Non-parametric Analysis." *The Economic Journal*, 99 (395, Conference Supplement): 1-37.

Deaton, Angus (1990), "Price Elasticities from Survey Data. Extensions and Indonesian Results", *Journal of Econometrics*, 44:281-309.

Deaton, Angus (1997), *The Analysis of Household Surveys: A Microeconomic Approach to Development Policy*, Washingtin D.C.:World Bank and The Johns Hopkins University Press.

Deaton, A. and J. Muellbauer (1980a), *Economics and Consumer Behaviour.* Cambridge University Press. New York.

Deaton, A and J. Muellbauer (1980b), "An Almost Ideal Demand System", *American Economic Review*, 70:312-329.

Deaton, A. and F. Grimard (1992), "Demand Analysis and Tax Reform in Pakistan", LSMS Working Paper, No. 85. Washington, D.C.: World Bank.

Deaton, A. and M. Grosh (2000), "Consumption," in M. Grosh and P. Glewwe (eds.), *Designing Household Questionnaires for Developing Countries: Lessons from Fifteen Years of the Living Standards Measurement Study*. Washington DC.: World Bank, pp. 91-133.

Deaton, A. and S. Zaidi (2002), "Guidelines for Constructing Consumption Aggregates for Welfare Analysis", LSMS Working Paper 135. Washington D.C.: World Bank.

Dordonu, C. K., (1997), "Enabling Conditions for Accelerated Agricultural Growth and Development in Ghana: The Macroeconomic Conditions". Strategy Paper presented at the discussion of Ministry of Food and Agriculture.

Friedman, J. and J. A. Levinsohn (2002), "The Distributional Impact of Indonesia's Financial Crisis on Household Welfare: A 'Rapid Response' Methodology", *World Bank Economic Review*, 16(3): 397-423.

Ghana Statistical Service (2000b), *Ghana Living Standards Survey Report on the Fourth Round (GLSS 4)*, Accra: GSS.

Ghana Statistical Service (2000a), *Poverty Trends in Ghana in the 1990s*, Accra: GSS,.

Gibson, J. and S. Rozelle (2002), "Prices and Unit Values in Poverty Measurement and Tax Reform Analysis," Mimeo, Department of Economics, University of Waikato.

Hutchful, Eboe (2002), *Ghana's Adjustment Experience: The Paradox of Reform*. Geneva.: UNRISD,.

ISSER (various years). *The State of the Ghanaian Economy Report*, University of Ghana, Legon: Institute of Statistical, Social and Economic Research.

Kedir, A. (2001), "Some Issues in Using Unit Values as Prices in the Estimation of Own-Price Elasticities: Evidence from Urban Ethiopia." CREDIT Research Paper No. 01/11, University of Nottingham.

Kedir, A. M. (2005) "Estimation of Own- and Cross-price Elasticities using Unit Values: Econometric Issues and Evidence from Urban Ethiopia", *Journal of African Economies*, Vol. 14(1):1-20.

McCulloch, N. (2003), "The Impact of Structural Reforms on Poverty: a Simple Methodology with Extensions", World Bank Policy Research Working Paper 3124.

McCulloch, N., Winters, A. and X. Cirera, (2001), *Trade Liberalisation and Poverty: A Handbook.* London: CEPR.

Minot, N., and Goletti, F. (2000), "Rice Market Liberalization and Poverty in Vietnam", Research Report 114, Washington DC :International Food Policy Research Institute,

Nicita, A. (2004a), "Who Benefited from Trade Liberalization in Mexico? Measuring the Effects on Household Welfare", World Bank Policy Research Working Paper 3265.

Nicita, A. (2004b), "Efficiency and Equity of a Marginal Tax Reform: Income, Quality and Price Elasticities for Mexico", World Bank Policy Research Working Paper 3266.

Niimi, Y. (2005), "An Analysis of Household Reponses to Price Shocks in Vietnam: Can Unit Values Substitute for Market Prices?", Poverty Research Unit Working Paper 30, University of Sussex.

Nyanteng, V. and A.W. Seini (2000), "Agricultural Policy and the Impact on Growth and Productivity 1970-95" in *Economic Reforms in Ghana, The Miracle and The Mirage*, edited by E. Aryeetey, J. Harrigan and M. Nissanke,Oxford and Accra:James Currey and Woeli Publishers,

Ravallion, Martin (1990), "Rural Welfare Effects of Food Price Changes under Induced Wage Responses: Theory and Evidence for Bangladesh," *Oxford Economic Papers*, 42: 574-585.

Ravallion, M. and Van De Walle, D. (1991), "The impact on poverty of food pricing reforms: A welfare analysis for Indonesia", *Journal of Policy Modelling*, Vol. 13(2), pp. 281-299.

Reimer, J.R. (2002), "Estimating the Poverty Impacts of Trade Liberalization", GTAP Working Paper 20, Center for Global Trade Analysis, Department of Agricultural Economics, Purdue University.

Stone, R. (1954), "Linear Expenditure Systems and Demand Analysis: An Application to the Pattern of British Demand", *The Economic Journal*, 64, 511-527.

Teal, F., and M. Vigneri (2004), "Production Changes in Ghana Cocoa Farming Households under Market Reforms", Centre for the Study of African Economies Working Paper 2004-16.

Winters, L.A. (2002), "Trade, Trade Policy and Poverty: What Are the Links", *The World Economy*, Vol. 25, pp. 1339-1367.

Winters, L.A., N. McCulloch, and A. McKay (2004), "Trade Liberalization and Poverty: The Evidence So Far", *Journal of Economic Literature*, 42(1): 72-115.

World Trade Organisation (2001), *Trade Policy Review – Ghana*, Report by the Secretariat, WTO, Geneva. http://www.wto.org/english/tratop_e/tpr_e/tp157_e.htm (accessed 21/11/2006).

Appendix

Table A1: Summary Statistics - Explanatory Variables (except prices)

	1992-93		1998-99	
Variable	Mean	Std. Dev.	Mean	Std. Dev.
Expenditure Variable (Cedis)				
Total Food Spending	330,690	228,862	2,271,279	1,637,836
Demographic variables				
Age of Head	44.3	15.3	45.8	15.4
Age ofHhead Squared	2195.9	1525.7	2336.9	1563.6
Log of Household Size	1.271	0.724	1.245	0.697
Geographical Variables				
Dummy Variables for -				
Urban Locality	0.349	0.477	0.367	0.482
Central Region	0.114	0.318	0.117	0.321
Greater Accra Rregion	0.140	0.347	0.143	0.350
Eastern Region	0.146	0.353	0.107	0.309
Volta Region	0.090	0.287	0.137	0.344
Ashanti Region	0.162	0.369	0.177	0.381
Brong Ahafo Region	0.100	0.301	0.090	0.286
Northern Region	0.075	0.263	0.060	0.238
Upper West Region	0.024	0.154	0.020	0.140
Upper East Region	0.042	0.201	0.043	0.204

Source: Authors' calculations from GLSS 3 & 4.

Table A2: Parameter Estimates for the AIDS Model, 1991/92

	Cereal		Tubers		Fish		Meat		Alcohol	
	coef-ficient	p-value	coef-ficient	p-value	coef-ficient	p-value	coef-ficient	p-value	coef-ficient	p-value
Intercept	0.224	0.000	0.186	0.028	0.755	0.000	-0.033	0.477	-0.187	0.000
Total Food Expenditure	-0.017	0.002	0.019	0.040	-0.083	0.000	0.016	0.000	0.016	0.000
Relative Prices (in logs)										
Cereals	0.010	0.002	-0.006	0.129	-0.003	0.311	0.000	0.961	-0.005	0.061
Tubers, roots & plantain	-0.006	0.129	-0.013	0.128	0.004	0.466	-0.007	0.012	-0.002	0.693
Fish	-0.003	0.311	0.004	0.466	0.007	0.545	0.005	0.396	0.020	0.000
Meat	0.000	0.961	-0.007	0.012	0.005	0.396	-0.014	0.100	0.001	0.749
Alcohol	-0.005	0.061	-0.002	0.693	0.020	0.000	0.001	0.749	-0.001	0.872
Demographic & geographic										
Age of Head	-0.001	0.211	0.000	0.717	0.002	0.000	0.000	0.182	0.003	0.000
Age of Hhead Squared	0.000	0.236	0.000	0.908	0.000	0.006	0.000	0.299	0.000	0.000
Log of Household Size	0.014	0.000	0.037	0.000	0.032	0.000	-0.008	0.000	-0.023	0.000
Urban Dummy	0.029	0.000	-0.083	0.000	-0.004	0.417	-0.008	0.001	-0.025	0.000
Central	0.034	0.000	-0.052	0.000	0.043	0.000	-0.016	0.000	-0.022	0.000
Greater Accra	0.067	0.000	-0.128	0.000	-0.004	0.690	-0.011	0.006	-0.024	0.000
Eastern	0.018	0.007	-0.006	0.578	0.007	0.323	-0.007	0.020	-0.017	0.002
Volta	0.096	0.000	-0.092	0.000	-0.027	0.002	-0.006	0.084	-0.002	0.682
Ashanti	0.033	0.000	-0.017	0.138	-0.030	0.000	-0.008	0.014	-0.025	0.000
Brong Ahafo	0.009	0.251	0.015	0.208	-0.038	0.000	-0.013	0.000	-0.006	0.292
Northern	0.147	0.000	-0.185	0.000	-0.096	0.000	-0.028	0.000	-0.012	0.138
Upper West	0.224	0.000	-0.295	0.000	-0.164	0.000	0.004	0.522	0.098	0.000
Upper East	0.333	0.000	-0.293	0.000	-0.168	0.000	0.012	0.028	-0.005	0.560
R-squared	0.34		0.30		0.29		0.05		0.11	

Source: Authors' calculations from GLSS 3.

Table A3: Parameter Estimates for the AIDS Model, 1998/99

	Cereal coefficient	p-value	Tubers coefficient	p-value	Fish coefficient	p-value	Meat coefficient	p-value	Alcohol coefficient	p-value
Intercept	0.363	0.000	0.116	0.037	0.711	0.000	-0.097	0.001	-0.056	0.084
Total Food Expenditure	-0.027	0.000	0.010	0.050	-0.043	0.000	0.006	0.001	0.007	0.004
Relative Prices (in logs)										
Cereals	0.005	0.103	-0.005	0.067	-0.008	0.001	0.011	0.000	-0.007	0.000
Tubers, roots & plantain	-0.005	0.067	-0.012	0.007	0.000	0.906	-0.004	0.020	0.008	0.000
Fish	-0.008	0.001	0.000	0.906	-0.018	0.000	-0.001	0.466	0.004	0.040
Meat	0.011	0.000	-0.004	0.020	-0.001	0.466	0.006	0.015	0.000	0.804
Alcohol	-0.007	0.000	0.008	0.000	0.004	0.040	0.000	0.804	0.000	0.930
Demographic & geographic										
Age of Head	0.000	0.692	0.004	0.000	0.001	0.009	0.000	0.157	0.001	0.056
Age of Head Squared	0.000	0.778	0.000	0.000	0.000	0.158	0.000	0.446	0.000	0.012
Log of Household Size	0.028	0.000	0.040	0.000	0.021	0.000	-0.003	0.008	-0.015	0.000
Urban Dummy	0.023	0.000	-0.073	0.000	-0.001	0.897	0.000	0.938	-0.008	0.006
Central	0.006	0.378	-0.031	0.001	0.011	0.102	0.000	0.889	0.003	0.474
Greater Accra	0.031	0.000	-0.081	0.000	-0.010	0.094	0.006	0.034	0.024	0.000
Eastern	0.052	0.000	-0.083	0.000	-0.009	0.139	0.004	0.127	0.023	0.000
Volta	-0.003	0.563	0.005	0.496	-0.014	0.020	0.010	0.000	0.010	0.011
Ashanti	0.007	0.241	0.010	0.216	-0.016	0.004	0.011	0.000	-0.007	0.059
Brong Ahafo	0.009	0.186	0.050	0.000	-0.041	0.000	0.003	0.311	-0.001	0.820
Northern	0.154	0.000	-0.158	0.000	-0.135	0.000	0.010	0.008	0.021	0.000
Upper West	0.263	0.000	-0.215	0.000	-0.216	0.000	0.013	0.013	0.152	0.000
Upper East	0.193	0.000	-0.272	0.000	-0.166	0.000	0.016	0.000	0.065	0.000
R-squared	0.25		0.31		0.30		0.05		0.13	

Source: Authors' calculations from GLSS 4.

181

Table A4: Expenditure Shares in Ghana, by Region in 1991/92

	Cereals	Tubers	Fish	Meat	Alcohol	Other Food
Region						
Western	0.08	0.29	0.23	0.02	0.05	0.22
Central	0.10	0.26	0.24	0.01	0.03	0.25
Greater Accra	0.14	0.13	0.15	0.02	0.03	0.43
Eastern	0.09	0.30	0.23	0.02	0.04	0.22
Volta	0.16	0.23	0.21	0.02	0.05	0.23
Ashanti	0.10	0.29	0.16	0.02	0.03	0.31
Brong Ahafo	0.08	0.34	0.17	0.02	0.04	0.26
Northern	0.26	0.15	0.07	0.01	0.04	0.36
Upper West	0.30	0.05	0.04	0.03	0.15	0.31
Upper East	0.41	0.06	0.03	0.04	0.06	0.29
Locality						
Rural	0.14	0.27	0.19	0.02	0.05	0.23
Urban	0.13	0.18	0.15	0.02	0.03	0.38
All Ghana	0.14	0.24	0.18	0.02	0.04	0.29

Source: Authors' calculations from GLSS 3

Table A5: Expenditure Shares in Ghana, by Region in 1998/99

	Cereals	Tubers	Fish	Meat	Alcohol	Other Food
Region						
Western	0.15	0.29	0.23	0.03	0.03	0.25
Central	0.13	0.26	0.27	0.01	0.03	0.28
Greater Accra	0.16	0.14	0.17	0.04	0.06	0.41
Eastern	0.20	0.22	0.24	0.02	0.05	0.25
Volta	0.14	0.29	0.24	0.03	0.04	0.24
Ashanti	0.14	0.28	0.21	0.03	0.03	0.29
Brong Ahafo	0.13	0.33	0.19	0.02	0.03	0.25
Northern	0.29	0.13	0.08	0.03	0.05	0.38
Upper West	0.43	0.08	0.04	0.02	0.18	0.21
Upper East	0.32	0.05	0.05	0.04	0.10	0.40
Locality						
Rural	0.17	0.26	0.21	0.02	0.04	0.25
Urban	0.17	0.18	0.18	0.03	0.04	0.37
All Ghana	0.17	0.23	0.20	0.03	0.04	0.30

Source: Authors' calculations from GLSS 4.

Table A6: Hicksian (Compensated) Demand Elasticity Matrix, 1991-92

Commodity	With Respect to the Price of					
	Cereals	Tubers	Fish	Meat	Alcohol	Other Food
Cereals	-0.908	-0.073	0.005	-0.014	-0.053	0.031
Tubers	0.025	-1.094	0.098	-0.005	-0.045	-0.049
Fish	0.001	-0.111	-0.776	-0.037	-0.008	-0.138
Meat	-0.109	0.387	-1.104	-1.973	0.545	1.744
Alcohol	-0.067	0.189	-0.015	0.082	-0.904	-0.195
Other Food	0.009	0.033	-0.144	0.061	-0.043	-0.920

Source: Authors' calculations from GLSS 3.

Table A7: Hicksian (Compensated) Demand Elasticity Matrix, 1998/1999

Commodity	With respect to the Price of					
	Cereal	Tubers	Fish	Meat	Alcohol	Other Food
Cereals	-0.951	-0.125	0.046	0.034	-0.050	-0.009
Tubers	-0.114	-0.729	-0.245	0.075	0.082	0.121
Fish	0.045	-0.262	-0.838	-0.096	0.003	0.016
Meat	0.202	0.496	-0.592	-0.711	0.093	-0.161
Alcohol	-0.229	0.408	0.012	0.071	-0.955	-0.244
Other Food	-0.005	0.068	0.009	-0.014	-0.028	-1.031

Source: Authors' calculations from GLSS 4.

Table A8: Expenditure (Income) Elasticity of Demand: 1998/99

Commodity	1991-92	1998-99
Cereals	0.966	0.876
Tubers, Roots & Plantain	0.723	1.439
Fish	0.781	0.699
Meat	2.556	1.742
Alcohol	1.306	1.146
Other Food	0.987	0.999

Source: Authors' calculations from GLSS 3 & 4.

Table A9: Demand Elasticities -1991/92, by Income Group and Locality

Commodity	Poor	Non-poor	Urban	Rural	All Households
Expenditure Elasticities					
Cereals	0.966	0.966	0.971	0.962	0.966
Tubers, roots & plantain	1.433	0.310	0.235	1.356	0.723
Fish	0.944	0.686	0.381	1.045	0.781
Meat	3.097	2.242	2.803	2.393	2.556
Alcohol	1.818	1.009	0.727	1.689	1.306
Other Food	0.986	0.987	0.990	0.985	0.987
Uncompensated Own-price Elasticities					
Cereals	-1.036	-1.022	-1.047	-1.014	-1.027
Tubers, roots & plantain	-1.089	-1.595	-1.782	-1.163	-1.409
Fish	-1.090	-0.749	-0.416	-1.177	-0.874
Meat	-2.349	-1.819	-2.174	-1.908	-2.014
Alcohol	-0.787	-1.074	-1.164	-0.840	-0.969
Other food	-1.273	-1.328	-1.417	-1.235	-1.308
Compensated Own-price Elasticities					
Cereals	-0.908	-0.907	-0.921	-0.899	-0.908
Tubers, roots & plantain	-0.773	-1.280	-1.522	-0.811	-1.094
Fish	-0.960	-0.670	-0.348	-1.059	-0.776
Meat	-2.316	-1.773	-2.133	-1.867	-1.973
Alcohol	-0.726	-1.007	-1.111	-0.767	-0.904
Other Food	-0.914	-0.923	-0.938	-0.908	-0.920

Source: Author's calculations using GLSS 3.

Table A10: Demand Elasticities -1998/99, by Income Group and Locality

Commodity	Poor	Non-poor	Urban	Rural	All Households
Expenditure Elasticities					
Cereals	0.896	0.867	0.877	0.874	0.876
Tubers, Roots & Plantain	1.541	1.396	1.606	1.337	1.439
Fish	0.740	0.681	0.698	0.699	0.699
Meat	1.817	1.709	1.706	1.764	1.742
Alcohol	1.161	1.140	1.149	1.145	1.146
Other food	0.999	0.999	0.999	0.999	0.999
Uncompensated Own-price Elasticities					

Commodity	Poor	Non-poor	Urban	Rural	All Households
Cereals	-1.148	-1.082	-1.099	-1.103	-1.102
Tubers, roots & plantain	-0.975	-1.064	-0.875	-1.137	-1.037
Fish	-1.032	-0.969	-0.965	-1.002	-0.988
Meat	-0.716	-0.776	-0.781	-0.744	-0.758
Alcohol	-1.001	-1.005	-1.002	-1.005	-1.004
Other Food	-1.337	-1.365	-1.423	-1.316	-1.356
Compensated Own-price Elasticities					
Cereals	-0.960	-0.947	-0.951	-0.951	-0.951
Tubers, roots & plantain	-0.686	-0.747	-0.621	-0.795	-0.729
Fish	-0.869	-0.825	-0.836	-0.839	-0.838
Meat	-0.681	-0.724	-0.727	-0.702	-0.711
Alcohol	-0.951	-0.957	-0.954	-0.955	-0.955
Other food	-1.033	-1.030	-1.024	-1.035	-1.031

Source: Authors' alculations using GLSS 4.

Table A11: Consumer Price Indices, 1991/92 – 1998/99 (September 1997=100)

Month	Food	Non-Food	Combined
GLSS 3 (1991/92)			
Sep-91	21.2	18.0	18.9
Oct-91	21.0	18.1	19.0
Nov-91	21.0	18.2	19.0
Dec-91	21.0	18.2	19.1
Jan-92	21.1	18.3	19.1
Feb-92	21.7	18.5	19.5
Mar-92	22.7	18.7	19.9
Apr-92	23.4	19.1	20.4
May-92	24.2	19.2	20.7
Jun-92	24.4	19.3	20.8
Jul-92	24.5	19.7	21.1
Aug-92	24.4	19.9	21.3
Sep-92	24.0	19.9	21.1
Average	22.7	18.9	20.0
GLSS 4 (1998/99)			
Apr-98	124.4	108.3	115.9

Month	Food	Non-Food	Combined
May-98	129.0	110.2	119.0
Jun-98	128.7	111.8	119.7
Jul-98	125.9	111.2	118.2
Aug-98	125.4	112.0	118.4
Sep-98	121.9	113.2	117.4
Oct-98	118.0	113.7	115.8
Nov-98	117.9	113.5	115.6
Dec-98	119.8	114.2	116.9
Jan-99	122.7	115.1	118.7
Feb-99	125.2	118.8	121.9
Mar-99	127.8	121.6	124.6
Average	123.9	113.6	118.5
% change in CPI between 1991/92 and 1998/99	415.8	471.3	461.5

Source: Statistical Service, Statistical Newsletter *(various issues)*

Table A12: Tariffs on Agricultural Food Imports

Commodity	1993	2000	% change
Meat			
Goat	20	20	0
Poultry	20	40	100
Pork	20	20	0
Beef	20	20	0
Mutton	20	20	0
Fish			
Herrings	20	0	-100
Cod	20	0	-100
Sardines (not tin)	20	0	-100
Haddock	20	0	-100
Mackerel	20	0	-100
Lobsters, shrimps & prawns	25	20	-20
Tubers & starchy roots (cassava)	25	20	-20
Cereals			
Rice (paddy or rough)	20	20	0

Commodity	1993	2000	% change
Sorghum	20	0	-100
Wheat	20	20	0
Millet	20	20	0
Other Cereals	20	20	0
Alcohol			
Beers	25	20	-20
Sparkling Wine	25	20	-20
Whiskies & Rum	25	20	-20
Gin & Brandy	25	20	-20
Vodka.	25	20	-20
Other spirits	25	20	-20

Source: Authors' calculations using HS 6–digit level tariff data from UNCTAD TRAINS Database.

(Endnotes)

1   See Deaton (1997); (Deaton and Grimard (1992); Friedman and Levinsohn (2002); Kedir (2001, 2005); and Nicita (2004a, b) for applications of how unit values have been used in place of market prices.
2   The compensating variation is derived from a second-order Taylor expansion of the minimum expenditure function.

The Effect of Import Liberalization on Import Tariff Yield in Ghana

William Gabriel Brafu-Insaidoo and Camara Kwasi Obeng

1. Introduction

Trade liberalization has formed a very important component of economic reform programs in Ghana since 1983. In terms of sequencing, Ghana did not go through the normal intermediary stage of translating quantitative restrictions into equivalent tariffs before gradually reducing the tariffs. Most quantitative restrictions, including import licensing, were eliminated at the same time as went ahead to reduce the level and range of tariffs.

The reason for import trade liberalization as part of this economic reforms was to reduce the the government spread between the official and parallel exchange rates, and to provide foreign exchange to ease import suppression with the aim of increasing output, particularly in the export sector. In this regard, the long term goal was to replace quantitative restrictions with price instruments.

However, the impact of the liberalization on trade tax revenue has been a subject of debate in recent times. There are concerns about existing ambiguity in both theory and empirical evidence on the relationship between trade liberalization and trade tax revenue in the global context. In theory, liberalization in the form of lower tariff rates and the simplification of rates causes direct trade tax revenue loss on one hand, but can also amount to an increase in volume of imports, and hence the tax base and revenue. The net effect depends on a host of factors, including the initial trade regime and the extent of increase in demand for imports. Empirical studies confirm this ambiguous relationship suggested in theory (see Tanzi, 1989; Ebrill et al., 1999; Glenday, 2000; Khattry *et al.*, 2002; Agbeyegbe *et al.*, 2003; Economic Commission for Africa, 2004; Suliman, 2005).

Oduro (2000) asserts that trade liberalization has been fiscally incompatible in Ghana for the 1990s even though Jebuni *et al.*, (1994) indicate that trade liberalization is fiscally compatible for the second half of the 1980s. Such studies only rely on descriptive analysis of changes in tax revenues. They do not apply testable models in investigating the exact impact trade liberalization has on trade tax revenues in Ghana.

To validate Oduro's assertion, this chapter used regression analysis, applied to testable models, in examining such relationships from observed data. The empirical purpose of this study was to quantitatively determine the impact of import liberalization on import tariff revenue in Ghana. Two steps were followed in the regression exercise to achieve the objective of the study. The first step involved an estimation of the import tariff yield in Ghana and an examination of the dynamics of the yield under conditions of import liberalization. The model was then extended to examine the quantitative effect of import liberalization on tariff revenue in Ghana.

The organization of the study is as follows: In the next section a brief discussion of trends in trade liberalization in Ghana is made. This is followed by an explanation of what the authors mean by import trade liberalization and a presentation of the approach to study in Section 3. Findings from the analysis are then reported in Section 4. Section 5 summarizes the findings and provides conclusions and policy implications of the study.

2. Trade Liberalization in Ghana

Until the inception of the Economic Recovery Programme in 1983, Ghana had operated alternating intermittent episodes of a fairly liberal trade regime. The first was between 1950 and 1961 as a member of the sterling zone, with virtually no restrictions on payments to and from member countries but imposed restrictions on payments to non-member countries. Interruption of the liberalization process was basically the result of fiscal indiscipline and depletion of the country's foreign exchange reserves. The country's second experience of a liberal import regime was between 1967 and 1971. Under this regime, the domestic currency was devalued by about 43 percent and import duties on some selected items were reduced. Again, the process of liberalization was interrupted with a resort to control measures in 1972 following the deterioration of the country's balance of payments position and depletion of its foreign exchange reserves due to fiscal indiscipline and huge import bills (Jebuni, Oduro and Tutu, 1994).

The current episode of trade liberalization has been an integral part of the structural adjustment programmes which began in 1983 and can be categorized into three phases: the period of attempted liberalization or transition to import liberalization; the period of import liberalization; and the period of liberalized trade regime (Oduro, 2000; Brafu-Insaidoo and Obeng, 2008).

The period of attempted liberalization or transition to import liberalization covers the years 1983–1986. This period is characterized by the introduction of a system of bonuses and surcharges, and their later replacement by frequent nominal devaluations. Import tariff rates were adjusted downward, but the range of rates with the import licensing system and import programming were maintained. Aside from these, the period witnessed a decline in export tax rates that was greater than the decline in import tariffs. The period of import liberalization *per se* ran from 1986 to 1989. This period was characterized by the introduction of a formal dual exchange rate system, which was later unified into a single exchange rate system based on auctioning and a further liberalization of the exchange rate. Other features of this phase of the liberalization process include a redefining of the import licensing categories, a reduction of the import tax schedule and a reduction in the sales taxes on imported goods by 10 percentage points. The foreign exchange retention scheme was liberalized in 1987, while the cocoa export tax rate (made up of the ratio of cocoa duties to cocoa export earnings) was reduced.

A liberalized trade regime has been in place since 1989. This period has been characterized by a replacement of retail auctioning with wholesale auctioning in the foreign exchange market in 1990, abolition of the import licensing system, decline in import tax rates on raw materials and capital goods, and reduction in sales tax on imported basic consumer goods. Over this same period, protective duty rates were introduced for specific goods in 1990 and 1994, and the export retention scheme was phased out.

The most favoured nation (MFN) tariffs apply on most imports, except those from the Economic Commission of West African States (ECOWAS) member countries, which have attracted duty-free rates since 1996.

Under the ECOWAS trade liberalization scheme established in 1990, Ghana initially provided preferential tariff reductions of 20 percent on imports of a few goods from some countries that had been granted community status. Products from member states that qualified for preferential treatment attracted rates of 8, 16 and 20 percent while similar items from other countries attracted duty rates of 10, 20 and 25 percent respectively.

However, since 1996 most imports from member countries have attracted duty free rates. Ghana provides duty-free preferences on a range of unprocessed agricultural products and several industrial products imported from enterprises sited within member countries, and that are eligible to receive such preferential treatment. Eligibility is based on whether the imports meet the ECOWAS rules of origin and have obtained at least, 60 percent of their raw materials from within the Community.

3. Concepts and Methods

Before discussing the approaches used in our analysis, our initial effort is to discuss the definition and concept of trade liberalization broadly, as well as those specifically considered in our analysis.

3.1 Concepts and Definitions

The definition of trade liberalization is fraught with ambiguity (Edwards, 1989). On a wider scale, the benchmark definition of trade liberalization indicates a change from the use of quantitative restrictions to the use of price instruments. This definition lends support to the assertion that quantitative restrictions must be replaced with equivalent tariffs (Krueger, 1986). Jebuni *et al.* (1994) regard this definition as second-best liberalization. A second definition of trade liberalization is frequently regarded as a move toward neutrality in relative prices. In this instance, trade liberalization is considered as the provision or increase in financial incentives for exports equivalent to some given proportion of custom duty on imports. An extensive definition of trade liberalization demands the elimination of quantitative restrictions and reduction in import tariff rates. This represents a move towards free trade.

Ghana's liberalization process could be described as one of a move toward free trade. Unlike in many developing countries, Ghana did not go through the intermediary stage of translating its quantitative restrictions into equivalent tariffs before steadily but progressively reducing the tariffs. Most quantitative restrictions, including import licensing, were eliminated at the same time as it went ahead to reduce the level and range of tariffs.

Trade liberalization basically consists of the liberalization of quantitative import restrictions, tariff liberalization, and the reduction or elimination of taxes on exports. Often, trade liberalization has been accompanied by exchange rate devaluation and liberalization and has in most cases been regarded as an integral component of the liberalization process. The liberalization of quantitative import restrictions consists of the relaxation or removal of the restrictions. Tariff liberalization involves reducing the average tariff rate, a unification of the range of import tax rates towards a single rate and the phasing out of tariffs. The focus of our estimation exercise is on the impact of import liberalization on tariff revenue from imports. Consequently, our measures of trade liberalization exclude changes in export taxes, but involve a brief consideration of the relative importance of exchange rate variations.

3.2 Buoyancy and Elasticity

Our analysis begins with evaluating the import tariff yield in Ghana. This is meant to determine the efficiency of the trade tax administration system and to find out whether revenue leakage remains a major problem for import tax after trade liberalization.

Two measures are usually used for this exercise. These are the buoyancy and elasticity of a given tax system. The buoyancy measures growth in duty revenue as a result of growth in income, reflecting the combined effects of tax base expansion and discretionary changes in tax rates, base definition and changes in collection and enforcement of the law. Elasticity, on the other hand, measures control for discretionary tax measures, implying that changes in duty revenues are attributed to automatic or natural growth of the economy (Osoro, 1993).

Generally, the buoyancy of a tax is obtained assuming the following functional form:

$$TR = \alpha Y^{\beta} \varepsilon \qquad (1)$$

This can be re-written in double log as follows:

$$\text{Log } TR_t = \text{Log}\alpha + \beta \text{Log} Y_t + \varepsilon_t \qquad (2)$$

where TR and Y are real import tariff revenue and income or GDP in aggregate level respectively, α and ε represent a constant and error term respectively. The parameter β then becomes the direct measure of buoyancy. It follows from equation 1 that, $(\partial TR/\partial Y)(Y/TR) = \beta$.

The buoyancy of a tax system, which generally, refers to the responsiveness of tax revenue to a change in income, is defined as:

$$E_{\tau,y} \quad = \quad (\partial TR/\partial Y)*(Y/TR) \quad = \quad [(\partial TR/\partial B)*(B/TR)][(\quad \partial B/\partial Y)*(Y/B)] \qquad (3)$$

where TR is tax revenue, Y is income (GDP) and ∂ denotes partial derivatives. The right hand side of equation 3 represents a decomposed version of the tariff buoyancy, interpreted as elasticity of tariff revenue with respect to tax base (imports in this case) and the elasticity of the base with respect to income (GDP). Overall, tax base-to-income elasticities can be determined by how the economic structure changes with economic growth. The tax-to-base elasticities, on the other hand, show the revenue growth that is within the control of customs administration or can be attributed to efficiency in customs administration.

To find out the responsiveness of tariff revenue to change in the tax base, we assume the following functional form:

$$TR = aB^{\beta}v \qquad (4)$$

This can be re-written in double log form as follows:

$$Log\, TR_t = Log\, a + bLogB_t + v_t \qquad (5)$$

where TR and B are import tariff revenue and the tax base (imports M, in this case) respectively, a and v represent a constant and error term respectively. The parameter b then becomes the direct measure of the responsiveness of import tax revenue to change in the tax base. It follows from equation 4 that, $(\partial TR/\partial B)(B/TR) = b$.

In determining elasticities, two main techniques are usually used for cleansing the revenue series of discretionary effects. One is that of proportional adjustment which involves use of historical time series-tax data adjusted for discretionary tax measures, as in Mansfield (1972), Osoro (1993 and Muriithi and Moyi (2003). The other is the use of unadjusted historical time-series tax data with time trends or dummy variables incorporated as proxies for discretionary tax measures, as in Singer (1968) and Artus (1974).

Lack of sufficient data made us opt for the dummy method, usually referred to as the Singer approach. Thus, we introduce dummy variables to control for discretionary tax measures and a lagged base variable into equation 5 as follows:

$$Log\, TR_t = Log\, a + b_1 LogB_t + b_2 LogB_{t-1} + \Sigma\, b_{3i}\, D_i + v_t \qquad (6)$$

where the dummy variable D takes on the value of one for discretionary tax measures and zero otherwise. The summation accounts for the multiple discretionary changes over the sample period. More specifically, three dummies are introduced. A liberalization dummy D_{1983} is introduced as a dummy for tariff reforms undertaken to accommodate import liberalization initiated in 1983 measures. A second dummy D_{slope}, which is an interactive term is a slope dummy introduced to capture any shift in the slope of the tariff revenue function as a result of the liberalization. D_{slope} is defined as $TR*D_{1983}$, where TR denotes tariff revenue. The third dummy D_{tar} is introduced to capture the impact of customs administration reforms in Ghana. Tax reforms in Ghana started with the establishment of the National Revenue Secretariat with an oversight responsibility of supervising the operations of revenue collection agencies, as well as the granting of autonomy to the agencies including customs administration in 1985. The regression exercise also examined the effect of the changes in the simple average official tariff rate *otr* on tariff revenue.

Data Sources and Definition of Variables
Annual data collected from various sources were used for the study. These include the International Monetary Fund database, the World Bank database, United Nations' Commodity Trade Statistics, Ghana Statistical Service, Customs, Excise and Preventive Service, and the Ministry of Finance and Economic Planning.

For this chapter, the following variable definitions applied. Real import tax or duty revenue was calculated by deflating nominal import duty revenues with the consumer price index. The values of real imports were obtained by deflating nominal imports with import price indices. Real GDP is nominal GDP deflated by GDP deflator. The average import duty rate variable used in the estimation exercises is the average of official duty rates for imports. The real exchange rate was computed by deflating nominal exchange rate by consumer price index. The study period is from 1965 to 2008.

4. Estimation Results
This section presents the findings from estimating import tariff buoyancy and elasticity and analyses the impact of import liberalization on import tariff revenue in Ghana. The direct and indirect effect of import tariff liberalization is also inferred from estimating a function for aggregate imports.

4.1 Import Tax Revenue Productivity – Buoyancy and Elasticity
Estimates of import tariff buoyancy and elasticity have been derived using the Cochrane-Orcutt iterative procedure which corrects for the problem of multicollinearity and auto-correlation.

A Report of the estimates on tariff buoyancy is presented in Table 1 below. The estimates indicate that activities towards the generation of revenue from taxing imports in the economy have been more fruitful during the liberalization period (post-1983) compared to the pre-reforms (pre-1983) period. By contrast however, Table 3 indicates that import tariff has become less elastic over the period of import liberalization compared to the pre-reforms (pre-1983) period. This could be attributed to leakages in the form of duty evasion and exemptions, and inefficiencies in customs administration and the collection system.

Table 1: Estimates of Import Tariff Buoyancy in Ghana

Period	Coefficient	DW
1965-2008***	0.703	1.559
1966-1982*	0.330	1.566
1983-2008**	2.530	1.750
Difference in coefficients	2.200	

Source: Computed by authors, using Stata 9.0

In particular, there has been widespread use of discretionary exemptions, often administered under poorly specified authority. It is estimated that about 14 percent of total imports in 1998 alone passed through bonded warehouses, including many duty-free goods. Bonded goods are estimated to be the single largest category of exempt imports, accounting for 35 percent of total exempt imports. This common use of bonded warehouses tends to contribute to duty evasion. Duty evasion also arises from under-invoicing of imports and outright smuggling, often with the connivance of corrupt customs officials.

Table 2: The Decomposed Tariff Buoyancies Over the Reform and Pre-reform period

Period	Coefficient	DW
A. Base-to-Income Elasticity		
1965 – 2008***	3.146	1.276
1965 – 1982	0.173	1.002
1983 – 2008***	4.449	1.771
Difference in Coefficients	4.276	
B. Tax-to-Base Elasticity		
1965-2008***	0.395	1.985
1965-1982***	0.771	1.540
1983-2008*** 0.713	1.803	
Difference in Coefficients	-0.058	

Source: Computed by author, using Stata 9.0

Estimates of the decomposed tariff buoyancies in Table 2 above indicate high growth of taxable imports over the liberalization period compared to the pre-liberalization (pre-1983) period. This supports earlier analysis that imports have grown substantially over the period of import liberalization following economic reforms initiated in 1983. However, the liberalization period has also witnessed comparatively slow growth in tariff revenue. This observation implies that the administration of collection of duties has remained weak, despite earlier efforts made to strengthen it. The estimates of the tax-to-base elasticity indicate that elasticity fell marginally from 0.771 during the pre-reforms period (pre-1983 period) to 0.713 during the liberalization period (post-1983). This suggests the need to further strengthen and improve duty collection administration in Ghana.

Table 3: Estimates of Overall Elasticity of Tariff Revenue

Period	Coefficient	DW
1966-2008***	0.237	1.926
1965-82*	0.527	1.792
1983-2008*	0.154	2.202
Difference in coefficients	-0.373	

Source: Computed by authors, using Stata 9.0

A comparison of duty buoyancy and elasticity presented in Table 4 indicates that duty buoyancy outweighed duty elasticity when considering the entire study period, a suggestion that discretionary tax measures (DTMs) have improved tariff revenue mobilization over the entire period. A comparison of regimes, however, indicates that the contribution of DTMs in improving tariff revenue mobilization has been positive during the period of import liberalization. Measures such as comprehensive reforms to customs duties (which includes reduction of the level and range of rates) and customs collection administration have improved efficiency in the import tax system over the liberalized period.

Table 4: Comparison of Import Tax Buoyancy and Elasticity

Period	Buoyancy	Elasticity	Difference
1965-2008***	0.703	0.237	0.466
1965-1982*	0.330	0.527	-0.297
1983-2008*	2.530	0.154	2.375

Source: Computed by authors, using Stata 9.0

Table 5 also confirms the positive impact of the liberalization in enhancing tariff revenue in Ghana. This is reflected in the statistically-significant and positively signed coefficients for the liberalization and interactive dummies in the estimation results. The significance of the interactive slope dummy in explaining tariff revenue suggests that the slope of the tariff revenue function has shifted upward. This is an indication of the fact that other events such as reforms to the tax collection system have contributed significantly to improving revenue generation from taxing imports. Although the coefficient for the reduction in the average official duty rate is correctly signed, its influence on improving tariff revenue is marginal. This suggests that reduction in average official duty rates has contributed only marginally to the improvement in import duty revenue.

Table 5: **Estimates of overall Elasticity of Tariff Revenue (1965-2008)**

logTR	Coefficient	Standard Error	t	P>{t}
logM	0.234	0.098	2.38	0.023
logy_1	-0.529	0.657	-0.81	0.426
Dslope	0.891	0.193	4.61	0.000
Dtar	0.001	0.106	0.02	0.990
D_{1983}	0.454	0.100	2.40	0.017
otr	-0.147	0.145	-1.01	0.319
D-W (original) 0.715	D-W (transformed)	1.858		

Source: Computed using Intercooled Stata 11.0

7. Conclusions and Policy Implications

Ghana has been hailed by the international community as one of the countries that have pursued deep economic reforms since 1983. As part of the programme, efforts were made to reform the external trade sector, with import liberalization as an important component. Among the instruments used were reductions in the level of tariffs, simplification of rates into more uniform rates, the removal or relaxation of quantitative restrictions and equilibrating role of a liberal exchange rate regime.

However, experiences with tax revenues from international trade, particularly over the 1980s and 1990s, raised concerns over whether import trade liberalization conflicts with the revenue generation objectives of economic reforms in Ghana. This has been important by virtue of the fact that fiscal discipline in the earlier part of adjustment was relaxed and the government was no longer discreet with its spending.

An attempt has been made in this study to address one of the prevailing issues by adopting a sturdy approach to quantitatively determine the exact impact import liberalization has on import tax revenue in Ghana.

A summary of the research findings from the analysis are as follows: first, activities towards the generation of revenue from taxing imports in the economy have been fruitful during the liberalization period (post-1983) as compared to the pre-reforms (pre-1983) period. Nevertheless, tariff revenue has become less responsive to growth in imports during the liberalization (post-1983) period. In addition, the results reflect continued inefficiencies in customs administration and collection system, and leakages in the form duty evasion and widespread exemptions. Furthermore, discretionary tax measures including tax administration reforms have improved tariff revenues, particularly during the liberalization (post-1983) period. Other events in addition to import tariff liberalization have improved tariff revenue in Ghana. Lastly, and in broad terms, import liberalization is fiscally-compatible in Ghana although the impact of the average official tariff rate reductions has been marginal.

In conclusion, this study invalidates Oduro's assertion that trade liberalization has been in conflict with the revenue objective of economic reforms.Consequently, the study provides useful insight for public policy. First, the continued inefficiencies in import tax administration in the country suggests the need for further strengthening of customs administration and improving on duty collection mechanisms in the country. This would enhance the capacity of the country to generate more revenue from taxing imports. Secondly, public policy should focus on the identification of the major sources of duty revenue leakage. The pervasive use of exemptions creates a gap in the tax base, especially through abuses of the exemptions offered. Consequently, a further review of the rationale for the duty exemption program and reduction in range of items exempt from duty payments in Ghana will be required. In addition, sustaining complementary measures such as the replacement of import tariff with the Value-Added Tax and maintaining a liberal exchange rate regime are likely to contribute to the enhancement of revenue from taxing imports.

References

Artus, K.K. (1974), "Tax Revenue Forecasting: A Methodological Study with application to Turkey". *Studies in Domestic Finance*, No.5

Brafu-Insaidoo, W.G. and Obeng, C. K., (2008), "Effect of import trade liberalization on import tariff revenue in Ghana", Nairobi:AERC Research Paper 180:

Ebrill, L., J. Stotsky and Gropp, R., (1999), "Revenue Implications of Trade Liberalization," International Monetary Fund Occasional Paper, 99/80

Edwards,S. (1989), "Openness, Outward Orientation, Trade Liberalization and Economic" Performance in Developing Countries», Policy, Planning and Research Working Paper *Series* No. 119, Washington D.C.: World Bank.

Glenday G., (2000), "Trade Liberalization and Customs Revenues: Does Trade Liberalization Lead to Lower Customs Revenues? The Case of Kenya," Development Discussion Papers, 764. Harvard Institute for International Development.

Jebuni, C.D., A.D. Oduro and K.A. Tutu (1994), "Trade, Payments Liberalization and Economic Performance in Ghana", AERC Research Paper 27: Nairobi.: African Economic Research Consortium. Khattry, Barsha and Rao, M. J., (2002), "Fiscal Faux Pas?: An Analysis of the Revenue Implications of Trade Liberalization", *World Development*, 30: 1431-1444.

Krueger, A., (1986), "Problems of Liberalization", in A. Choksi and Papageorgiopu (ed.) *Economic Liberalization in Developing Countries,* Oxford: Blackwell.

Mansfield, C.Y. (1972),"Elasticity and Buoyancy of a Tax System: A Method Applied to Paraguay," *IMF Staff Papers*, Volume 19.

Muriithi, M.K. and E.D. Moyi, (2003), "Tax Reforms and Revenue Mobilization in Kenya," AERC Research Paper 131: Nairobi: African Economic Research Consortium, Nairobi.

Oduro, A.D. (2000) "Performance of The External Trade Sector Since 1970", in E. Aryeetey, J. Harrigan and M. Nissanke (eds.) *Economic Reforms in Ghana*. Oxford. Accra. Trenton. : James Currey, Woeli Publishing Servicesand Africa World Press.

Osoro N. E. (1993) "Revenue Productivity Implication of Tax Reform in Tanzania," AERC Research Paper 20: Nairobi: Africa Economic Research Consortium.

Singer, N.M. (1968), "The Use of Dummy Variables in Estimating the Income Elasticity of State Income Tax Revenues", *National Tax Journal*, 21: 200-4.

Suliman, K.M. (2005), "The Impact of Trade Liberalization on Revenue Mobilization and Stability in Sudan," Global Development Network.

Tanzi,V. 1989, "The Impact of Macroeconomic Policies on the Level of Taxation and the Fiscal Balance in Developing Countries". IMF Staff Papers 36(3): Washington D.C

United Nations Economic Commission for Africa (2004), *Economic Report on Africa 2004*, Addis Ababa

World Trade Organization, (2001), *Trade Policy Review Ghana*, No. 81.

Appendix: Import Duty Revenue Productivity

Table A1: Import Tax Buoyancy (1965-2008)

logTR	Coefficient	Standard Error	t	P>{t}
log y	0.703	0.052	13.50	0.000
D-W (original)	0.176	D-W (transformed)	1.559	

Source: Computed using Intercooled Stata 9.0

Note: The estimates are obtained after applying the Cochrane-Orcutt iterative process to correct for the problem of autocorrelation and multi-collinearity.

Table A2: Base-to-Income Elasticity (1965 – 2008)

Log M	Coefficient	Standard Error	t	P>{t}
Log Y	3.146	0.883	3.56	0.001
D-W (original)	0.229	D-W (transformed)	1.365	

Table A3: Tax-to-Base Elasticity (1965-2008)

Log TR	Coefficient	Standard Error	t	P>{t}
log M	0.395	0.111	3.57	0.001
D-W (original)	0.414	D-W (transformed)	1.987	

Source: Computed using Intercooled Stata 8.0

Table A4: Estimates of Overall Elasticity of Tariff Revenue (1965-2008)

Log TR	Coefficient	Standard Error	t	P>{t}
Log M	0.237	0.097	2.45	0.003
Log y_1	-0.399	0.618	-0.65	0.523
Dslope	0.933	0.186	5.02	0.000
Dtar	-0.032	0.099	-0.32	0.749
D_{1983}	0.401	0.110	2.10	0.017
D-W (original)	0.712	D-W (transformed)	1.926	

Source: Computed using Intercooled Stata 8.0

Table A5: Import Tax Buoyancy (1965-1982)

Log TR	Coefficient	Standard Error	t	P>{t}
Log y	0.771	0.030	25.89	0.000
D-W (original)	0.666	D-W (transformed)	1.540	

Source: Computed using Intercooled Stata 9.0

Note: The estimates are obtained after applying the Cochrane-Orcutt iterative process to correct for the problem of autocorrelation and multi-collinearity.

Table A6: Base-to-Income Elasticity (1966 – 1982)

logM	Coefficient	Standard Error		t P>{t}
logY	0.173	0.425	0.41	0.690
D-W (original)	0.236068	D-W (transformed)	1.001621	

Table A7: Tax-to-Base Elasticity (1966-1982)

logTR	Coefficient	Standard Error	t	P>{t}
Constant (dropped)				
logM	0.614	0.224	2.74	0.015
D-W (original)	0.725932	D-W (transformed)	1.815719	

Source: Computed using Intercooled Stata 9.0

Table A8: Estimates of Overall Elasticity of Tariff Revenue (1965-1982)

logTR	Coefficient	Standard Error	t	P>{t}
Constant (dropped)				
logM	0.527	0.207	2.55	0.023
log y_1	-0.941	1.253	-0.75	0.466
D-W (original)	0.895	D-W (transformed)	1.792	

Source: Computed using Intercooled Stata 9.0

Table A9: Import Tax Buoyancy (1983-2008)

logTR	Coefficient	Standard Error	t	P>{t}
Constant (dropped)				
Log y	2.530	0.943	2.68	0.013
D-W (original)	0.243	D-W (transformed)	1.750	

Source: Computed using Intercooled Stata 9.0

Note: The estimates are obtained after applying the Cochrane-Orcutt iterative process to correct for the problem of autocorrelation and multicollinearity.

Table A10: Base-to-Income Elasticity (1983 – 2008)

Log M	Coefficient	Standard Error	t	P>{t}
Constant (dropped)				
Log y	4.449	1.136	3.91	0.001
D-W (original)	0.275 D-W	(transformed)	1.892	

Table A11: Tax-to-Base Elasticity (1983 - 2008)

Log TR	Coefficient	Standard Error	t	P>{t}
Constant (dropped)				
Log M	0.714	0.017	41.36	0.000
D-W (original)	0.958	D-W (transformed)	1.803	

Source: Computed using Intercooled Stata 9.0

Table A12: Estimates of Overall Elasticity of Tariff Revenue (1983-2008)

Log TR	Coefficient	Standard Error	t	P>{t}
Log M	0.154	0.143	1.08	0.292
Log y_1	1.345	0.996	1.35	0.191
Dtar	0.187	0.106	1.76	0.093
D-W (original)	0.762	D-W (transformed)	2.209	

Source: Computed using Intercooled Stata 8.0

Cash Cropping, Gender and Household Welfare: Evidence from Ghana

Charles Ackah and Ernest Aryeetey

1. Introduction

Trade and agricultural liberalisation were the main focus of Ghana's economic reform programme as discussed in Aryeetey *et al.* (2000). Like the vast majority of African countries, Ghana had extremely restrictive and distortionary agricultural policies from independence until the 1980s, motivated by the desire to protect domestic producers in order to (1) increase food production, (2) provide raw materials and inputs to the other sectors of the economy, and (3) to ensure food security and adequate nutrition by improving the availability of food for consumers (Brooks *et al.* 2006). Such policies included price controls, input and credit subsidies, obligatory credit allocations, and heavy state involvement in production, distribution and marketing.

The reforms from 1983 onwards involved the removal of price distortions on crops, eliminating subsidies for agricultural inputs including fertilizer, and reducing the role of parastatals (Sarris and Shams, 1991; Nyanteng and Seini, 2000). Yet, reforms were introduced gradually, and only gained momentum with the Agricultural Services Rehabilitation Project initiated in 1987. This joint Ghana government/World Bank project aimed at improving the institutional capacity of the country's agricultural policy bodies mainly through privatisation. A number of successes were recorded in the area of agricultural research, extension and irrigation (Brooks *et al.* 2006).

In the cash crop sector, the parastatal monopoly in cocoa marketing has not been eliminated (World Bank, 1995; IMF, 2000) although reforms have ensured that cocoa farmers receive a higher share of world market prices (Kanbur, 1994). In fact, an upward trend in cocoa output since 2002 has been attributed in part to improved agronomic practices as well as price incentives.

In agricultural production, trade policies often encourage shifting staple foods production for domestic consumption to products for export. In Ghana, while men are often viewed as being responsible for producing cash crops, women are allotted the responsibility for producing subsistence food crops for home consumption. Consequently, agricultural development programmes and market liberalization have been often criticized for focusing on men's crops rather than women's crops. Consideration of gender accessibility of land and the type of crops grown by small producers as well as large producers are important in poverty assessment in rural agricultural locations. Failure to consider these issues, especially the gender concerns into trade and market liberalization may affect the outcomes of these reforms.

We use data from the most recent household survey conducted in 2005/06 to examine the role of cocoa production in improving household welfare by (1) examining differences in cocoa supply responses between female- and male-headed rural households, (2) assessing the independent effects of participation in cocoa on household income, (3) isolating the impact of participating in cocoa on food security, and (4) analyzing the impact of cocoa income on household consumption patterns. The rest of this paper proceeds as follows. The next section briefly reviews the literature on gender roles in Ghanaian agriculture and the effects of agricultural liberalization from a gender perspective. In Section 3, we present a latent welfare framework for analyzing the nexus between cash cropping and household welfare, while in Section 4 we present an overview of the data and descriptive statistics. Section 5 reports and discusses the econometric results. Section 6 concludes and draws some implications for policy.

2. Gender and Agriculture

It has long been recognized that the organisation of agricultural production has important implications for gender relations and vice versa in the Sub-Saharan Africa (SSA) context. Often, it is claimed that cash crops fall under the domain of men, while food crops are controlled by women. The following review of the empirical evidence on gender roles in Ghanaian agriculture, with special focus on female farmers, demonstrates that while there is some justification in the characteriation of cash crops as 'male' it oversimplifies Ghanaian rural reality and the changing political economy. This is particularly true in the cocoa-producing regions of the country.

In pre-colonial traditional, subsistence-agriculture-based Ghana, men and women farmed together on the same plot of land, producing exclusively for home consumption. Specific agricultural tasks were confined to certain age and gender groups. While men were responsible for the production of food crops, women had to do the weeding and assisted during harvest. Most domestic tasks, including cooking, fetching water, gathering firewood and taking care of the many children were also taken care of by women.

While these domestic tasks remained in the female domain until today, the advent of cash crops, principally cocoa, and, more generally, the increasing importance of market exchange in agriculture, significantly impacted on gender roles in agriculture. It was primarily men who became cash crop producers initially, while women's responsibility shifted towards the production of food crops for home consumption and the main traditional food crop, yam, was replaced by the less labour-intensive maize and cassava. As the proceeds from cocoa production accrued to men, women soon started to sell part of their production to ensure cash income for themselves. In fact, most authors claim that the rise of the market economy went along with the establishment of separate male and female agricultural income accounts.

The review so far draws a picture of rural households with "men and women tending to have separate income and expenditure streams" with "conventional divisions of responsibility for household expenditure" (Baden *et al, 1994*). Yet, the assumption of separate income and expenditure streams seems to be exaggerated. Most importantly, the household survey datasets used in this study suggest that the majority of male-headed rural households do not run more than one farm and if they do, other farms are in most cases controlled by the (male) household head. If reported control over a farm were to imply exclusive access to agricultural income, women in those households would not have any access to agricultural income. This seems fairly unrealistic and, more likely, household members bargain over access to income and the related allocation of expenditures between male or female private goods as well as over expenditure on household public goods.

To sum up the discussion on gender roles in agriculture, the evidence presented suggests that a model of households with complex bargaining processes on expenditure as well as production (and certainly further non-economic ones) seems more adequate to describe the reality of decision making in rural Ghana than a simple neoclassical household model. Apparently, income is often not being pooled, and males and females sometimes even appear to manage their own farms independently. Certainly, understanding the resource allocation processes within rural households seems an important prerequisite to understanding the impact of agricultural reforms and the increasing importance of cash crops.

The gendered consequences of agricultural and trade reforms have been addressed in a number of policy documents and reports (Baden, 1993; Baden *et al, 1994*; Brown and Kerr, 1997; World Bank, 1999). These assessments have either focused on women as a vulnerable group or on gender-linked constraints in responding to changing price incentives (Baden *et al, 1994*). While the former have stressed the increased workload of women without adequate compensation, the latter have highlighted women's limited access to productive resources in the process of reallocating resources, especially land, from non-tradable to tradable sectors. Intra-household issues have received relatively little attention in this literature.

For Ghana, the prevailing view on the effects of the reforms from a female farmer's perspective is summarized by Baden *et al* (1994): "In agriculture, the benefits of adjustment have largely accrued to medium and larger farmers in the cocoa sector, of whom few are women. There is limited evidence as yet of women own-account producers switching to cocoa production under the influence of adjustment; the benefits of female producers under adjustment may be largely confined to those women already in the cocoa sector".

Generally, access to resources, including land, labour, capital and complementary agricultural inputs, is an essential condition to respond to improved incentives. For Ghana, the issue of female access to land has received quite some attention in the literature (Quisumbing *et al*, 2001; Goldstein and Udry, 1999 and 2005). Inheritance rules are very complex, in particular among the matrilineal Akan. Eventually, the transfer of land rights depends, among other factors, on an individual's land use history (e.g. planting of cocoa trees), her or his contribution to land improvements, and the status within the family (Goldstein and Udry, 2005). Structural adjustment seems to have caused a shift towards more individualized land rights (Baden et al., 1994; Quisumbing *et al*, 2001). There are conflicting views on whether these developments favour men (Mickell, 1986) or whether they increasingly allow women to gain access to land (Quisumbing *et al*, 2001).

Investigating the adoption of modern maize varieties and chemical fertilizer, Doss and Morris (2001) find important gender differences that they attribute to differential access to complementary inputs, in particular land, labour, and extension services. In other words, once one controls for resource access, gender *per se* does not play a role in explaining adoption patterns. Furthermore, Doss and Morris (2001) find that female-managed plots within the same household are not disadvantaged compared to male plots, a finding that cannot be confirmed by Quisumbing *et al* (2001).

In sum, this review presents strong evidence of discrimination against females in terms of access to productive resources. What is common to most gender policy documents is their focus on female farmers. Despite this focus, relatively little is known on the supply response of female vis-à-vis their male counterparts. Finally, the policy-oriented studies pay little attention to intra-household issues.

3. Empirical Methodology

This section assesses the determinants of cocoa adoption and the effects of adoption on household welfare and gender resource allocation. The analysis of the effects of cocoa adoption has two main purposes: first, to evaluate the impact of export crop production on household welfare (using total expenditures and food spending per adult equivalent and as proxies); and secondly, to assess the effects of the nature of the income stream on the composition of consumption expenditures. Of specific interest are questions such as, "What happens to welfare and the composition of expenditures once households earn more income from export crops?" and, "Does more income from export crops bias household spending towards 'male goods' than 'female goods'?"

3.1. Determinants of cocoa adoption and its impact on household welfare

Farm households that are eligible to grow cocoa are likely to engage in cocoa production when the expected returns exceed those from engaging the household's factor endowments in subsistence food crops. With perfect foresight, cocoa adoption would always be welfare-enhancing: that is, a household would only engage its resources in the production of cocoa if the marginal returns from cocoa are more than the returns from food crop production. A smallholder farmer elects to grow cocoa if the expected welfare after growing cocoa is at least as great as the expected welfare under the alternative of growing food crops. However, because realized returns from cocoa production can vary greatly from expected returns, the *ex post* impact of cocoa adoption on welfare may be positive or negative. In this paper, we use two broad categories of measures of welfare: income (proxied by total household expenditure per equivalent adult) and food security (proxied by total food consumption per equivalent adult).

A suitable measure of the impact of cocoa adoption should compare outcomes in farm households that received income from cocoa production to what those outcomes would have been had the same households not participated in cocoa production. The construction of this unobserved counterfactual has long been the focus of impact evaluation. Measuring impact as the difference in mean outcomes between all households receiving income from cocoa and those not receiving cocoa income may give a biased estimate of the treatment. This bias would arise if there are unobserved characteristics that affect the probability of adoption that are also correlated with household welfare.

Let D be an indicator variable equal to 1 if the household receives income from cocoa production and 0 otherwise. In the treatment literature, D is an indicator of receipt of the "treatment." The potential outcomes are then defined as $W_i(D_i)$ for each household i, where $i = 1, ..., N$ and N denotes the total population. Following Caliendo and Kopeinig (2008), the treatment effect for a household can be written as

$$\tau_i = W_i(1) - W_i(0) \tag{1}$$

The fundamental evaluation problem arises because only one of the potential outcomes is observed for each household i. Since the counterfactual outcome is unobserved by the microeconometrician, estimating the individual treatment effect τ_i is not straightforward. For most evaluation studies, the focus lies on constructing an estimate of the (population) average treatment effect on the treated (ATT) and therefore we will focus on this parameter, too.[49] In this specific case, we will concentrate on constructing an estimate of the average impact of cocoa income on those households that receive it. It can be defined as

$$\tau_{ATT} = E(\tau \mid D = 1) = E[W(1) \mid D = 1] - E[W(0) \mid D = 1] \tag{2}$$

The expected value of *ATT* is defined as the difference between the expected outcome values with and without treatment for those who actually participated in the treatment. Since this parameter focuses directly on actual treatment participants, it could be used to measure the realized gross gain from participation (Heckman *et al* 1999).

The true parameter τ_{ATT} is only identified if

---

49   See Becker and Ichino (2002); Gilligan and Hoddinott (2006); Becker and Caliendo (2007); and Caliendo and Kopeinig (2008).

$$E[W] - E[W(0) | D = 0 = 0]$$ (3)

Estimation based on the matching involves matching treated and untreated households based on their observable characteristics X, and comparing how the outcome differs depending on treatment. Exact matching involves comparing individuals for whom the values of X are identical. This estimator is rarely an option in practice. With continuous variables in X, and/or many explanatory variables, we resort to inexact matching - instead of requiring the households across which we compare outcomes to have identical values of X, we now require them to have similar values of X.

Propensity score matching has become a popular approach to estimate causal treatment effects and will be employed in this paper for estimating the counterfactual outcome for cocoa participants. The estimator constructs a plausible comparison group by matching households with treatment to similar households without treatment using a set of control variables.[50] Let $P(X) = \Pr(D = 1 | X)$ be the probability of a household participating a treatment (cocoa) given its observed covariates X. We use propensity score matching to construct a statistical comparison group by matching observations on cocoa income recipients to observations on non-recipients with similar values of $P(X)$.

3.2. The effects of cocoa income on gender resource allocation

In this section, we attempt to examine the influence of cocoa income, which is often considered to be male-controlled, on intra-household resource allocation. The income pooling assumption of the neoclassical household model can be empirically tested by detecting an influence of individually earned income on expenditure patterns. If such an influence can be found, income is not being pooled. As it is difficult to identify individually earned income in poor agricultural economies, the income pooling test typically relies on anthropological evidence that assigns income from certain crops to male or female individuals (Haddad and Hoddinott, 1995; Duflo and Udry, 2004). Given that households bargain over expenditure allocation, the effect of income from a presumably male or female crop on the allocation can be considered to reflect the extent of control over this income source.

A number of factors determine how scarce resources are allocated by households to food consumption versus other consumer goods. To test the extent to which the source of income along with other factors impinges on the budget share allocated to different expenditure categories, a model is specified for estimation of Engel curves that includes the share of income earned from cocoa (*cocoash*) as an explanatory variable together with the level of total income. Also, household

---

50   For details on propensity score matching, the interested reader is referred to Gilligan and Hoddinott (2006); Rosenbaum and Rubin (1983); Becker and Ichino (2002); and Caliendo and Kopeinig (2008).

size is controlled for to account for potential scale effects. The hypotheses to be tested are that income earned under men's control is spent relatively less on "necessary (female) goods" such as food, than general household income. The expectation is that reatively more income from cocoa is relatively spent on "luxury (male) goods" such as alcohol and tobacco. Total expenditure is used as a proxy for expected permanent income in this analysis.

The Engel curve specification follows Deaton (1989) and Deaton *et al.* (1989) to examine the influence of the cocoa income on expenditure patterns.

$$w_i = \frac{p_i q_i}{x} = \alpha + \beta_i \ln\left(\frac{x}{n}\right) + \eta_i \ln(n) + \sum_{j=1}^{J-1} \gamma_{ij}\left(\frac{n_j}{n}\right) + \delta_i z + \lambda_i cocoash + u_i \qquad (4)$$

where total household expenditure is expressed as x and the number of people in the same household as n. w_i is the expenditure share on good i, which is linearly related to the logarithm of the household per capita expenditure (see Deaton and Muellbauer, 1980). The vector z comprises additional information expected to influence the overall expenditure pattern, in particular the sex of the household head, the age of the head, and information on the educational level of the household head. The primary variable of interest on the right-hand side of the equation is the household's income share from cocoa. Following the literature, we hypothesize that household members have different preferences with regard to consumption of some categories of goods. With egoistic preferences, relative bargaining power determines the allocation of expenditure. If cocoa income is controlled by men it proxies for male bargaining power. We then expect the share of cocoa income in total income to have an impact on household consumption choices in favour of male consumption goods, suggesting that incomes are not being pooled.

4. Data and Some Descriptive Statistics

We use data from the Ghana Living Standards Survey (GLSS), conducted by the Ghana Statistical Service in collaboration with the World Bank. We use the 2005/06 round, which is the most recent of the five rounds of surveys conducted since 1987. The 2005/06 (GLSS5) survey covered a sample of 8,686 households containing 36,481 household members, giving an average household size of 4.2.[51] The survey follows a two-stage sampling process. At the first stage of the selection process, a predetermined number of enumeration areas (EAs) was randomly selected with probability proportional to estimated size from which a fixed number of households was systematically selected from each selected EA to give the total of households. Both rounds collected information on households and community characteristics and reproductive histories of one randomly selected woman of childbearing age in each household. Our working sample consists of all rural households residing within the six cocoa growing regions in Ghana.

---

51 For more information on the GLSS, including more details on the sample design, strata weights, and fieldwork, see GSS (2000) and Coulombe and McKay (2003).

To explore the impact of participation in cocoa on welfare, the following variables are considered: dummy variables are included for two ecological zones and six regions in which cocoa is cultivated: the forest zone and savannah zone (a third zone, the coastal zone, serves as the reference). The purpose of the zonal dummy variables is to control for agro-climatic differences that could affect the profitability of cocoa production. Several characteristics of the household are included as controls. The key variable of interest is the gender dummy for the household head. This allows us to examine the behaviour of female-headed and male-headed households. The household head's age is also included, as is the educational level expressed as dummies for whether the head's highest educational qualification is primary, junior secondary or secondary (no formal education serves as the reference). The size of land owned by the household, measured in hectares, is included because wealthier rural households (i.e. those with more land) are more likely to adopt high-value crops such as cocoa. Access to credit may also affect the adoption decision, so a dummy was created to indicate whether the household has access to formal credit. Another dummy was created to indicate the type of land ownership as a simple measure of the security of the land – whether the household possesses a title deed to the land. Household size is included as a simple measure of labour availability. We also include a set of five regional dummies – Central, Volta, Eastern, Ashanti and Brong Ahafo (a sixth region, Western, serves as the reference). The regional dummies are included to purge the regression of regional effects that may confound the effects of the other covariates, which might or might not be conducive to higher cocoa adoption.

Table 1(a) provides some general trends in cocoa farming from a gendered perspective. In the group of female-headed households, 13 percent grew cocoa in 2006 compared to 25 percent of male-headed households. When the sample is restricted to farm households only, the share of cocoa-growing households among the female-headed households, increases to 26 percent while the share of cocoa-growing households among the male-headed households increases to 37 percent. The average share of household income earned from cocoa farming stood at 36 percent for female-headed households, compared with 41 percent for the male counterparts. Much stronger are the differences in terms of cocoa output and yield: male-headed households on average produce about double the amount of cocoa produced by female-headed ones. The main reason for the huge difference in cocoa output is due in part to the much smaller farm size of female-headed households. In 2006, female-headed households held farms that average about half the size of male-headed farms. This difference applies similarly for value of the land held by the two groups. Not only do female-headed households own less land; those women who own some land do actually own less valuable lands, than to their male counterparts. The value of the land owned by female-headed households is only about a third that of the male-headed households. Table 1(b) confirms that these gender differences in inputs and outputs persist in every region in the country – in each of the six cocoa growing regions, female-headed households own smaller and less valuable lands and their output is smaller than that of their male counterparts.

Table 1(a): Characteristics of rural cocoa-farming households, by gender of head

	Male-headed households	Female-headed households	Total Average
Cocoa farming-household (% of all hhs)	0.25	0.13	0.22
Cocoa farming-household (% of farm hhs)	0.37	0.26	0.34
Land size (hectares)	6.00	3.28	5.55
Value of farm land (Ghana cedis)	7,780	2,840	6,970
Household size	6.64	4.59	6.30
Farm labour (persons)	3.50	2.90	3.41
Area harvested (hectares)	1.81	0.93	1.66
Cocoa harvested (kg)	1,553	930	1,452
Cocoa yield (kg/ha)	286	146	264
Total household income (Ghana cedis)	1,540	1,000	1,450
Revenue from all crops (Ghana cedis)	997	545	924
Revenue from cocoa (Ghana cedis)	574	314	531
Share of household total income from cocoa	0.41	0.35	0.40
Education of household head (years)	6.84	3.60	6.31

Source: Authors' calculations. Note: Figures are mean values.

Table 1(b): Characteristics of rural cocoa-farming households, by region

	Western	Central	Volta	Eastern	Ashanti	Brong Ahafo	Average Total
Land size (ha)							
Male	8.7	5.9	4.1	2.8	6.2	4.4	6.0
Female	3.8	4.6	1.0	1.4	3.5	2.7	3.3
Area harvested (ha)							
Male	2.0	0.7	2.4	2.2	1.4	3.6	1.8
Female	1.2	0.2	0.7	1.3	0.8	1.5	0.9
Farm value (Ghana cedis)							
Male	17,400	2,770	3,510	3,240	4,230	7,030	7,780
Female	4,450	1,520	674	1,340	2,340	5,240	2,840
Cocoa harvested (kg)							
Male	2,600	2,786	205	515	401	689	1,553

Table 1(b): Characteristics of rural cocoa-farming households, by region							
	Western	Central	Volta	Eastern	Ashanti	Brong Ahafo	Average Total
Female	584	3,234	76	129	366	286	930
Cocoa yield (kg/ha)							
Male	491	231	134	288	184	222	286
Female	242	135	107	91	99	176	146

Source: Authors' calculations. Notes Figures are mean values.

5. Empirical Results

Determinants of participation in cocoa

Table 2 presents results from a probit regression of factors that influence the likelihood that a farm household will grow cocoa. Several aspects of the results are noteworthy. First, the gender variable has significant explanatory power - this result is consistent with our *a priori* expectation, considering that men and women farmers are known to adopt export crops at different rates. Secondly, many of the other explanatory variables have the expected signs and are statistically significant: regressors that increase the probability that a household will grow cocoa are the amount and security of land controlled by the household and the age of the household head. In addition, residing in the forest and savannah zones, compared with the coastal zone, and the Central Region, compared with the Western Region, are positively associated with the probability of adoption. Two factors decrease the likelihood that a household will choose to grow cocoa: female-headed household dummy and the educational qualification of the household head (measured by years of schooling).

Table 2: Probit Estimates of Propensity Score for Adoption of Cocoa

Determinants:	Estimated coefficient	Standard error
Female-headed household	-0.532***	0.0714
Years of schooling - Head	-0.151**	0.0066
Age - Head	0.0430***	0.0112
Age squared - Head	-0.00025**	0.00011
Household size	0.0134	0.0117
Land size per capita	0.0204***	0.00742
Titled land dummy	0.571***	0.0719

Determinants:	Estimated coefficient	Standard error
Access to credit	-0.00242	0.111
Central region	0.425***	0.118
Volta region	-1.559***	0.13
Eastern region	-0.801***	0.101
Ashanti region	-1.057***	0.0906
Brong Ahafo region	-0.859***	0.11
Forest zone	1.898***	0.115
Savannah zone	0.850***	0.16
Constant	-2.785***	0.292
No. of Observations	2,837	
Pseudo R-squared	0.27	

Source: Authors' calculations.
Notes: Robust standards errors in parentheses. * significant at 10%; ** significant at 5%; *** significant at 1%.

Overall, the analysis of the cocoa participation decision suggests a fair amount of discrimination against female farmers. Differential access to land plays an important role in explaining these results. Wealth is often positively associated with the adoption of high-value crops, because wealthier farmers are better able to bear risk and, therefore, are more likely to venture into export markets. In rural Ghana, land ownership provides a good measure of wealth. Clearly, there is some sort of association between land ownership and gender: female-headed households tend to own smaller plots than male-headed households. Similarly, households headed by women tend to cultivate plots that are less valuable than those of households headed by men (Table 1a and b). The determinants of land ownership were explored using a tobit approach. Controlling for the age, education, household size and the ecological zone, we find that female-headed households on average have significantly less access to land (Table 3). In other words, households headed by women need to gain more land if they are to participate more in export crop farming.

Table 3: Determinants of Household Land Ownership (Tobit Estimates)

Determinants	Estimated coefficient	Standard error	Significance level
Female-headed household	-0.897	0.216	***
Years of schooling - Head	0.072	0.020	***
Age - Head	0.078	0.006	***
Household size	-0.009	0.035	
Forest zone	0.421	0.258	
Savannah zone	-0.109	0.392	

Determinants	Estimated coefficient	Standard error	Significance level
Central region	-0.094	0.323	
Volta region	-2.123	0.349	***
Eastern region	-1.923	0.303	***
Ashanti region	-1.254	0.295	***
Brong Ahafo region	-0.810	0.369	**
Constant	-4.448	0.476	***
Log likelihood = -5774.22			

Source: Authors' calculations.
*Note: Dependent variable is land per capita. ** denotes significant at 5%; *** denotes significant at 1%.*

5.2 Effects of cocoa income on welfare

The logic underlying cash crop liberalization is that it would increase household income which, in turn, would allow households to shore up food spending and welfare. Therefore, we investigate the contribution of cocoa income to household welfare. Table 4 reports the effects of cocoa income on total expenditure and food spending per adult equivalent in cocoa-growing households. Results show that all else being equal, as cocoa income increases, the welfare of the household also improves. In addition, welfare seems to rise with the level of education of the head of the household, land ownership and access to credit while it falls with the family size.

Table 4: Effects of Cocoa Income on Household Welfare and Food Security

Explanatory Variables:	Real per capita expenditure (log)	Real per capita food spending (log)
Female-headed household	0.0367	-0.00194
	(0.0226)	(0.0248)
Years of schooling - Head	0.0138***	0.00135
	(0.0021)	(0.0024)
Age - Head	0.00523	0.00521
	(0.0035)	(0.0039)
Age squared	-5.07E-05	-4.82E-05
	(3.43E-05)	(3.76E-05)
Household size	-0.111***	-0.126***
	(0.0038)	(0.0042)
Land size per capita	0.0169***	0.0133***
	(0.0029)	(0.0031)

Explanatory Variables:	Real per capita expenditure (log)	Real per capita food spending (log)
Titled land dummy	0.143***	0.109***
	(0.024)	(0.0264)
Access to credit	0.255***	0.164***
	(0.0363)	(0.0399)
Cocoa income share	0.0828**	0.111**
	(0.0396)	(0.0434)
Central Region	-0.0899**	-0.123***
	(0.035)	(0.0384)
Volta Region	-0.160***	-0.206***
	(0.0379)	(0.0416)
Eastern Region	0.0214	0.0337
	(0.0324)	(0.0355)
Ashanti Region	-0.127***	-0.259***
	(0.0325)	(0.0357)
Brong Ahafo Region	-0.120***	-0.106**
	(0.039)	(0.0429)
Forest zone	-0.0522*	-0.0924***
	(0.0273)	(0.03)
Savannah zone	-0.0914**	-0.104**
	(0.0391)	(0.0429)
Constant	14.49***	14.19***
	(0.087)	(0.0955)
Observations	2,837	2,837
R-squared	0.31	0.32

Source: Authors' calculations.
Notes: Robust standards errors in parentheses. * significant at 10%; ** significant at 5%; *** significant at 1%.

5.3 Average impacts of participation in cocoa on welfare

Although the preceding results are informative, the coefficient of the cocoa income share can be estimated by OLS without bias only if households that who receive cocoa income are a random sample of all farm households. This bias would arise if there are unobserved characteristics that affect the probability of adoption that are also correlated with household welfare. A suitable measure of the impact of cocoa adoption should compare outcomes in farm households that received income from cocoa production to what those outcomes would have been had the same households not participated in cocoa production. Table 5 reports results of the propensity score estimates of the average impact of participation in cocoa on welfare. A detailed interpretation of the propensity score estimates is not undertaken in this paper. However, the results of the treatment effects (ATT) show that participation in cocoa exerts positive and significant impacts on household income and food security. Using estimated propensity scores from the model, we generated samples of matched cocoa participants and non-participants using the kernel matching algorithm. The results show a significant effect of participation on both average total consumption per adult equivalent and on average food consumption per adult equivalent in 2006.

Table 5: Treatment Effects

	Real per capita expenditure (log)	Real per capita food spending (log)
Mean impact		
Average outcome, cocoa participants	14.2	13.7
Average outcome, non-cocoa participants	14.1	13.6
Difference in average outcomes, ATT	0.1	0.1
	(2.69)	(2.48)

Source: Authors' calculations.
Notes: Absolute values of t statistics on ATT are in parentheses.

5.4. The effects of cocoa income on gender resource allocation

We estimate Engel curves for three goods that can be thought of as representing either private male or female goods or household public goods that females might have a preference for. Alcohol and tobacco are primarily consumed by males, while clothing can be considered a female good. Household public goods that have been shown in the literature to be preferred by females include food. As most of the expenditure categories in the data are left-censored, we estimate the Engel curves using a Tobit model (with robust standard errors). The results for two different samples are reported in Table 6.

Table 6: Determinants of Budget Shares to Food, Alcohol and Clothing

Explanatory variables:	Food	Alcohol and Tobacco	Clothing
Expenditure per capita (log)	-0.0245***	-0.0762***	0.00578***
	(0.00417)	(0.0226)	(0.00169)
Expenditure per capita squared (log)	0.00205***	0.00455***	-0.00040***
	(0.0002)	(0.00122)	(0.0000)
Cocoa income share	-0.00493*	-0.0118	-0.000426
	(0.00299)	(0.0297)	(0.00115)
Female-headed household	0.00426***	-0.0725***	-0.00108*
	(0.00165)	(0.0255)	(0.00065)
No. of children (<15 years)	0.00228***	-0.00294	-0.00014
	(0.00084)	(0.0096)	(0.00030)
Primary -Head	-0.00460**	0.014	0.00108
	(0.00215)	(0.0178)	(0.00082)
Junior secondary - Head	-0.00265	-0.0186	0.00200***
	(0.00172)	(0.0167)	(0.00067)
Senior secondary - Head	-0.0105***	-0.570	0.00247**
	(0.00295)	(0.0000)	(0.00104)
Household size	0.00114*	-0.0019	-0.00011
	(0.00059)	(0.00665)	(0.00021)
Central Region	0.00586**	0.0199	0.0011
	(0.00253)	(0.0225)	(0.00098)
Volta Region	0.0044	-0.0092	-0.00067
	(0.0027)	(0.0234)	(0.00103)
Eastern Region	0.00619***	0.00676	0.00112
	(0.00235)	(0.0228)	(0.00091)
Ashanti Region	0.00212	-0.0223	-0.00042
	(0.00237)	(0.0239)	(0.00090)
Brong Ahafo Region	0.00229	-0.016	-0.0011
	(0.00272)	(0.0251)	(0.00104)
Constant	0.0123	0.114	-0.0262***
	(0.0216)	(0.095)	(0.00804)
Pseudo R-squared	0.44	0.30	0.07
No. of Observations	3,170	3,170	3,170

Source: Authors' calculations.
Notes: Robust standards errors in parentheses. * significant at 10%; ** significant at 5%; *** significant at 1%.

Food expenditures as a proportion of total expenditures increase significantly, but not rapidly, with increased income. The dummy variable for female-headed households is statistically significant. Thus, *ceteris paribus*, gender seems to have a distinct effect on shifting expenditure patterns in favour of food. On the contrary, having a woman as head of the household significantly reduces the budget shares to alcohol and tobacco and clothing. The cocoa income share significantly decreases the food budget share beyond the total income effect. The effect is, however, not highly statistically significant. Similarly, the cocoa income share negatively correlates with the budget shares of alcohol and tobacco and clothing but the effects are not statistically significant. Thus, the cocoa income share does not seem to systematically affect gender resource allocation. Overall, while we find the female-headed dummy to bias household expenditure patterns towards female-preferred and household public goods such as food, cocoa income *per se* does not seem to be used primarily for male consumption purposes.

6. Conclusion and Policy Implications

This paper has examined ways in which participation in cash cropping differs among women and men, and the ensuing implications for household welfare and food security among farm households in Ghana. We have done so by first analyzing the determinants of participation in cocoa by female-headed vis-à-vis male-headed households. The study also points to traces of discrimination of females in terms of access to productive resources and assets. More specifically, we find that female-headed households are considerably less likely to engage in cocoa farming activities, primarily due to their limited access to land. This implies that getting the incentives right can have much higher payoffs for women when they are provided with the means to respond to these incentives. From a policy perspective, our results thus underline the scope for and the importance of policy interventions aimed at female empowerment.

The paper also examined the impacts of cocoa adoption on farm household income and food security status using a propensity score matching model to account for selection bias that normally occurs when unobservable factors influence both participation and outcomes such as household income and food security status. Results of the propensity score matching show that cocoa participation exerts a positive and statistically significant effect on household income and food security status. These findings are generally consistent with the widely held view that income from commercial farming is crucial to food security and poverty alleviation in rural areas of developing countries.

Finally, to shed some light on gender resource allocation, we then examined whether cocoa income is controlled by males and whether this in turn causes gender inequalities to be reinforced by the promotion of cash cropping in rural areas. We investigated whether higher cocoa incomes influence household resource allocation by estimating Engel curves for a number of more or less gender-specific goods including the share of cocoa income as an explanatory variable. The conjecture of cocoa income being controlled by males cannot be confirmed for the Ghanaian case. Put somewhat more cautiously, we find that cocoa income is not being spent primarily on male consumption goods. As in Ackah and Lay (2009), the analysis of intra-household allocations suggests that one has to be careful with generalizations with regard to control over (increased) proceeds from cash crops. At least for cocoa production in Ghana, it does not seem to be true that cash crop production is a male domain and that reforms that lead to its expansion would therefore disproportionately favour males.

Our findings make two contributions to the related literature. We generate direct evidence that commercial farming matters for poverty reduction: farmers who are able to adopt high-yield export crops such as cocoa are on average better off than farmers more oriented towards subsistence activities. Further, we provide some evidence of gender bias in access to the most productive resource needed for participation in cash cropping in Ghana – land. The analysis reveals traces of discrimination against women in accessing larger and higher quality plots of land.

On the whole, these results from Ghana suggest that cash cropping decisions depend primarily on access to resources, rather than on gender *per se*. This conclusion should not be interpreted to mean that cash crop adoption is gender-neutral. If participation in cash cropping depends on access to land, labour, or other resources, and if men tend to have better access to these resources than women, then cash crop liberalization will not benefit men and women equally. Our analysis suggests that improvements in female access to land are cardinal to female-headed cocoa-farming households responding as well to the market incentives in export crop adoption as their male counterparts. The challenge for policymakers may thus be to increase women's access to the key resources. Given that women normally face entry barriers to participation in cash crop production, policy measures could target them by lowering the entry barriers. In particular, land reforms must have the objective of allowing increased acquisition of land by women.

References

Ackah and Lay (2009), "Gendered Impacts of Agricultural Liberalisation: Evidence from Ghana" .A World Bank Netherlands Partnership Program (BNPP)-funded project.

Aryeetey, E., Harrigan, J. and M.Nissanke, (eds.) (2000) "Economic Reforms in Ghana: The Miracleand the Mirage". Oxford: James Currey and Accra: Woeli Publishers.

Baden, S. (1993) "Gender and adjustment in Sub-Saharan Africa". BRIDGE Report No. 8, Brighton: Institute of Development Studies.

Baden, S., Green, C. Otoo-Oyortey, N., Peasgood, T. (1994), "Background paper on gender issues in Ghana." Report prepared for the West and North Africa Department, Department for Overseas Development (DFID), UK.

Becker, S. and A. Ichino. (2002), "Date Correct Estimation of Average Treatment Effects Based on Propensity Scores". *Stata Journal* 2 (4): 358-377.

Becker, S. and M. Caliendo (2007), "Sensitivity analysis for average treatment effects", *The Stata Journal*, 7(1), 71-83.

Brooks, J., Croppenstedt, A. and E. Aggrey-Fynn (2006), *Distortions to Agricultural Incentives in Ghana*. Unpublished Manuscript, FAO, Rome.

Brown, L.R. and J. Kerr, (1997) *The Gender Dimensions of Economic Reforms in Ghana, Mali, and Zambia*. Ottawa: The North-South Institute.

Caliendo, M. and S. Kopeinig (2008), "Some Practical Guidance for the Implementation of Propensity Score Matching," *Journal of Economic Surveys*, pg 22 (1), 31–72.

Coulombe, Harold and Andrew McKay (2003), "Selective Poverty Reduction in a Slow Growth Environment: Ghana in the 1990s", January 2003, mimeo., University of Bath. Paper presented at ISSER-Cornell International Conference on Ghana at the Half Century, Accra, July 2004.

Deaton, A. (1989), " Looking for Boy-Girl Discrimination in Household Expenditure Data." *The World Bank Economic Review*, 3(1), pp. 1-15.

Deaton, A. and Muellbauer, J. (1980) *Economics and Consumer Behaviour* (Cambridge: Cambridge University Press).

Deaton, A., Ruiz-Castillo, J. and Thomas, D. (1989), "The Influence of Household Composition on Household Expenditure Patterns: Theory and Spanish Evidence." *The Journal of Political Economy*, 97(1), pp. 179-200.

Doss, C.R., and M.L. Morris (2001), "How does gender affect the adoption of agricultural innovations?: The case of improved maize technology in Ghana." *Agricultural Economics*, 25 (1), pp. 27-39.

Duflo, E. and C.Udry (2004), "Intrahousehold Resource Allocation in Cote d'Ivoire: Social Norms, Separate Accounts and Consumption Choices." NBER Working Papers 10498, National Bureau of Economic Research.

Ghana Statistical Service (2000), *Poverty Trends in Ghana in the 1990s*, (GSS, Accra, Ghana)

Gilligan, D. and J. Hoddinott (2006), "Is There Persistence in the Impact of Emergency Food Aid? Evidence on Consumption, Food Security and Assets in Rural Ethiopia", forthcoming *American Journal of Agricultural Economics.*

Goldstein, M. and C.Udry, (1999) "Agricultural Innovation and Resource Management in Ghana." Final Report to IFPRI under MP17. Washington D.C.

Goldstein, M. and C. Udry, (2005) "The Profits of Power: Land Rights and Agricultural Investment in Ghana." Yale University Economic Growth Center Discussion Paper, No. 29.

Haddad, L. and J. Hoddinott, (1995) "Does Female Income Share influence Household Expenditures? Evidence from Cote D'Ivoire." *Oxford Bulletin of Economics and Statistics*, 57 (1), pp. 77-96.

Heckman, J, LaLonde, R. and J. Smith, (1999) "The Economics and Econometrics of Active Labor Market Policies." In *The Handbook of Labor Economics Volume 3*, eds. Orley Ashenfelter and David Card., 1865-2097. Amsterdam: Elsevier.

International Monetary Fund (2000), *Ghana: Selected Issues.* IMF Staff Country Report No.2, Washington: IMF.

Kanbur, R. (1994) "Welfare Economics, Political Economy, and Policy Reform in Ghana." Policy Research Working Paper, No. 1381. Washington D.C.: World Bank

Mikell, G. (1989) *Cocoa and Chaos in Ghana.* New York: Paragon House,

Nyanteng, V. and A. W. Seini, (2000) "Agricultural Policy and the Impact on Growth and Productivity" 1970-95. In: Aryeetey, E., Harrigan, J. and Nissanke, M. (eds.) (2000), *Economic Reforms in Ghana: The Miracle and the Mirage.* Oxford and Accra: James Currey and Woeli Publishers.

Quisumbing, A.R., Payongayong, E., Aidoo, J.B. and K.Otsuka, (2001) "Women's Land Rights in the Transition to Individualized Ownership: Implications for Tree-Resource Management in Western Ghana." *Economic Development and Cultural Change*, 50 (1), pp. 157-181.

Rosenbaum, P.R., and D.B. Rubin (1983) "The Central Role of the Propensity Score in Observational Studies for Causal Effects", *Biometrika* 70(1), 41-55.

Sarris, A. and H. Shams, H. (1991) *Ghana under structural adjustment : the impact on agriculture and the rural poor.* International Fund for Agricultural Development. New York University Press.

World Bank (1995), *Is Growth sustainable? Ghana Country Assistance Review: A Study in Development Effectiveness,* Washington: The World Bank.

World Bank (1999) "Ghana – Gender Analysis and Policymaking for Development." World Bank Discussion Paper, No. 403, Washington D.C.

Chapter 11

The Transmission of World Commodity Prices to Domestic Markets: Household Welfare Effects in Ghana

Charles Ackah, Ernest Aryeetey, David Botchie and Robert Osei

1. Introduction

The pace of globalization has generated conditions that allow developments in one country to easily affect another. Such is the case for food prices. Tradable food commodities do have cross-border connectivity, such that happenings in one end influence the outcomes in another. Analytically, the significant role that exchange rates and tariff regimes play when assessing price transmission mechanisms across borders cannot be overemphasized. This is because tariffs and exchange rates are the main variables that determine the extent to which prices will change in the domestic market. Furthermore, the efficiency in the level of friction between two markets is determined mainly by tariffs and exchange rates. An increase in tariffs on imported commodities will cause domestic prices of those commodities to also increase, *ceteris paribus*. At two extremes, one may assume that a full transmission of price shocks can indicate the presence of a frictionless and well-functioning market, while at the other extreme, a total absence of transmission may make the very existence of a market questionable. Therefore, the degree of price transmission can provide at least a broad assessment of the extent to which markets are functioning and price signals are passing through consistently between different markets, say international and domestic markets (Conforti, 2004).

The effects of commodity price shocks on developing countries receive considerable emphasis whenever there are major international commodity price booms or slumps, such as the global food price increases during the mid-1970s and the more recent price hike that started around 2007. Using the recent period of rising food prices, this paper attempts to provide an assessment of the short- run impacts of higher global food prices on welfare in Ghana. It does this by first establishing how much and how fast domestic prices change in response to changes in international prices. We are particularly interested in computing the pass-through elasticities. The second major objective of the paper is to attempt to measure the impact of international and domestic price shocks on household welfare in Ghana in the short run. The rest of the paper is organized into six sections. The next section presents a brief review of the literature on price transmission and household welfare. Section 3 presents the data sources and some descriptive statistics. The empirical approach to the study is discussed in Section 4. In Section 5 the results from the analyses are presented and discussed for each commodity. The sixth and final section draws conclusions and makes recommendations for policy.

2. Literature Review

The most contentious issue in most developing countries over the past two decades is the implementation of market reforms as the major channel for price transmission between local and international agricultural markets (see Rashid, 2004; Bediane and Shively, 1997). A critical factor considered in trade liberalization studies is the significance of transport cost in determining the price differences at two different market locations. The differences in prices are best demonstrated by the *special arbitrage condition*, which is explained by Listorti (2008) that the difference between prices in two different markets will not exceed the cost of transport. Actually, the *special arbitrage condition* forms the basis for the Law of One Price (LOP), which also states that prices of similar commodities in two different markets will be the same if and only if it is less transport cost. It further explains that prices will be the same for similar commodities in different markets if prices are expressed in the same currency (see Dolado *et al*, 1999). However, there can be a co-movement of prices at different locations due to factors other than commercial integration factors such as seasonality. This explains the concept of *spatial market integration* which is more restrictive than the LOP. This also implies that even if the LOP is satisfied with a high and volatile transport cost, it may not be enough for prices to co-move. Thus, LOP can still hold if the price transmission ratio is less than one (see Listorti, 2008).

Undoubtedly, the concept underlying the LOP remains a very vital ingredient in market efficiency and its integration as well as in international trade as a whole, particularly in the agricultural sector. However standard literature remains skeptical about the LOP. Miljkovic (1999) concludes that relative to other economic laws, several empirical tests have violated the LOP mainly due to factors such as market power, the pass-through of exchange rate on output prices as well as border and domestic policies such as increases in tariffs (see Conforti, 2004). Therefore the role of exchange rates and tariffs in determining price transmission signals from the international market to domestic markets is cardinal in national policy formulation as well as examining price stability in developing economies. This is one of the reasons why a small shock in commodity price changes receives major attention in developing economies such as that of Ghana where a floating exchange rate regime operates.

The increased level of integration of national and international markets means that a change in world prices will affect domestic food prices, whether or not the country exports or imports food staples. The changes in domestic food prices, whether resulting from trade policy such as changes in tariffs or changes in international food prices, could affect household welfare and hence incomes of the poor. These effects are transmitted through changes in the price of tradable products demanded and supplied by the poor – the price transmission effects (Winters, McCulloch and McKay, 2004). Thus, trade liberalization affects the poor by changing the prices at which they buy as consumers and sell as producers (Matusz and Tarr, 1999). In this way, trade liberalization reduces poverty by lowering prices of imported goods and keeping prices of import substitutes low, and thus increasing real incomes of the poor.

In the case of rising domestic food prices due to high world food prices, the exact impact on household welfare and poverty depends on how households are able to take advantage of the potential opportunities arising from high food prices, or how they cope with the threat of increasing prices and the degree of transmission of world prices to domestic prices. One major direct effect of higher food prices[52] on developing countries is that as high international prices of food push up local prices, food becomes less affordable for consumers but provides an incentive for local farmers to increase their production of foodstuffs. In both cases, real incomes and welfare of the population, including the poor, are affected (Plan, 2008). Thus, standard literature indicates that the first-order approximation of the change in welfare for households, also referred to as 'before response' effect of higher food prices depends on the status of households either as net food consumers or net producers. While higher food prices will benefit net food producers, net food buyers will suffer.

Higher food prices will hurt the poor and worsen poverty if the majority of poor households are net food buyers (Byerlee, Myers and Jayne, 2006; Christiaensen and Demery, 2007; Ivanic and Martin, 2008 and Hoekman and Olarreaga, 2007). Many studies such as Jaumotte *et al* (2008) and Aksoy and Isik-Dikmelik (2008) posit that developing countries will benefit from agricultural trade liberalization as it reduces inequalities by facilitating higher exports of agricultural commodities which in turn creates jobs and increases the income of poo people. The availability of cheaper imports associated with reduction in tariffs also reduces inequality in developing countries. Thus, agricultural trade liberalization is viewed as pro-poor in low-income developing countries and hence justified in terms of social welfare and treasury costs (Bakhshoodeh and Akbari, 2002).

Simler (2010) uses more recent price data to estimate the impact of higher food prices on consumption poverty in Uganda. The paper finds that poor households in Uganda tend to be net buyers of food staples, and therefore suffer welfare losses when food prices increase. This is most pronounced in urban areas, but holds true for most rural households as well. The diversity of staple foods has not been an effective buffer because of price increases across a range of staple foods. The paper estimates that both the incidence and depth of poverty increased—at least in the short run as a result of higher food prices in 2008, increasing by 2.6 and 2.2 percentage points,

---

52   The other effect which is indirect is the higher cost of imported food which ultimately leads to trade deficits that depress the level of activity in the economy ,hence unemployment and lower government revenues that might depress spending on public services as well.

respectively. The increase in poverty was highest in the northern region, which was already the poorest in Uganda. These studies utilized domestic prices with the assumption that international prices are fully transmitted to domestic prices. If changes in world prices are not fully transmitted or over-transmitted to domestic prices, then those studies may arrive at skeptical conclusion about the impact on welfare.

The paper computes a simple measure of short-term change in welfare following an increase in tradable staple food prices and relates it to a range of household characteristics in a cross-section of developing countries. The results of the paper indicate that poorer households and those with the least means to cope are the most likely to be adversely affected by an increase in the price of basic tradable staple food commodities in all countries considered. Households in the lower expenditure quintiles, households with little land and education, and larger households are all found to be systematically associated with larger estimated percentage losses from rising food prices. The poor households that gain from the increase in prices appear to be linked to having access to the key resources needed to turn farming into a profitable activity with reasonable levels of productivity: land in sufficient quantity, and modern inputs such as fertilizers and pesticides.

3. Empirical Approach

Price transmission elasticity shows the extent to which changes in world prices are transmitted onto domestic markets. Thompson and Bohl (1999) argue that price transmission elasticity can indeed be interpreted as a measure of the degree of market insulation, or the extent to which border policies are transmitted onto the domestic market. Price transmission is affected by trade liberalization and by trade policies. Tariffs are mostly the policy variables that can be used by countries to insulate the domestic market from cheap imports of competing products. It is therefore imperative to check the extent to which tariffs on food prices from the international market affect prices on the domestic market. Exchange rate is another variable that influences prices of imported food commodities on the domestic market. An appreciating exchange rate regime will cause prices of imported food commodities to decline on the domestic market and rise when the exchange rate depreciates. Thus exchange rate as an explanatory variable will be crucial in this study.

Generally speaking, increased trade liberalization will contribute to greater price transmission elasticity. The existence of a stable relationship between two prices has been assumed as a necessary condition for integrated markets (see Ardeni, 1989). In a system with n prices, the number of co-integrating vectors can be taken as an index of the degree of integration of the markets. We employ time-series econometric techniques to investigate these relationships. In particular the use of co-integration analysis allows us to explore the long-run elasticities. In this study, we consider domestic prices for imported commodity i at time t (PD_i) as a function of international price of commodity i at time t (PW_i), exchange rate (E) and Tariff (T) imposed on commodity at a particular time. We outline a pass-through model which quantifies the extent to which the international prices affect domestic market prices from 1990 to 2008. The pass-through model is as follows:

$$PD = \alpha + \beta PW \quad PD_i = \mu PW_i^{\beta_1}(E)^{\beta_2}(1+T)^{\beta_3} \tag{1}$$

This is a general form of the standard purchasing power parity (PPP) equation in which μ, β_1, β_2, and β_3 are all equal to 1.

Taking the logarithm of Equation 1

$$\ln PD = \alpha + \beta \ln PW + \varepsilon \quad \ln PD = \ln(\mu) + \beta_1 \ln PW + \beta_2 \ln E + \beta_3 \ln(1+T) + \varepsilon \tag{2}$$

where $lnPD$, $lnPW$, lnE and $ln(1+T)$ are the log of domestic prices, international prices, exchange rate and tariff respectively. β_1, β_2, β_3 and μ are the coefficients of the international prices, exchange rate, tariff and the constant term respectively. ε is the error term. The commodities that are considered in this paper are rice, maize, and groundnut.

One could think of β_1 as capturing the 'price effect' of the pass-through. By price effect, we mean the effect which is due only to international prices and cannot be influenced by policy. The effect of the policy variables will be captured by β_2 and β_3. In other words these policy variables also impact on the domestic prices of these commodities and can reinforce or counteract the price effects depending on what policy relation these variables are. The pass-through is labeled "full" or "complete" if $\beta = 1$, "incomplete" if $\beta < 1$ and more than complete if $\beta > 1$ (see Nicita, 2009).

Time series data in levels are usually non-stationary and can result in spurious results if not used appropriately. It is therefore imperative that the stationarity or otherwise of the series is tested before they are employed in regression analysis (see Gujarati, 2006). We employ the Augmented Dickey-Fuller tests to establish the order of integration of the series. The autoregressive distributive lag (ADL) model of Inder (1993) is used to test for co-integration. This procedure involves estimating a general dynamic equation or ADL model of the form

$$
\begin{aligned}
\ln PD_t &= \ln(\mu) + \beta_1 \ln PD_{t-1} + \beta_2 \ln PD_{t-2} + ... + \beta_p \ln PD_{t-p} + \delta_1 \ln PW_{t-1} + \\
&\quad \delta_2 \ln PW_{t-2} + ... + \delta_q \ln PW_{t-q} + \lambda_1 \ln E_{t-1} + \lambda_2 \ln E_{t-2} + ... + \lambda_x \ln E_{t-x} + \\
&\quad \eta_1 \ln(1+T)_{i-1} + \eta_2 \ln(1+T)_{i-2} ...... + \eta_z \ln(1+T)_{i-z} + \varepsilon_t
\end{aligned}
\tag{3}
$$

where $lnPD_t$ and $lnPW_t$ represent domestic and international prices at time t respectively. β, δ, λ and η are the coefficients of domestic prices, world prices, exchange rate and tariff respectively; μ a constant term. The implied long-run solution is obtained by noting that in the long run

$$\ln PD = \ln PD_t = \ln PD_{t-1} = \ln PD_{t-2} = ...\ln PD_{t-p}, \tag{4}$$

$$\ln PW = \ln PW_t = \ln PW_{t-1} = \ln PW_{t-2} = ... = \ln PW_{t-q}, \tag{5}$$

$$\mathrm{h}\,E = \mathrm{h}\,E_t = \mathrm{h}\,E_{t-1} = \mathrm{h}\,E_{t-2} \ldots\ldots = \mathrm{h}\,E_{t-x} \tag{6}$$

$$\ln(1+T) = \ln(1+T)_t = \ln(1+T)_{t-1} = \ln(1+T)_{t-2} = \ldots\ldots = \ln(1+T)_{t-z} \tag{7}$$

From equation 3 the domestic price can be expressed as

$$\ln PD\,1 - \beta_1\!\left(-\beta_2 - \ldots - \beta_p\right) = \mu + \delta_1 + \!\left(\delta_2 + \ldots + \delta_q\right)\ln PW +$$
$$(\lambda_1 + \lambda_2 + \ldots + \lambda_x)\,\mathrm{h}\,EXCH + (\eta_1 + \eta_2 + \ldots + \eta_z)\ln(1+T) + \varepsilon_t, \tag{8}$$

This implies that

$$\ln PD = \frac{\mu}{(1 - \beta_1 - \beta_2 - \ldots - \beta_n)} + \frac{(\delta_1 + \delta_2 + \ldots\ldots + \delta_q)}{(1 - \beta_1 - \beta_2 - \ldots\ldots - \beta_n)}\ln PW +$$
$$\frac{(\lambda_1 + \lambda_2 + \ldots + \lambda_x)}{(1 - \beta_1 - \beta_2 - \ldots \beta_p)}\ln E + \frac{(\eta_1 + \eta_2 + \ldots + \eta_z)}{(1 - \beta_1 - \beta_2 - \ldots - \beta_P)}\ln(1+T) + \frac{\varepsilon_t}{(1 - \beta_1 - \beta_2 - \ldots - \beta_p)} \tag{9}$$

The coefficients of the prices in equation 9 can be read as the long-run degree of pass-through of price changes on the international market to the domestic market. The interpretation is that changes in international prices do impact on domestic prices if the pass-through coefficient is significant. A re-parametisation of equation (9) is the Error Correction Model (see Davidson *et al.* 1978 and Lloyd *et al.* 2001). In this study, the short-run pass-through effects are measured using the ECM.

Effects of international food price changes on household welfare

Changes in international prices of tradable goods are important in determining the level of household welfare. In determining the effect of international price changes on household welfare, we quantify the welfare impact of a change in international prices using the following household indirect utility function linking welfare in household h with prices and household monetary incomes:

$$U_h = u_h(Y_h P_h) \tag{10}$$

where Y_h and $P_h\,P_h$ represent the money income of household h and prices respectively. Following Singh *et al* (1986), for households involved in agricultural or any other entrepreneurial activities, Y_h can be defined as the sum of earnings and profits

$$Y_h = \sum_i P_i(Q_i^s - Q_i^d) - \sum_j w_j(V_j^d - V_j^s) \tag{11}$$

where P_i is commodity prices, Q_i^s commodities sold in the market, and Q_i^d the household's consumption; V_j^d are the inputs demanded by the household, V_j^s is the household's inputs supply (including labour) and w_j represents the input prices. Now, assuming homogeneity of domestic and foreign-owned tradable food commodities, domestic prices of food items can be defined as the function of tariff, exchange rate and international price (see Nicita, 2004). Under these simplified assumptions we model a simple econometric specification linking changes in international prices, tariffs and exchange rate to domestic prices. By so doing, we combine equations 1 and 11

$$Y_h = \sum_i PD(PW, TARR, EXCH)(Q_i^S - Q_i^d) - \sum_j w_j (V_j^d - V_j^S)$$
$$Y_h = \sum_i (PW_i)^{\beta_1} (EXCH)^{\beta_2} (1+T)^{\beta_3} (Q_i^s - Q_i^d) - \sum_j w(V_j^d - V_j^s) \qquad (12)$$

Combining equations 10 and 12 and taking the first differential resulted in the first-order effect of welfare as a result of changes in international prices.

$$U_h = u_h((P) \sum_i PD(PW, TARR, EXCH)(Q_i^S - Q_i^d)) \frac{du_h}{dPW_i} = \varphi(Q_i^s - Q_i^d) \qquad (13)$$

where φ is the marginal utility of money income. Most empirical literature on welfare impacts of food price changes assumes full pass-through of changes in international prices to domestic prices. If that is so then the effect on household welfare can be expressed as

$$du_h = \varphi(Q_i^s - Q_i^d) dPW_i \qquad (14)$$

where dPW_i represents the change in international prices of the commodities in question.

However, it is possible that changes in international prices may be partially or over-transmitted to domestic prices. This makes the assumption of full transmission very problematic, particularly when at least two factors (the non-competitive behavior of intermediaries and poor physical connectivity) which can dilute the impact of rising international food prices on the domestic prices in Africa are taken into consideration (Benson, 2008). In this paper, we depart from the existing studies that assume full pass-through and utilize the pass-through elasticities computed from equation 9 to measure the actual impact of international price changes on household welfare. The estimating equation is of the form:

$$du_h = \varphi(Q_i^s - Q_i^d) dPW_i * \delta T \qquad (15)$$

where δ is the pass-through elasticity of changes in international prices. Measuring welfare changes using equation (15) is relatively straightforward. Nevertheless, given that it assumes that agents' behaviour is constant, the results will only be meaningful for marginal changes in prices and/or for measuring short-run effects. Therefore, in order to determine whether households are net producers (sellers) or net consumers (buyers) as a result of changes in international prices, the Net Benefit Ratio (NBR) was employed (see Deaton, 1989). Thus, in terms of budget shares, the first-order "before response." welfare impacts of international price changes is derived by modifying the NBR as

$$\Delta W_h = dPW(PR_h - CR_i) \qquad (16)$$

where PR_b and CR_i are the food production ratios and food consumption ratios respectively. ΔW_b is the welfare effect of price changes expressed as a proportion of the baseline income.

4. Data Sources and Descriptive Statistics

The analysis in this study is done for rice, maize, and groundnuts. The main variables of interest here are domestic prices, world prices, exchange rates and tariffs. Household expenditure data on the three commodities is obtained from the Ghana Living Standards Survey data (GLSS 5). The basis for selecting these commodities is that the Food and Agricultural Sector Development Policy (FASDEP), which is the main agricultural sector policy document for Ghana, gives cardinal focus to these food commodities though the policy has made room for all other food crops that show good prospects for the future. International monthly prices of rice, maize and groundnuts for 1990 to 2008 were obtained from FAOSTATS. Data on domestic prices for the same period were obtained from the Statistical, Research and Information Directorate (SRID) of the Ministry of Food and Agriculture (MOFA). In addition, monthly exchange rate figures and tariff rates for the same period were obtained from the Bank of Ghana and Ghana Customs Excise and Preventive Service (CEPS) respectively.

4.1 Trends in prices of rice on the international and domestic markets

Figure 1 shows that international prices for imported rice remained fairly stable from 1990 to 1994 but rose steadily from 1996 to 2008. The rise in international prices was very sharp between 2007 and 2008. This sharp rise may be attributed to the global food crisis that was experienced during that period. With the global food crisis easing, the prices on the international market dropped significantly during the latter parts of 2008, but started rising again before the close of 2008. The domestic price of imported rice also rose steadily from 1994 to 2007. The rise became more pronounced from the last quarter of 2007 to the second quarter of 2008. On the domestic front, the sharp rise may also be attributed to the global food and oil crises that hit the country at that time.

Despite the importance of rice as a staple, domestic supply is inadequate, making Ghana a net importer of rice. Total rice imported into Ghana exceeded production levels by 20 percent in the 1990s (Codjoe, 2007). As of 2002, the self- sufficiency ratio of rice was fluctuating within the range of 26 percent to 65 percent, with an average production level of 178,000 metric tons per annum, a figure far below the country's potential production capacity. Though Ghana has the potential to produce an average of 6.5 mt/ha, the current yield is about 2 mt/ha (FASDEP, 2002).

It is intriguing to note that while imported rice is heavily subsidized by governments of their countries of origin, the policies of successive Ghanaian governments since the mid-1970s have consistently focused on removal of input subsidies, removal of support or guaranteed producer prices, trade liberalization and food aid. The effects of these policies are the surges in rice imports, particularly since 2001. This situation is also making local production unattractive especially when the two markets are uneven in terms of support for production and marketing. In addition, consumer preferences are also seen to be shifting from the more nutritious local rice to the imported milled white polished rice. Also, it is increasingly becoming a cliché that imported rice is gradually becoming a staple food for Ghanaians compared to the locally produced rice, mainly because of the taste, aroma and attractiveness of the imported rice variety.

Figure 1: Monthly Price Trends of Rice for the International and Domestic Markets

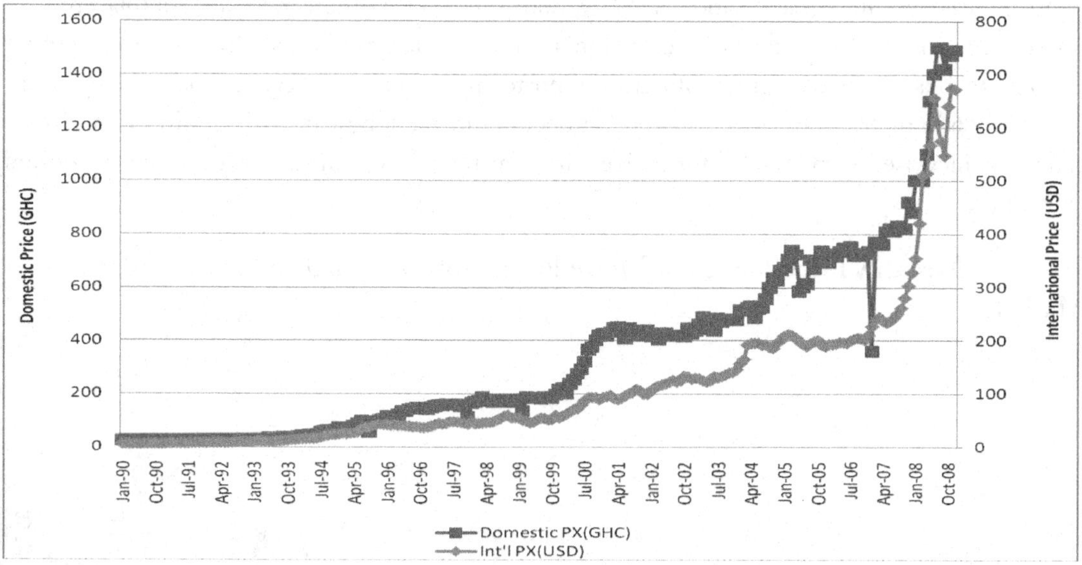

Source: FAOSTATS and Ministry of Food and Agriculture, Ghana

4.2 Price trends for maize on the international and domestic markets

Maize is the basis of several local dishes and the main feedstuff for poultry as well as other livestock in Ghana. It is cultivated by 1.75 million (64 percent) of the 2.74 million households operating farms in Ghana (FASDEP, 2002). Compared to domestic prices, international prices of maize remained fairly stable from 1990 to 2008. The increase in 2008 was purely due to the food price hikes on the international market. Prices of maize on the domestic front have been on the rise and highly volatile. Very sharp increases occurred in 2005, 2006 and 2008. These periods were the periods when demand for maize in the poultry industry was very high due to the support government provided to the poultry industry at that time. Furthermore, an increase in tariffs on imported chicken was also an incentive for poultry farmers to produce more chicken for the local market since importers were finding it difficult to import larger quantities of chicken from the international market. As a result, demand for maize shot up causing prices to also increase on the domestic market during those periods. Maize imports constituted 0.9 percent and 1.0 percent of production levels in the 1990s and 2000s, respectively (Codjoe, 2007). The author further indicates that a metric tonnes of maize imported onto the domestic market decreases its production locally by 6 metric tonnes.

On the other hand, exports of maize have been on the rise in recent times, with export volumes increasing from 367 metric tonnes in 2007 to 1,097 metric tonnes in 2008; a 200 percentage point increase within these periods (ISSER, 2008). However, one cannot be complacent as a result of the potential and adverse effects of maize importation. If Cudjoe's findings are anything to go by, then a 100 metric tonnes of maize imported into Ghana will cause production levels to decline by 600 metric tonnes (a 600 percent decline) in the long run. This implies that Ghana can easily increase its import bill for maize within a short period of time if this scenario occurs (Figure 2).

Figure 2: Monthly Price Trends of Maize for the International and the Domestic Markets

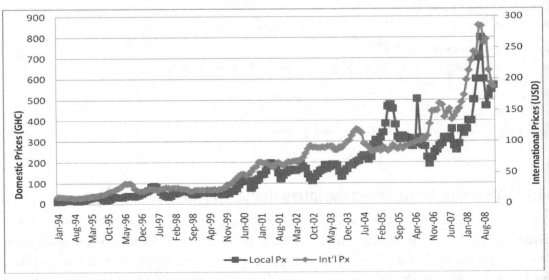

Source: *FAOSTATS and Ministry of Food and Agriculture*

4.3 Trends in monthly prices of groundnut

Both domestic and international prices of groundnut have not been stable for the entire period of the study. The most interesting part is that it is only groundnut that has prices on the international market higher than that on the local market. The possible reason is that international trade for groundnut has been growing steadily since 1970 due to the growing demand for groundnut in the confectionary industry. Though some few firms in Ghana import groundnut, the price of groundnut on the local front seems to be on the lower side compared to that of the international prices. This may be due the fact that Ghana is self sufficient in groundnut consumption. Groundnut is mostly consumed as a complement to other foodstuffs present on the local market. Figure 3 gives a clear illustration on the trends in the prices of groundnuts from 1990 to 2008.

Figure 3: Monthly price trends of groundnut for international and domestic markets

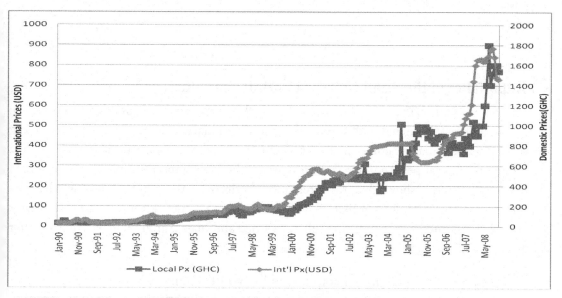

Source: FAOSTATS and Ministry of Food and Agriculture

4.4 Production and trade of the major staples

Maize is the most produced and consumed commodity among the three commodities considered in the study. Its production and consumption levels are 1,171 and 925 thousand tonnes respectively (Table 1). This implies that Ghana produces more maize than it consumes. However, Ghana still remains a net importer of maize. Maize imports recorded an average of 57,000 tonnes and the level of exports was only 1,000 tonnes. The level of rice consumption, on the other hand, far outweighs the level of production in Ghana. Ghana produces an average of 191 thousand tonnes of rice, as against a consumption level of 453, 000 tonnes. This attests to the fact that Ghana is a net importer of rice. In addition, Ghana imports 482,000 tonnes of rice a year and does not export any at all. Among the three commodities, groundnuts are the least consumed. A total of 120,000 tonnes of groundnuts consumed every year as against a production level of 294,000 tonnes. Ghana does not import groundnuts but exports 7,000 tonnes a year. This is so because groundnut is always not the major constituent of Ghanaian dishes relative to rice and maize.

Table 1: Production and Trade of Major Food Staples in Ghana in 2007 (000 tonnes)

Food item	Production	Consumption	Imports	Exports
Rice	191	453	482	0
Maize	1,171	925	57	1
Groundnut	294	120	0	7

Source: FAOSTATS

4.5 Importance of the major staples in the Ghanaian diet

In terms of importance, maize can be assumed to be the most important commodity among the three commodities considered in this study. The quantity of maize consumed per capita is 41.1kg per year. In terms of daily calories, maize produces 357 kcal per person. This is far more than a per capita of 192 kcal per day for rice. Furthermore, the per capita quantity of rice consumed per year is 20.1kg. This shows that, the international price pass-through for maize will have an impact on more households than that of rice. Groundnuts are the least important commodity. This may be attributed to the fact that relative to rice and maize, groundnuts are not a major constituent of household diets in Ghana (Table 2).

Table 2: Importance of the major staple food in diet of Ghana in 2007

Commodity	Quantity consumed (kg/person/year)	Daily caloric intake (Kcal/person/day)
Rice	20.1	192
Maize	41.1	357
Groundnut	5.3	82

Source: FAOSTATS

4.6 Household expenditure on food during the 2007/2008 food crisis

Overall, expenditure on rice, maize and groundnuts accounts for approximately 23 percent of total household expenditure on food. Clearly, household expenditure on maize was the highest (13%) compared to rice (8 percent) and groundnuts (2.2 percent). This is associated more with rural households than with urban households. Rural households spend 16 percent of their total food expenditure on maize whereas urban households spend only 7.4 percent on maize. This is also due to the fact that most rural households produce maize for domestic consumption as opposed to rice and groundnuts. Another interesting aspect of the story is that Greater Accra and Ashanti regions where poverty is on the lower side compared to the other regions spend a little more on rice than on maize (see GSS, 2007). This also confirms the point that richer households gravitate towards the consumption of rice relative to maize and groundnuts. In the Greater Accra Region, households spend on average 6.3 percent of their total expenditure on food on rice, followed by maize 5.8 percent. Similarly, the average expenditure on rice for households in the Ashanti Region was 8.6 percent and expenditure on maize was 7.8 percent.

Table 3: Household Total Food Expenditure Shares (%) in 2005/2006

	Rice	Maize	Groundnuts	All 3 foods
National	0.0797	0.1275	0.0220	0.2292
Locality				
Urban	0.0756	0.0767	0.0100	0.1624
Rural	0.0825	0.1620	0.0302	0.2746
Region				
Western	0.1007	0.0740	0.0089	0.1836
Central	0.0859	0.1373	0.0068	0.2301
Greater Accra	0.0631	0.0589	0.0045	0.1265
Volta	0.0678	0.2006	0.0240	0.2924
Eastern	0.0685	0.1452	0.0107	0.2243
Ashanti	0.0857	0.0783	0.0141	0.1781
Brong Ahafo	0.0730	0.1116	0.0139	0.1985
Northern	0.0836	0.2822	0.0800	0.4458
Upper East	0.1122	0.1766	0.1019	0.3907
Upper West	0.0815	0.2363	0.0703	0.388
Socio-Economic Group				
Public	0.0806	0.0771	0.0115	0.1691
Wage-priv-formal	0.0706	0.0706	0.0096	0.1508

	Rice	Maize	Groundnuts	All 3 foods
Wage-priv-informal	0.0783	0.091	0.0104	0.1796
Self-agro-export	0.0829	0.1167	0.0124	0.2119
Self-agro-crop	0.0845	0.1815	0.0361	0.3022
Self-bus	0.0759	0.0986	0.0156	0.1901
Non-working	0.0664	0.0668	0.0065	0.1398
Gender –Head				
Male	0.0804	0.1369	0.0252	0.2424
Female	0.0777	0.0994	0.0125	0.1896

Source: Authors' own computation

5. Empirical Results

The series for our analysis are subjected to unit root tests to determine whether they are stationary or otherwise. We employed the Augmented Dickey Fuller test (ADF) to test for the stationarity or otherwise of the series. The test statistics show that all the variables are integrated in order I (see Appendix 1).

5.1 Long-run elasticities

In testing for the long-run relationships between the variables of interest, we estimate two different models to explain the determinants of domestic prices of the different crops. In the first model (Model A) we include the world prices and exchange rate as our explanatory variables. In the second model (Model B), we include world prices, exchange rate and tariff as our explanatory variables. Generally, the results show that tariffs have not been important in explaining the long-run movements in domestic prices for the three crops. For all the three crops we do find cointegration for the model in which domestic prices are explained by international prices and exchange rate (Model A). It is only in the case of maize that we find cointegration in both Model A and Model B.

We note from the results of the long-run estimates (Table 4) that for all the three crops, the international price is important in explaining domestic prices. Indeed, for rice and maize, the long-run elasticity of the international price is about unity, suggesting complete pass-through. However, the same cannot be said of groundnuts for which we find a long-run elasticity of between 0.7 and 0.8 for Models B and A respectively. This is not surprising as imports of groundnuts tend to absorb only a relatively small proportion of the total demand in Ghana. We also note from the results that it is only in the case of maize that we find a robust and significant effect of exchange rate on domestic prices in the long-run. For rice, and in the model for which we find evidence of long-run co-movements, the exchange rate variable is not significant. Interestingly, in the estimated ECM (shown in the Appendix) we find that the exchange rate has a contemporaneous and positive effect on domestic prices. In other words, for rice we find that the exchange rate has an instantaneous effect on domestic prices. However in the long run, it is international prices which tend to drive domestic prices.

In the case of maize, both the exchange rate and world prices are significant in explaining long-run movements in domestic prices. As with the model for rice, there seems to be a complete pass-through of international prices to domestic prices. The elasticities of world prices seem to be higher than that of exchange rate, both with respect to domestic prices. For maize, we note that exchange rates are not important in driving domestic prices in the short run (from the estimated ECMs shown in the Appendix). We suspect that very little imported maize may be going into direct consumption. Rather, it may be going into the brewery or poultry industry. Therefore , domestic prices are going to be dominated by factors which influence supply constraints. In that case exchange rates will not feed in directly. However, these supply-side factors are important enough for maize so that the exchange rate effects persist in the long run (through fertilizer, pesticides, etc.).

What these results are suggesting is that policy variables are important in explaining domestic price changes for some food items in Ghana. We would argue that a policy variable such as exchange rate may be important in explaining short-run movements in rice of which Ghana is a net importer. Another important observation from the results is that tariffs do not seem to have much of an influence in explaining movements in domestic prices of food in Ghana – neither in the short-run nor in the long run. This result, therefore, challenges the reasoning behind government's policy of reducing import duties of selected food products in the wake of the 2007 food crisis. However, it is also important to mention here that tariffs have limited variability over the period of the study and so one should discuss this result in the light of this limitation. We also find that elasticities in the groundnuts models are much lower than the estimates in the rice and maize models. We argue that this may be because the net imports of groundnuts are much lower than those of maize and rice. As a result, exchange rate depreciations and/or tariff increases will hurt domestic consumers of groundnuts less (if at all) than they do for maize and rice.

Table 4: Long Run Estimates and Co-Integration Test

	RICE		MAIZE		GROUNDNUT	
	Model A	Model B	Model A	Model B	Model A	Model B
Constant	-7.4725***	-7.3198***	1.8841**	2.2057***	0.27	-0.0883
LNPW$	0.9953***	0.9957***	1.0149***	1.0588***	0.7754**	0.6698***
LNEXCH	0.8326	0.7925***	0.8996***	0.8929***	0.2248	0.2909
LNTARR		0.0349***		0.0643		0.0661
ECM test for cointergration	-3.4862**	-3.4556	-3.81**	-3.925**	-3.6258**	-3.6312

*Notes: Numbers in parentheses represent standard error. *; *** and ** show rejection of null hypothesis at 10%, 5%, and 1% level respectively. The ECM Test is the Banerjee, Dolado and Mestre (1998) test for co-integration.*

5.2 Patterns of food consumption and production

Tables 5 to 8 provide summary data on rice and maize consumption in Ghana. We observe considerable heterogeneity in the weight of the two staples in the overall consumption basket of the population. The average annual household consumption of rice in the population as a whole is roughly 758,000 cedis (about $505 at the current exchange rate). On average, rice accounts for approximately 10 percent of total food consumption expenditure for a household. As a nation, rice is consumed by about 71 percent of households but it is the preferred choice of the richer households – about 84 percent of households in the richest income quintile consume rice, compared with only about half of the households in the poorest quintile. On a geographical basis, we see that rice consumption is rather less frequent in the three northern regions and the rural savannah in particular. However, in terms of budget shares, these poorer regions spend more on rice as a share of total food spending. For maize, consumption is higher, at 1,300,000 cedis per year (about $867 at the current exchange rate). About two thirds of maize consumption is from auto-consumption. The consumption patterns for maize and rice are quite similar. About 73 percent of the population consumes maize, but again there are important regional differences. Like rice, maize is also heavily patronized by the relatively better off households. In terms of consumption shares, among the population as a whole, maize accounts for approximately an average of 25 percent of total food consumption expenditure in Ghana. Again, the consumption share of maize is much higher for the very poor and poor than for other income groups. The poor tend to consume on average much more maize than rice. Thus, on the consumption side an increase in the price of maize would likely hurt the poor more than an increase in the price of rice, because for the poorest 40 percent of the population, the share of their consumption allocated to maize is substantially (more than thrice) higher than that allocated to rice.

We now turn to the production side to assess who earns income from rice and maize production and their weights in household total incomes. Table 5 shows that very few households (4 percent of the population) derive incomes from rice production. Rice production is concentrated in the savannah ecological zone, in the three northern regions (Northern, Upper East and Upper West), among male-headed households and among the poorer households. The average income from rice sales in the population as a whole is just 61,000 cedis (about $41 at the current exchange rate) per year, accounting for less than 1 percent of total household income. Table 6 presents the same information for maize. The share of maize-producing households in the population is much higher, at about 28 percent. Unlike rice production that is concentrated in the rural savannah zone, maize production is more evenly spread among the rural coastal, rural forest, and rural Savannah areas. Average income from maize production is more than five times that of rice production, 320,000 cedis compared with 61,000 cedis.

Table 5: Rice Consumption for Different Household Groups, 2006

	% of House-holds consum-ing rice	Average consumption for all house-holds			Budget share (% of total food spending)
		Purchase	Auto	Total	
Residence area					
Urban	81.6	920,000	2,700	922,700	7.6
Rural	74.1	530,000	140,000	670,000	10.6
Locality					
Accra (GAMA)	73.1	930,000	0.0	930,000	6.8
Urban Coastal	87.1	1,100,000	1,900	1,101,900	8.6
Urban Forest	88.1	940,000	0.0	940,000	8.0
Urban Savannah	76.4	670,000	17,000	687,000	7.2
Rural Coastal	79.4	570,000	130,000	700,000	6.9
Rural Forest	87.3	670,000	13,000	683,000	8.9
Rural Savannah	55.9	330,000	300,000	630,000	14.3
Region					
Western	90.0	990,000	3,200	993,200	10.2
Central	86.5	770,000	1,700	771,700	8.6
Greater Accra	74.2	870,000	0.0	870,000	6.3
Volta	81.8	500,000	10,000	510,000	7.0
Eastern	82.2	700,000	110,000	810,000	7.4
Ashanti	88.5	780,000	15,000	795,000	8.7
Brong Ahafo	76.1	510,000	100,000	610,000	10.1
Northern	56.7	410,000	200,000	610,000	11.5
Upper East	61.2	380,000	610,000	990,000	22.7

	% of House-holds consum-ing rice	Average consumption for all house-holds			Budget share (% of total food spending)
		Purchase	Auto	Total	
Upper West	34.5	210,000	170,000	380,000	12.2
Sex of head					
Male	75.0	680000	110000	790000	9.8
Female	83.2	660,000	16000	676000	8.2
Poverty Quintile					
Poorest	55.3	260,000	140,000	400,000	11.7
2	77.0	470,000	110,000	580,000	10.2
3	83.1	670,000	70,000	740,000	9.4
4	85.5	870,000	120,000	990,000	8.9
Richest	84.0	1,100,000	5,200	1,105,200	7.2
National	71.7	670,000	88,000	758,000	9.5

Source: Authors' calculations using 2005-06 GLSS.

Table 6: Maize Consumption for Different Household Groups, 2006

	% of households consuming maize	Average consumption for all house-holds			Budget share (% of total food spending)
		Purchase	Auto	Total	
Residence area					
Urban	84.1	580,000	270,000	840,000	9.2
Rural	69.0	420,000	1,200,000	1,600,000	34.2
Locality					
Accra (GAMA)	85.6	540,000	19,000	550,000	4.6
Urban Coastal	84.8	700,000	150,000	850,000	9.5
Urban Forest	84.5	440,000	280,000	710,000	6.6
Urban Savannah	78.9	920,000	900,000	1,800,000	26.0
Rural Coastal	83.4	540,000	1,100,000	1,600,000	22.2
Rural Forest	77.2	340,000	670,000	1,000,000	16.0
Rural Savannah	52.4	460,000	1,800,000	2,300,000	61.8
Region					
Western	80.8	440,000	220,000	660,000	7.9
Central	82.8	530,000	700,000	1,200,000	16.6
Greater Accra	86.4	560,000	110,000	670,000	6.0

	% of households consuming maize	Average consumption for all households			Budget share (% of total food spending)
		Purchase	Auto	Total	
Volta	75.8	660,000	1,300,000	1,900,000	34.5
Eastern	80.9	500,000	970,000	1,500,000	18.4
Ashanti	83.1	310,000	420,000	730,000	10.2
Brong Ahafo	70.3	340,000	650,000	990,000	21.5
Northern	43.9	550,000	2,300,000	2,900,000	73.2
Upper East	63.7	570,000	950,000	1,500,000	37.4
Upper West	56.5	470,000	1,500,000	2,000,000	67.6
Sex of head					
Male	72.1	490,000	940,000	1,400,000	28.0
Female	83.1	450,000	470,000	920,000	14.5
Poverty Quintile					
Poorest	55.0	290,000	1,000,000	1,300,000	47.5
2	72.2	410,000	1,000,000	1,500,000	30.6
3	78.8	530,000	870,000	1,400,000	22.0
4	82.9	570,000	760,000	1,300,000	15.6
Richest	84.6	590,000	430,000	1,000,000	8.7
National	73.4	480,000	830,000	1,300,000	24.9

Source: Authors' calculations using 2005-06 GLSS.

Table 7: Rice Incomes for Different Household Groups, 2006

	% of HHs receiving income from rice	Average Income for all HHs	Income share (% of total HH income)
Residence area			
Urban	0.9	31,000	0.3
Rural	6.5	80,000	0.9
Locality			
Accra (GAMA)	0.0	0.0	0.0
Urban Coastal	0.4	31,000	0.1
Urban Forest	0.3	11,000	0.2
Urban Savannah	5.3	150,000	1.4
Rural Coastal	0.0	0.0	0.0
Rural Forest	1.6	26,000	0.2

	% of HHs receiving income from rice	Average Income for all HHs	Income share (% of total HH income)
Rural Savannah	15.5	180,000	2.0
Region			
Western	1.1	29,000	0.1
Central	0.2	4,200	0.0
Greater Accra	0.0	0.0	0.0
Volta	2.7	16,000	0.3
Eastern	0.9	30,000	0.3
Ashanti	1.0	14,000	0.2
Brong Ahafo	6.0	180,000	1.2
Northern	12.3	220,000	1.7
Upper East	29.1	140,000	4.0
Upper West	10.7	47,000	0.8
Sex of head			
Male	5.5	79,000	0.8
Female	0.9	2,900	0.1
Poverty Quintile			
Poorest	10.2	76,000	1.7
2	5.6	110,000	0.7
3	3.4	64,000	0.5
4	2.1	40,000	0.3
Richest	0.8	17,000	0.1
National	4.0	61,000	0.6

Source: Authors' calculations using 2005-06 GLSS.

Table 8: Maize Incomes for Different Household Groups, 2006

	% of HHs receiving income from maize	Average Income for all HHs	Income share (% of total HH income)
Residence area			
Urban	9.4	120,000	1.1
Rural	38.3	450,000	5.1
Locality			
Accra (GAMA)	0.2	6,400	0.1
Urban Coastal	6.8	44,000	0.6

	% of HHs receiving income from maize	Average Income for all HHs	Income share (% of total HH income)
Urban Forest	15.7	210,000	1.8
Urban Savannah	14.9	230,000	2.1
Rural Coastal	38.9	390,000	4.9
Rural Forest	38.4	420,000	5.1
Rural Savannah	37.8	500,000	5.1
Region			
Western	20.5	190,000	1.6
Central	33.2	270,000	2.9
Greater Accra	3.5	32,000	0.5
Volta	31.8	290,000	4.4
Eastern	29.4	310,000	3.7
Ashanti	32.3	440,000	5.6
Brong Ahafo	39.5	570,000	5.6
Northern	42.7	520,000	5.4
Upper East	16.3	130,000	1.9
Upper West	17.7	510,000	2.7
Sex of head			
Male	30.1	380,000	4.1
Female	18.4	140,000	2.0
Poverty Quintile			
Poorest	31.5	330,000	5.1
2	34.4	380,000	4.6
3	31.6	380,000	4.1
4	23.9	280,000	2.4
Richest	15.4	250,000	1.7
National	27.3	320,000	3.6

Source: Authors' calculations using 2005–06 GLSS.

5.3 Impact of international food prices on poverty

In Table 9 we present the short-run impact of changes in international food prices on poverty. The simulation results are presented individually for the three crops and then for the aggregate crops in the study. The measures of poverty are then compared to the base line poverty measures stipulated by the Ghana Statistical Service and the World Bank. At the national level, the global food price increases for the three commodities were estimated to increase household poverty by 0.9 percent, forcing approximately 20,0000 persons below the national poverty line. In addition, poverty increased in both rural and urban localities of Ghana, when the estimates were compared with the national average.

At the national level, the commodity that showed the highest impact on poverty as a result of increases of its prices on the international market is rice (followed by maize). Considering the GSS base poverty line, rice alone contributed to poverty increases among rice consumers by 2.3 percent. This may be due to Ghana' being a net importer of rice. Maize recorded a marginal increase in poverty by 0.1 percent. On a regional basis, the Upper West Region was the least affected region in terms of poverty increase as a result of increase in international food prices. In addition, across all the 10 regions, rice impacted most in increasing poverty as a result of the increases in global food crisis.

Male-headed households were less affected than female headed households. Male-headed households were pushed into poverty by 2.2 percent whereas female-headed households were pushed into poverty by 2.2 percentage points. In addition, rice affected both male- and female-headed households than the other two food commodities. Male- and female-headed households were actually pushed into poverty for consuming rice by 2.2 and 2.5 percentage points respectively. However, male-headed households were taken out of poverty for consuming maize and groundnuts during the global food crisis, by 0.2 and 0.001 percentage points respectively. On the other hand, maize pushed female-headed households into poverty by 1.2 percentage points. Female-headed households maintained a neutral position for consuming groundnuts. With the foregoing, it can be deduced that the impact of poverty on female-headed households was higher than on male-headed households during the international food price hikes.

In terms of the socioeconomic status of households, crop farmers (self-agro-crop) gained marginally from the international food price increases. This may be attributed to the fact that they are net producers. However, exporters of the food commodities were pushed into poverty by 4.2 percentage points. This may be due to their exposure to the international market as well as the fact that they are net consumers.

Table 9: Impact of Increases in International Food Prices on Poverty

	Base	Rice	Maize	G'nut	All 3
National	0.2855	0.308	0.2868	0.2854	0.2943
Locality					
Urban	0.1074	0.1178	0.1153	0.1084	0.1187
Rural	0.3932	0.4229	0.3905	0.3923	0.4004
Region					
Western	0.1857	0.2295	0.1894	0.1857	0.2156
Central	0.1994	0.2302	0.2061	0.1994	0.2283
Greater Accra	0.1179	0.1237	0.1231	0.1179	0.1244
Volta	0.3171	0.3472	0.3188	0.3133	0.3370
Eastern	0.1473	0.1686	0.1362	0.1473	0.1537
Ashanti	0.2051	0.238	0.1975	0.2059	0.2132
Brong Ahafo	0.2968	0.3076	0.303	0.2968	0.295
Northern	0.5215	0.5421	0.5357	0.5219	0.508
Upper East	0.7050	0.7137	0.7130	0.7048	0.7183
Upper West	0.8789	0.8798	0.8685	0.8783	0.8740
Gender-Head					
Male	0.3145	0.3363	0.3126	0.3144	0.3193
Female	0.1896	0.2145	0.2017	0.1896	0.2117
Socio-Economic Group					
Public	0.0782	0.0863	0.0799	0.0802	0.0858
Wage-private-formal	0.1015	0.1108	0.0979	0.1015	0.1083
Wage-private-informal	0.1707	0.2064	0.1906	0.1707	0.2029
Self-agro-export	0.2412	0.2829	0.2559	0.2412	0.2829
Self-agro-crop	0.4573	0.4843	0.4522	0.4568	0.4533
Self-business	0.1668	0.1818	0.1709	0.1666	0.1824
Non-working	0.1304	0.1401	0.1366	0.1304	0.1379

Source: Authors' own computation

6. Conclusion and Policy Implications

This study has attempted to shed some light on the important linkages between higher world food prices, domestic prices and poverty in Ghana. Using a simple stylized methodology of calculating the first-order welfare changes of households covered in the most recent Living Standards Survey (GLSS5), we were able to provide some detailed assessment of the impact of higher food prices on national welfare and poverty in Ghana. While the methodology employed in the paper is simple, it provides a fairly good approximation of the poverty impacts of changes in food prices. The globalised nature of the world implies that what happens in one part of the world has implications for other parts of the world. This is indeed true for food prices. The degree of openness determines the degree of price transmission from the world to a given economy. Food price changes affect the welfare of households and the nature of the effect is a function of whether households are net buyers or sellers. In this study, therefore, we tried to investigate the nature of price transmission from world markets to domestic markets for three main food crops namely, rice, maize, and groundnuts. We also went further to investigate what the welfare implications are for households in terms of these price changes. We find a long-run relationship between domestic prices, world prices and exchange rates.

We find that the effect of world prices on domestic prices is significant and positive. In the long-run there is complete pass-through for rice and maize. For groundnuts however, the degree of pass-through is much lower. The welfare simulations demonstrate that a substantial number of households in Ghana are vulnerable to food price shocks and have likely suffered significant welfare losses from rising food prices. The paper has been able to show that the average impact of the past and recent food price increases may have resulted in an increase in both the incidence and depth of poverty in Ghana.

At the national level, the commodity that showed the highest impact on poverty as a result of increases of its prices on the international market is rice (followed by maize). Considering the GSS base poverty line, rice alone contributed to poverty increases among rice consumers by 2.3 percent. This may be due to Ghana being a net importer of rice. Maize recorded a marginal increase in poverty by 0.1 percent. On regional basis, the Upper West Region was the least affected region in terms of poverty increase as a result of increase in international food prices. In addition, across all the 10 regions, rice had the most impact in terms of increasing poverty as a result of the increases in global food crisis.

Male-headed households were less affected than female-headed households. Male headed households were pushed into poverty by 2.2 percent whereas female headed-households were pushed into poverty by 2.2 percentage points. In addition, rice affected both male and female headed households than the other two food commodities. Male- and female-headed households were actually pushed into poverty for consuming rice by 2.2 and 2.5 percentage points respectively. However, male-headed households were taken out of poverty for consuming maize and groundnuts during the global food crisis, by 0.2 and 0.001 percentage points respectively. On the other hand, maize pushed female-headed households into poverty by 1.2 percentage points. Female-headed households maintained a neutral position for consuming groundnuts. With the foregoing, it can be deduced that the impact of poverty on female-headed households was higher than on male-headed households during the international food price hikes.

In terms of the socioeconomic status of householsd, crop farmers (self-agro-crop) gained marginally from the international food price increases. This may be attributed to the fact that they are net producers. However, exporters of the food commodities were pushed into poverty by 4.2 percentage points. This may be due to their exposure to the international market as well as the fact that they are net consumers. The increased level of integration of national and international markets means that a change in world prices will affect domestic food prices, whether or not the country exports or imports food staples. While it is possible that higher prices of staple foods could lower poverty by raising the incomes of some poor farmers, this effect was, in the case of Ghana, offset by adverse impacts on poor net-buyer households. Although the food price increases have had differential effects on the population, the general experience has been that, for the vast majority of urban and female-headed households, the higher food prices brought severe hardship. The commodity with the greatest poverty impact is rice.

A key policy implication of the study results is that since the poor include both net consumers and net sellers of food commodities, a change in price in either direction will inevitably hurt some of the poor and benefit some of the poor at the same time. With respect to the net impact on national poverty (i.e., on summary measures such as the headcount ratio and the poverty gap ratio), our findings for Ghana are consistent with available evidence that suggests that among the poorest households, the decline in living standards of net consumers caused by higher food prices far outweighs the benefits accruing to net sellers. It is, therefore, imperative for developing country governments and their development partners to be seen to be making efforts to improve smallholder agricultural productivity in the rural areas, even if the farmers produce for home consumption mainly. Sufficient attention should be given to maintaining or even improving the levels of social protection and poverty reduction expenditures.

References

Ackah, C., E. Aryeetey and E. B. D. Aryeetey (2009), 'Global Financial Crisis', ODI Discussion Series Paper 5: Ghana, London: OverseasDevelopment Institute.

Aksoy, A., Isik-Dikmelik, A. (2007). "Are Low Food Prices Pro-Poor? Net Food Buyers and Sellers in Low-Income Countries." Policy Research Working Paper N. 4642. Washington DC:. World Bank.

Ardeni, P.G. (1989), "Does the Law of One Price really hold for commodity prices?" *American Journal of Agricultural Economics*, 71: 303-328.

Badaine, O. and Shively, G.E (1998), "'Spatial Integration, Transportation Costs and the Response of Local Prices to Policy Changes in Ghana." *Journal of Development Economics*, Vol. 56, 411-431

Bakhshoodeh and M. Piroozirad (2003), "Effects of rice price change on welfare: Evidence from households in Fars Province, Iran", Paper for presentation at the International Conference on Policy Modeling, EcoMod2003, Istanbul, 3-5 July 2003.

Bautista R. Hans Lofgren and M. Thomas (1998), "Does Trade Liberalization Enhance Income Growth and Equity in Zimbabwe? The Role of Complementary Policies", Wahington DC:Trade and Macroeconomics Division International Food Policy Research Institute

Benson T. (2008), "An Assessment of the Likely Impact of Rising Global Food Prices on Ugandan Households", Kampala: IFPRI.

Chen, S., Ravallion, M., (2001). "ow did the world's poorest fare in the 1990s?" Policy Research Working Paper Series 2409, Washington DC:. World Bank.

Codjoe, S. N. A. (2007). "Supply and utilisation of food crops in Ghana, 1960–2010". *African Journal of Food Agriculture Nutrition and Development, 7*(2), 1–15.

Conforti P. (2004). "Price transmission in selected agricultural markets" FAO Commodity and Trade Policy Research Working Paper No. 7.

de Janvry, A. and Sadoulet (2009), *'The impact of rising food prices on household welfare in India'*, University of California at Berkeley.

Deaton, A (1989), "Rice Prices and Income Distribution in Thailand: A non parametric analysi." *Economic Analysis Journal*, Vol 99, no 395

Deaton, A. (1997), "The Analysis of household Surveys: A macroeconomic approach to Development Policy'", Washington DC.:World Bank and Johns Hopkins University Press.

Dolado, J., Felgueroso, F. and J. Jimeno (1999), "The Causes of Youth Labour Market Problems in Spain: Crowding-Out, Institutions or Technology Shifts", mimeo.

FASDEP (2002), "Food and Agricultural Sector Development Policy', A Ministry of Agriculture document.

Ghana Statistical Service (2007), Ghana Living Standards Survey 5 Report. Accra: GSS.

Gujarati (2006),"Essentials of Econometrics", Third Edition. New York: McGraw -Hill

Ianchovichina and N. Martin (2002), "Economic Impacts of China's Accession to the WTO", World Bank.

Inder, B. (1993), "Estimating Long-Run Relationships in Economics: A Comparison of Different Approaches", *Journal of Econometrics*, 57, 53-68.Ivanic, M and W. Martin (2008), 'Implication of higher global food prices for poverty in low income countries', World Bank Policy Research Working Papers No. 4594, Washington D.C: World Bank.

Lancon and H. D. Benz (2007), "Rice imports in West Africa: trade regimes and food policy formulation" Poster prepared for presentation at the 106th seminar of the EAAE(Pro-poor development in low income countries: Food, agriculture, trade, and environment) 25-27 October 2007 – Montpellier, France

Listorti G. and (2008) "Price Transmission Mechanisms: A Policy Investigation of International Wheat Markets", *Quaderno di Ricerca* No 114.

Lloyd T., Oliver M, and R. Osei (2001), "Aid, Exports and Growth in Ghana", CREDIT Research Paper No. 01/01, University of Nottingham.

Matusz, S.J. and D. Tarr (1999), "Adjusting to Trade Policy Reform", World Bank Policy Research Working Papers 2142.

Miljkovic, D. (1999). "The Law of One Price in international trade: A critical review." *Review of Agricultural Economics*, 21 (1999), 126–139.

Nicita, A. (2004). "Who benefited from trade liberalization in Mexico? Measuring the effects on household welfare," Policy Research Working Paper Series 3265, World Bank.

Nicita, A. (2009) "The price effect of tariff liberalization: Measuring the impact on household welfare", *Journal of Development Economics* 89 (2009) 19–27, Development Research Group, Trade (DECRG-TR), World Bank. 1

Polaski, S., A. Ganesh-Kumar, S. McDonald, M. Panda, and S. Robinson 2008.,"India's Trade Policy Choices: Managing Diverse Challenges". Washington, DC: Carnegie Endowment for International Peace..

Rapsomanikis G. and A. Sarris (2008), "Market Integration and Uncertianty" , Rome:Food and Agricultural Organization, Volume 44 No. 9 1354-1381.

Rashid, S., (2004), "Spatial Integration of Maize Markets in Post-Liberalized Uganda". Markets, Trade and Institutions Division (MTID) of IFPRI Discussion Paper No. 71.

Ravallion, M. and Van De Walle, D. (1991) "The impact of poverty on food pricing reforms: A welfare analysis in Indonesia," *Journal of policy modeling*, Vol. 13, No. 2.

Simler, (2010)," The Short-Term Impact of Higher Food Prices on Poverty in Uganda", World Bank Policy Research Working Paper 5210.

Singh, I., L. Squire and J. Strauss, (eds.) (1986)."gricultural Household Models, Extensions, Applications and Policy". World Bank and The Johns Hopkins University Press.

ISSER (2008) State of the Ghanaian Economy Report, Legon:Institute of Statiscal, Social and Economic Research.

Thompson, S.R.,and Bohl M.T. (1999). "International Wheat Price Transmission" , *Discussion Paper No 53, Institute of Agricultural Policy and Market Reasearch, University of Glessen.AP

Winters, L.A., McCulloch, N. and A. Mckay,. (2002), "Trade Liberalization and Poverty: The Empirical Evidence", CREDIT Research Paper No. 02/22, University of Nottingham.

Wodon, Q., C. Tsimpo, P. Backiny-Yetna, G. Joseph, F. Adoho and H. Coulombe (2008)," Measuring the potential impact of higher food prices on poverty: summary evidence from West and Central Africa", mimeo, May, Washington D.C. :World Bank,

Appendix

Table 1: ADF Unit Root on the Series

Variable	ADF	Lag Length	Inference
LNEXCH	-1.848*	12	I(1)
	(-1.616)		
LNTARR	-1.732*	12	I(1)
	(-1.616)		
RICE			
LNPD	-1.904*	12	I(1)
	(-1.616)		
PNPW$	-2.463*	12	I(1)
	(-1.616)		
Maize			
LNPD	-2.681*	12	I(1)
	(-2.575)		
PNPW$	-1.964*	12	I(1)
	(-1.616)		
Groundnuts			
LNPD	-2.222**	12	I(1)
	(-1.942)		
PNPW$	-3.896**	12	I(1)
	(-2.575)		
Sorghum			
LNPD	-2.101**	12	I(1)
	(-1.942)		
PNPW$	-2.381**	12	I(1)
	(-1.942)		

Note: Critical values in parenthesis. *, **, and *** are 10%, 5% and 1% significant levels respectively.

INDEX